## THE BACK STAGE GUIDE TO

# Casting Directors

### WHO THEY ARE,
### HOW THEY WORK, AND
### WHAT THEY LOOK FOR IN ACTORS

## HETTIE LYNNE HURTES

BACK STAGE BOOKS
An imprint of Watson-Guptill Publications

Copyright © 1992 Hettie Lynne Hurtes
First published 1992 by Back Stage Books, an imprint of Watson-Guptill
Publications, a division of BPI Communications, Inc., 1515 Broadway,
New York, NY 10036.

**Library of Congress Cataloging-in-Publication Data**
Hurtes, Hettie Lynne.
The Back Stage guide to casting directors: who they are, how they work,
and what they look for in actors/ Hettie Lynne Hurtes.
    p. cm.
ISBN 0-8230-7576-1

1. Motion pictures—Casting. 2. Theater—Casting.
3. Acting—Vocational guidance. 4. Casting directors—United States—
Interviews. 5. Casting directors—United States—Directories.
I. Title. II. Title: Casting directors.
PN1995.9.C34H87   1992                    91–39507
791.43'0233—dc20                              CIP

Manufactured in United States of America
First printing, 1992

1 2 3 4 5 6 7 8 9 / 96 95 94 93 92

*To my Dad*

# Contents

## PART ONE:
## THE CASTING DIRECTORS

# PART TWO:
# THE CASTING PROCESS

# PART THREE:
# CASTING DIRECTORS STATE BY STATE
*177*

# Acknowledgments

Writing one's first book is not only a challenge. It takes support from colleagues, friends, and family.

I wish to acknowledge all the above, including Wolf Schneider, editor of *American Film* magazine, for having given me the opportunity to write the initial article, "An Actor's Guide to Casting," which appeared in her publication and ultimately led to this undertaking.

I also wish to thank Breakdown Services in Los Angeles for having put up with my constant barrage of phone calls, seeking the whereabouts of a host of casting directors who weren't listed in any of the directories.

Thanks, too, to Sara Scribner, without whom this book would have been nearly impossible to complete. Her dedication and meticulous work in the transcription process was invaluable—a true lifesaver.

I express my gratitude to all the casting directors who took their valuable time to talk to me either in person or on the phone, especially those who weren't aware of my journalistic integrity and yet allowed me access to their quite personal thoughts and processes.

And, of course, my gratitude goes to my family: my husband, Ron, and our two daughters, Jennifer and Aubrey, for allowing me the many hours at my computer to churn out this year-long project. You're the best family a writer could ever hope for!

Thank you, one and all.

# Introduction

Once upon a time there were no casting directors. Prior to the onset of television, during the heyday of the Hollywood studio system, the studio selected the stars, carefully groomed them, and placed them before the cameras to determine their ultimate fate. The era of the studio system came to an end in the 1950s, but even as late as the 1960s, an established casting profession didn't exist.

"It was like ordering a Chinese meal: one from column A and one from column B," explains Marion Dougherty, Vice President of Casting for Warner Bros., recalling her early days in the business. The studios, she remembers, would simply recycle from their ranks. "That's why you'd always see the same actor cast in the same kind of role—cliché casting." Dougherty was a pioneer: she was the first casting director to set up her own office in 1965 on Manhattan's East Side, where apparently no one in show business had previously set foot.

She started casting in the late forties, while employed by the advertising agency that was producing the acclaimed Kraft Television Theater. "No one knew what we were doing. I did what seemed to work for me, which was calling people in and reading them for something, and then whittling it down to a couple of people I thought were right, and then bringing them in to read for the director." Marion found these actors on Broadway, where, at the same time, another casting director, Shirley Rich, was helping Rodgers and Hammerstein increase their roster of actors.

Most producers and directors in those days did their own casting, Rich recalls, but Rodgers and Hammerstein, along with the imperious Broadway producer David Merrick and a few others, hired someone else to undertake the task. "I always had an open-door policy," she explains. "I met all the actors, went to all the auditions, and kept extensive files."

It wasn't until Rich was hired by MGM as a talent scout that she became involved with film, and even then she didn't cast specific projects but found talent the studio might be interested in placing under contract for future films. In 1969, Shirley Rich opened her own office in New York and was able to cast for individual producers. Prior to that, the majority of filming was done on the West Coast. When Marion Dougherty was hiring actors for television projects in New York, most had only stage experience.

In the early 1960s, Dougherty was asked to cast "The Naked City," one of television's first dramatic series. "It became the New York actor's screening place for Hollywood," she recollects fondly. "They'd see these new faces and would immediately bring them to Hollywood." These faces belonged to actors like Alan Alda, Robert Redford, and Dustin Hoffman.

Dougherty began to establish an impressive reputation in her fledgling field. She was hired in 1964 to cast a feature film for director George Roy Hill—the first motion picture to be shot in New York since the days of D. W. Griffith's Biograph studios. Titled *The World of Henry Orient*, the movie marked Peter Sellers' American film debut.

The following year, Dougherty was brought to Los Angeles to cast *Hawaii*, not an easy task. Since there wasn't an established casting system and no filing cabinets of pictures and resumes, Dougherty had an uphill battle trying to find Polynesian actors. She turned to MGM, which had hired Polynesian cast members for *Mutiny on the Bounty*, but unfortunately they hadn't kept files on the film. Dougherty had to start from scratch.

A decade later, in 1976, Dougherty set up a casting office in Los Angeles. She didn't know it at the time, but she had cast the die, so to speak. Her rudimentary system has since evolved into a sophisticated, highly competitive, and lucrative business. Today, casting directors are not only one of the first creative forces to be brought aboard a project, but their title cards are prominently featured in the opening credits—in Hollywood at least, a definitive indication of the value of these professionals.

Some casting directors are still hired by major studios and television networks, but most are independent, hired either by the production company or by the producer of a particular film, television show, or theatrical production. Before a deal is inked, the casting director is sent a script. David Rubin, for one, believes it is essential that he have an emotional tie to a screenplay. "I have declined work on a fairly high-profile project because I did not have a connection with the material," he reports.

Once the casting director has read the script, the next step is a meeting with the producer and director to discuss the nuances of each character to be cast. The casting director will offer suggestions as to who might fit the bill. Most casting directors readily admit that casting must be a collaborative effort. "I think you develop a certain communication in terms of understanding a director's approach to a film," observes Lynn Stalmaster, whose clients have included Sidney Pollack, Mark Rydell, and Brian DePalma. "It is a process of continuous discussion and reexploration," explains Rubin, a former Stalmaster protégé. He feels that the initial exploration of the characters is one of the most critical periods in the casting process. It is vitally important, he observes, "to take all the existing elements into consideration."

The casting director discusses the essential elements of each character during arduous sessions with the producer and director. Following the discussions, the director informs the casting director which actors he or she would prefer to read. This brings us to the question of who really casts a project. The truth is, there is no definitive answer. It depends on the project, and it depends on the director. The actors for the leading roles are, for the most part, selected by the director or producer, or, in the case of a major network production, the network itself. The supporting cast, however, is usually the bailiwick of the casting director.

There are times when a casting director has a great deal of influence on the selection of an actor for a major role. Take the movie *Night Shift*, for example. Jane Jenkins explains that Brian Grazer and Ron Howard were intent on John Belushi for the lead, but after auditioning Michael Keaton for another project the three were working on, she was determined to give him a shot at *Night Shift*. "So when Ron and Brian were still contemplating Belushi," recalls Jenkins, "I did half an hour on why I thought it would be much more exciting to hire Keaton and discover somebody new." Her persistence paid off—Keaton won the role.

*The Back Stage Guide to Casting Directors* explores the various methods used by many of the entertainment industry's prominent casting directors when casting a play, film, or television project. It does this through interviews with many of the leading professionals in the field. They describe the different techniques employed to cast a

Broadway musical, a sitcom, or a feature film, and explain what qualities and acting experience they look for in the actors they consider.

The fifty-plus interviewees reveal how they expect actors to conduct themselves during an interview and/or audition, and what actors should expect from a casting director when they're being considered for a particular part. Accompanying each interview is a sampling of the casting director's credits, along with the medium or media in which he or she is involved.

Most producers and directors enthusiastically endorse the importance of casting directors in the creation of any contemporary production. Frank Marshall, a producer and director with Steven Spielberg's Amblin Productions, states that "it's the casting director who works with all the agents. I would never have enough time." But casting directors bring much more to a project than administrative support. Academy Award-winning director Robert Wise pays homage to the casting director's creative prowess. "Their biggest contribution to most pictures is the supporting cast. They bring you the whole range." And actor/director Sondra Locke gives the casting director credit for providing the director with the best talent available. "I've always said you can take the exact same film and make it the exact same way with six different sets of actors, and you'll have six different films. It's just that critical what an individual actor brings to the screen and to the role."

*The Back Stage Guide to Casting Directors* is an attempt to shed light on a profession that has heretofore been unexamined in book form. To directors, producers, agents, and other artists in the entertainment business, the insights shared by these casting directors will shed light on a fascinating and important part of the creative process of film, theater, and television production. Actors wanting to eliminate some of those gnawing anxieties all too prevalent in the continuous business of landing a job should find these casting directors' opinions especially valuable. But any reader interested in the entertainment business may be assured of finding this book to be an eye-opening, behind-the-scenes glimpse into the creation of this country's best motion pictures, television shows, and theater productions.

PART ONE

# The Casting Directors

# Joseph Abaldo

**INDEPENDENT**

The reason Joseph Abaldo made the transition from actor to casting director was that he wanted to improve the casting process for the actor, to make it fun. "That's been my philosophy," he says. "The more knowledge you can give an actor before he comes in, the more you can alleviate the tension. I do everything I can to break tension. If I see someone's really nervous, I won't bring him in right away. I'll give him more time. I try to be as flexible as I can. And I always say to actors, right to their faces: this is not important. You just have to come in and have a good time, and if you do that, they're going to love you."

Joseph attends theater showcases all the time and discovers talent along the way. He also conducts many open calls, which, he suggests, is the best way to meet him since he rarely schedules general auditions.

He remembers one project where several open calls were scheduled for a workshop he was casting for composer Cy Coleman (*City of Angels, The Will Rogers Follies*). Because they needed a lot of young people of all races and types, they held a number of mass auditions, both Equity and non-Equity. "The turnout was phenomenal," he remembers. "What was most exciting was that they [the producers/-creators] were willing to take a risk on brand-new talent. One of the leading girls, in fact, was non-union, and it's changed her life. I mean, every agent in New York has met her." The girl is Lorie Fischer. The production: *The Life*. It's about the life of pimps and prostitutes on

SPECIALTY:
Off-Broadway and regional theater

CREDITS INCLUDE:
*And the World Goes 'Round*
*A Change in the Air*
*The Rothschilds*
*Nunsense*
*The Life*

42nd Street, not an easy show to cast. "How many black actors at this stage are going to want to portray pimps and hookers? It was a very risqué show to be involved with," says Abaldo. No one was allowed to read the script or hear the music before the audition, which made his job even tougher. It also paid badly: $400 for about eight weeks of work. Moreover, the actors not only had to act, but to sing and dance as well.

Although Abaldo was not allowed to pass out any scripts before auditions for *The Life*, that's not his standard method of operation. "We try to make scripts and tapes available to everybody ahead of time," he stresses. "We often try to give them scenes to learn in advance so that when they come in, they have as much information as they can conceivably need before they walk in the door. Then it's up to them to do the best job."

When actors do come in for the audition, Joseph has a reader to read with them, or sometimes he'll pair people up, giving them plenty of time to work on the scene. When actors are auditioning for Abaldo, they're usually auditioning for the director at the same time.

Abaldo is impressed with quality training. He feels the best theater schools in the country are Yale, Juilliard, the Neighborhood Playhouse, Carnegie-Mellon, and Northwestern. "They change all the time, however," he admits. "And even with these schools, there are directors who'll say, 'Oh, I can't stand working with people who went to Yale.' So it's very difficult for me to second-guess them."

He suggests that actors study—not only acting, but voice and movement as well. "Your voice is your life. You need to be able to project, and there are constantly calls for actors who sing. It's ridiculous in this day and age, when there are so many musicals, for actors not to be working on their craft. If you're an actor, your body, your voice is what you've got!"

When an actor is auditioning for a musical, Joseph advises selecting songs that haven't been done to death. "Right now, *Les Miz* is very popular, as is *Phantom*. It doesn't bother me, but a lot of directors will refuse to hear them."

He also suggests picking tunes that show sufficient range. "There are certain numbers that actors who can't sing insist on singing. That's such a big mistake, because it doesn't show any range." He cites "Tonight at Eight" from *She Loves Me* as an example. He would prefer a more vocalized song. "I say do whatever you do, but make sure you do it well. I hate hearing 'Anyone Can

Whistle,' which is done all the time, because it's usually done so badly. If an actor does it well, fine, but it takes a lot of skill."

Another no-no from Abaldo: never tell a director you've tried to make your reading interesting. "That's a negative because what you're saying is that the playwright couldn't make it interesting. That's ridiculous. Obviously the director wants to do this play. If you don't, don't bother coming in." Actors, he says, can also lose an audition even before it starts, by being obnoxious, by spending forty-five minutes talking to the pianist about the music. "I see it happen. Before they even start, the director will cross out an actor's name. It's important to realize that your audition begins the moment you walk through the door."

Memorizing a scene is not important to Abaldo. In fact, it can even be a hindrance, "because often actors are concentrating so hard on the lines, they're not doing the character, and it's more important to get a feeling for the character." He does say, however, that if an actor is over fifty, directors may feel more at ease with a polished performance. "When we were casting *Our Town*, we were worried about the older actors, especially the stage manager, who has tons of lines to learn. At his callback, one actor memorized his scene and won the audition because of that. If there was any concern about him learning the lines, he proved he could do it."

A "star" to Joseph Abaldo is an actor who "loves to perform and can't wait to come in, and there's a spark there. It's almost infectious." Abaldo once made a concerted effort to pinpoint just what it takes to have "star" quality. "I went to see all the stars I could who were performing on Broadway, and I rented a lot of films to see if I could find out what all these people had in common, and let me tell you, I saw a lot of them. It was unanimous, right down the line. They loved what they were doing. When they stepped on the stage, you would go, 'My God, they love being here!' That's what makes a star."

---

*Joseph Abaldo accepts outside submissions excluding videocassettes; no generals.*

# Julie Alter

**INDEPENDENT**

Julie Alter has just recently altered her situation. Since the demise of "thirtysomething," she's now handling individual projects, hoping another gem like the last will appear. Alter has also gone solo, after a partnership with Susan Young for several years. She's currently working on a project for director Arthur Penn.

Alter started out in New York as an actress. When she decided to make the transition to casting, she naturally gravitated to the theater, where she learned her craft from such noted casting directors as Lynn Kressel and Johnson-Liff. Prior to her departure for the West Coast, she worked as the in-house casting director for the Manhattan Theatre Club. To Alter, theater is the best training ground for a young actor: compared to film and television, theater puts greater emphasis on the craft and offers many more opportunities, especially in New York.

That's one of the reasons Julie Alter was delighted with the responsibility of casting "thirtysomething," which was a phenomenon on network television because of the quality of its cast and scripts. Although Julie and Susie were not responsible for selecting the original primary players, they had the monumental task of rounding out each week's cast.

Casting "thirtysomething" was not like casting your usual TV sitcom. Alter and Young looked for the highest-caliber actor with good theater or film credits. "We never had trouble getting quality actors because of the quality of the show,"

SPECIALTY:
TV

CREDITS INCLUDE:
"thirtysomething"
"Sunday Dinner" (pilot)
"Chips"
"A Soldier's Story" (cable)
*The Last Temptation of Christ* (Alter)

explains Alter. The primary requisite is realism. "We sought out intelligent actors—not well-known or recognizable names." In fact, one of their main challenges was finding qualified actors who hadn't as yet been discovered.

That's where Alter's theater expertise comes in handy. She's always attending plays, hoping to find a refreshingly bright prospect, and it frequently pays off. Even if an actor hasn't had a great deal of experience, it's not critical. She'd rather see someone with an interesting background who can bring that quality to a character than a veteran performer who lives and breathes acting.

In fact, desperation is one quality that goes against her grain. Julie recalls an actor who came in for an audition several years ago when she shared her office space with Susie and her pet dog. Susie, it seems, always kept a dish of dog biscuits on her desk. This young actor was reading for the part of a homeless person, and to communicate that person's hunger, to show just how down and out he was, in the middle of the reading he reached out and snatched a dog biscuit from Susie's desk and proceeded to wolf it down. Well, needless to say, that ended the audition. Susie lost her composure, and the actor was never called in to read again. "It just went beyond what was appropriate in a professional situation," Alter explains. "This wasn't a scene study class. This was an audition."

In a similar vein, Alter recollects the casting of the pilot for "Poochinski" with Peter Boyle. At most auditions, Julie got to play the dog opposite the actors reading for other roles. "I tried to talk and act like a dog to the best of my ability to help the actors. One actor, however, just went crazy. He petted me, rubbed my nose. It was really difficult for me, and it destroyed it for him." It's quite risky, she believes, for an actor to cross that boundary, although she finds it impossible to define exactly where the boundary falls. On "thirtysomething," for instance, actors sometimes crossed the line during a love scene and kissed her. While it didn't always cost them the part, it was awkward for Julie, and she prefers that actors find another way to convey their emotions.

Julie delights in casting children, which she's frequently called upon to do. She'll never forget trying to explain to a five-year-old actor how different "thirtysomething" was from other television shows. She found it difficult to convey to the youngster the need to tone down his performance; like many young children, this one was overacting. "I tried to explain that this show was more earth tones than primary colors, but I don't think he quite got the picture."

Speaking of earth tones, Alter likens casting to interior decorating. "If you're working for someone who wants a yellow couch, even though you think a plaid one would look better, you have to find out what he means by yellow. Does he want mustard yellow? How much gold does he want in it? If you've worked with someone before, you can often change his mind, but it doesn't always work that way." She admits she's been able to convince several directors to consider actors about whom they were hesitant, as happened on *The Last Temptation of Christ*. Apparently Martin Scorsese had seen an actor on stage exude a certain quality that he found annoying. It turned out, however, that the very quality that annoyed him in one context worked beautifully once Scorsese heard him read. "You need an open-minded director," admits Alter, "who will occasionally take a chance and bring someone in despite a director's preliminary reluctance."

But, says Alter, casting directors themselves are often the culprits. "When casting directors close themselves off to actors, prejudging them and assuming they won't fit a certain role because they've played entirely different characters, that presents the biggest hazard to this job and to actors, and runs the risk of cheating a director out of meeting someone interesting." Alter says she strives to be open. "An actor may have an interesting look for one role, and if I haven't seen that 'color' or that sense of humor but I think he or she may be bright, if there's that certain *gestalt*, I'll want to read that actor again or take a chance bringing him or her in to read for the director."

Due to Julie's experience as an actress, she's able to help coach actors, both young and old, through auditions. If she believes in someone, she'll work with him or her to try to improve the reading for the director. She'll also have an actor read more than once to see if the actor is able to take direction. "If they can't take direction from me, then how will they be able to take direction on the set?"

One suggestion Alter offers actors is to forget the glamour and present what's underneath the make-up. "I'm not interested in the latest fashions, so don't ask me how you should wear your hair," says Alter. "I don't care." What's vital are the actor's choices. "I do admire training, but an actor can also click into a role, and if the part speaks to you and is close to you, then wonderful things can come out, training or not."

Julie stresses the importance of going for a role that you know you're right for: "It's the only time I think it's appropriate for someone to keep calling until he or she reaches me or gets a message to me." And if you're in a play that's worth seeing, she also recommends a few phone calls to make sure the casting director knows about it. If not, she suggests simply sending a photo or postcard about three times a year.

Rarely will Alter use videotape at auditions. "I don't feel video is the best judge of an actor's acting ability." She prefers a face-to-face audition, which is also less intimidating to the actor. She's had to use videotape on certain projects as specified by the director, but she believes videotape has been harmful to many actors who've come across as stiff and artificial, when under other circumstances they'd probably shine. "With video, it's an unreal situation," says Julie. "There's no time to work on a scene—you simply shoot it and move on to the next person." She's also opposed to actors memorizing their sides unless they feel absolutely comfortable with the material. "It only makes the director expect more from your reading. It puts an onus on the actor to deliver a polished performance."

Julie Alter is very supportive of talented actors, and encourages them to keep on going even when they don't get the roles. She does suggest, however, that if after five years or so they're still trying to make ends meet, they should possibly consider another field. "Just don't be discouraged by negative feedback from casting directors," she offers.

One of the nicest things about this particular casting office is its unpressured ambiance. "I'm often told by actors how comfortable they feel when they come in here," says Julie. "We try to be encouraging and friendly, rather than intimidating." And the simple, sunny office on the second story of a West Hollywood building will continue, she hopes, to be a safe haven for actors pounding the pavements of L.A.

---

*Julie Alter accepts photos and resumés, but will accept only professional videotapes of an actor's work. She schedules generals in the morning.*

# Deborah Aquila

**D**eborah Aquila is a trained actress, having studied for four years with the celebrated Stella Adler in New York. To Deborah, training is essential. "It's as important to me as law school would be to a law firm." When she decided to make the transition to casting, her belief in the proper training led her to work with Bonnie Timmerman, whom she calls "the Godmother of Casting." Says Aquila of her mentor, "She's a wonderful woman, and I learned from her the process of booking, and how to go for the interesting and not the obvious." These are the qualities she now passes along to her associates.

Aquila believes that training doesn't stop with school. She feels the best way to continue to study the craft is to do as much theater as possible. "I go to the theater every night," she confesses. And her associates may cover two or three additional plays. "All the actors in *Last Exit to Brooklyn* came out of the theater, except for Jennifer Jason Leigh." Referring to her casting of *sex, lies, and videotape.*, Aquila continues, "Laura SanGiacomo came out of the theater—I saw her in a play called *Beirut*. And Peter Gallagher was out of the theater. That's just how I work."

Trying to avoid using the word "discovered," Deborah says she was probably the first casting director to hire Laura SanGiacomo for feature film when she did *sex, lies, and videotape*. She was also responsible for casting John Costello in *Last Exit*, his first feature. "I don't like to use the word *discover*. Actors discover their own talent—we just happen to come

SPECIALTY:
Feature film and TV pilots

CREDITS INCLUDE:
*Dream Street*
*sex, lies, and videotape*
*Last Exit to Brooklyn*
*Wild Orchid*
*Pump Up the Volume*
(New York casting)
*The Rapture*
"thirtysomething" (first year)

9

across it. I think the definition has changed over the past decade. I think it's unfair, because if they didn't recognize their own wonderful talent, we wouldn't know it."

Aquila expects every actor at an audition to be completely prepared. "I think that's very important to the process. If I'm prepared and have done my homework, I expect the same from any actor who walks through the door." She expects the actor to understand the material fully. "I think it's important that actors create a situation in their mind's eye, so that when they come in, they have a total sense of what the script is." She also feels it imperative that actors read the script, whether they are up for a feature or a television pilot.

Most actors who make it past Aquila's pre-screening are put on videotape. Because so many directors are in Los Angeles, she has to send them the ones she's pre-selected so that they, in turn, can tell her the ones in which they're interested. And while Deborah doesn't expect an actor to dress for the part at such a preliminary audition, "if they're going on tape, then I expect them to dress as close to the character as possible. If they have questions about that, then they should always ask me or my associates."

She doesn't expect an actor to know his lines by heart, but "what's important to me is that the characterization be complete. If that means memorizing, sure, I'm grateful for that." Memorization is also recommended if actors are going on tape. "It may be the only thing NBC is going to see of them before they decide to fly them out for a test, so it's very important for them to be so familiar with the material that they're at least close to being off-book."

Deborah Aquila likes to talk to actors before an audition. "Sometimes I'll ask an actor about what his take of the character is. First I'll ask him if he's read the script, and what he thinks about it. Then I'll ask what the character's role in the story is." She may also try to get a feel for what the actor understands about the character by asking him where the character is from, what he does for a living, the relationship between that character and one of the others in the script, maybe the protagonist. "Then, if the answers are just a bit off, I'll adjust that, because I know what the director has in mind."

Deborah doesn't always follow the script to the letter. She enjoys trying to cast against type. The casting of Jennifer Jason Leigh is a good example. "Jennifer probably had never done a role like TraLaLa in *Last Exit* in her career, and it was difficult in the preliminary auditions to envision that total transformation." The producers apparently had some questions as to the physicality of Jennifer's presence. "But she's able to metamorphosize into so many different characters. And here was a case in point where TraLala was headed in a very different direction in our minds, and then when Jennifer showed us her version, she got the role."

When asked to explain her idea of "star quality," Aquila uses Jennifer Jason Leigh as a prime example. "I don't know if you can learn it," she offers, "but I think once you relax enough in your talent, and you can let that go, other elements of your personality can come through."

David Ducobney, whom she cast in *The Rapture*, is another example of a "star," according to Deborah's definition. "It's a charisma, sex appeal, an amazingly nice person, completely relaxed in his own body, and a talented actor. He's also very spontaneous and creative. Right there. Right in the moment."

Seeing a lot of stage actors, Aquila knows that some can easily make the transition to film, others can't. "I guess it comes down to the word *truth*. You can see truthfulness. It's there or it's not, and you can sometimes help a person adjust that. Because the theater is so big, you want to adjust that to the level of film and television. You have a lot to do in a very specific part of your body. Sometimes it's all in the face. In the theater it's broader. You have to reach across the proscenium with every cent you have, often reaching out to a thousand people a night." She believes a film director can help an actor through that process, and a casting director can aid the transition as well.

If an actor wants to schedule an interview with Deborah Aquila she asks that he or she send in a picture and resume, and when she's not very busy, she'll try to set up either a meeting or a reading, depending on the project. A two-and-a-half-minute monologue may be requested. No Shakespeare, please!

*Deborah Aquila encourages the submission of pictures and resumés; no videotapes; she schedules generals frequently.*

# Breanna Benjamin

**B**reanna Benjamin is one of the more accessible casting directors in New York. She is delighted to receive photos and resumes from actors, whether or not they are represented or even in the unions. "If they're right, I'm more than happy to see them."

Breanna, in fact, discovered the leading man in *True Love* from a picture he had submitted to her. "Neither the director nor producer thought he was right, but I convinced them to see him a second time and talk to him about changing his appearance just a bit." Ron Eldard was cast in the lead; he has since signed with Triad Artists, and has landed a television series.

Benjamin believes one of the most important attributes for actors is "a positive attitude about themselves. I find the ones who make it most of the time like themselves and like the people around them—they like the world they live in. They're involved in the world they live in." A lot of actors walk through her door every day, but sometimes she can't get past their attitude to find out if they can even act.

If Benjamin sees someone with potential she'll gladly pass along any advice the actor might seek. "I tell them that acting is the same as working at IBM. It's a job. It's their career, but if it's the only thing in their life, they're not going to make it. You've heard of a banker mentality or an

SPECIALTY:
Feature film and theater;
occasional TV

CREDITS INCLUDE:
*Outpost*
*True Love*
*Joker's Wild*
*South Philadelphia Story*
*Joseph and Emma*
*Tony and Tina's Wedding*
Nebraska Rep.
Soho Rep
"Maintenance Men's Lounge" (TV)

accountant mentality, and how boring it is? Well, an actor mentality is just as boring. There have to be other sides to your life. That's what makes you interesting. That's what makes people want to know you and be with you and give you a shot at showing your talent."

At an interview, Breanna expects to get to know the actor as a person, but at the audition, she wants to see the character. "I want to see the change that takes place. There's nothing more frightening than an actor auditioning for a street hoodlum who comes in for an interview with that persona. It's scary. And this," she admits, "happens more times than you know." When an actor only shows her "the hoodlum," she isn't sure if this is his real demeanor or not, and if it is, she questions whether he also has the technique to sustain a performance.

Benjamin offers another pointer for actors interviewing with a casting director. Be prepared for the most common question: Why don't you tell me about yourself? "If they're smart, they should know that question will be asked of them, and it's just like learning a role. They should keep a little one-minute set of notes in their daily diary on what they're going to talk about, so they don't just sit there and stutter and stammer." She suggests they keep updating those notes, especially if they've added something new to their lives.

A positive attitude should also be apparent at the audition. "In New York alone, there are fifty thousand actors. If you go in with the attitude 'Oh my God, there are twenty-nine other actors here, I don't have a chance,' you're right—you don't. You might as well go home." She prefers the alternate reaction. " 'Oh my God, she thinks I'm one of the thirty best in the city for this role. I've already beaten out 4,970 other people. My chances are pretty good.'"

She also tells the actor to think of the audition as a performance. "We [the casting directors] probably don't even know what we want. We've got a general idea in our heads, and we're waiting for an actor to come in and show us, perform for us, and that's how we usually make our decisions."

If there is one pet peeve that Breanna Benjamin has at an audition, it's an actor who fails to listen to direction. After she or the director tells the actor something, the actor will very often continue doing exactly what he or she did before or something else altogether, "because they're usually so busy trying to think of what to say next to impress us, they're not hearing what we said." And if actors don't listen to direction during an audition, chances are they won't respond on the set either, so there goes the opportunity.

Benjamin prides herself on providing plenty of opportunity to minority actors. On a recent production of *Romeo and Juliet*, she cast a black man in the role of Capulet simply because she believed the actor was right for the part.

There are certain actors she'll consider for stage productions but not for features. "It's a physical difference," she explains. "There are some actors who can do very nicely on stage and possibly even on television, but who couldn't make it on film for a variety of reasons, the main one being that some actors haven't learned to control their faces. If they do too much with their facial muscles, it may work on stage, but no one wants to see a rubber face fifteen feet high on screen, unless it's a real character part."

Eyes are also very important on screen, whereas on stage they're barely noticeable. Can an actor learn to control his face? "Absolutely," she believes. "If you take some kind of on-camera audition course, or even if you have your own video camera, you can monitor yourself."

Breanna Benjamin understands the pressures besetting an actor. She herself started out acting, but she opted to take the proverbial path of least resistance. She doesn't think of herself as a failed actor, and hopes that actors don't feel they've failed just because they've chosen to follow a different pursuit. "Acting, to me," she recalls, "was a carrot dangling out there that I was trying to catch. Once I caught it and started to work regularly, I found I didn't even like it! I spent all day saying someone else's words and all night learning them. I had to get out, because I'd lost me. And I really think that's why there are so many actors in this world, because they're all chasing that carrot and don't really want it once they've caught it. And it's okay to walk away from it. It doesn't mean you've failed."

---

*Breanna Benjamin encourages the submission of photos and resumés, but no videocassettes; she only schedules generals when working on a specific project.*

# Jack Bowdan

## JAY BINDER CASTING

T he most important element in casting to Jack Bowdan is who the actors are as people. That's aside from their preparation, presentation, and theatrical training. "If we don't get a sense of who these people are, as individuals, it doesn't mean much, no matter how well prepared they are or what work they're doing."

Jay Binder Casting tries to help actors be themselves by providing as comfortable an environment as possible. Then it's up to each individual actor. "Actors need to be prepared," stresses Jack. "If they come in with prepared material, they need to have spent as much time as necessary with it. Memorization isn't important, but they do need to be familiar with the script. That way," he adds, "they don't get locked into one way of doing something, and they can be open to any adjustments a director may give them." That shows the powers-that-be a flexibility and an ability to work in a give-and-take situation. "Most directors," Jack believes, "are pretty insecure themselves. They want to come away from an audition knowing that they're going to be able to work with the actor, and that the actor is imaginative enough and well-trained enough to handle different directions. They also need to get a feel for what the actor will be like to work with for an extended period of time."

While Bowdan believes it imperative that an actor reveal who he or she is, it can be carried to extremes. He recalls an episode in which an actor talked herself right out of a part. She apparently

> SPECIALTY:
> Broadway, TV, regional theater,
> and occasional Off-Broadway
>
> CREDITS INCLUDE:
> *Lost in Yonkers*
> *Jerome Robbins' Broadway*
> *Rumors*
> *Meet Me in St. Louis*
> *Hyde in Hollywood*
> (American Playhouse)

had done a lovely audition, and the director was impressed, but after it was over she got a bit carried away. "She just started chattering about everything and nothing and her entire life history, and in about ten minutes totally ruined her chances." The director came to the realization that spending four weeks in rehearsal with this woman was about the last thing he wanted to do.

Training is another important element to Binder and Bowdan. Bowdan feels it's less important for television, where personality and physical qualities are primarily the focus, but on the stage, actors really need to have the training. "A director has to know that the actors can deliver night after night, that they're trained vocally as well as physically to work on the stage." The best young theater actors, he adds, are the ones who come out of such well-known programs as Juilliard, Yale, N.Y.U., U.C./San Diego, and A.C.T. One of the wonderful things about these schools, Jack explains, is that upon completion of training, actors can be seen in presentations by every casting director and agent in New York and many in L.A. "It's never a guarantee," he admits, "but they have a real headstart on other young actors who don't have that kind of training, and those in the theater will respond to that."

Showcases are another source of talent for the Binder Agency. They try to see as many as possible, as long as they are reputable and seem interesting. "Barbara [Hipkiss] will not go to a Shakespeare showcase," explains Bowdan, "because they're usually quite terrible, and the actors are not really trained enough to handle the language." She prefers a contemporary play, which allows the actors to show themselves off in a better light. "Jay, on the other hand, has this thing against so-called Southern plays," says Hipkiss. "They're highly emotional, and there's a lot of bad language and heated stuff going on, and he got so tired of seeing them, he just decided against them."

When they do discover talent, they respond immediately. Bowdan recalls a play about six years ago that the agency was casting for European film director Lina Wertmuller. It was called *Love and Magic in Momma's Kitchen*. Unfortunately, it never opened, but the story is interesting. One of the characters in the play was a sixty-year-old woman dying of cancer. A much younger actress had come in to read for another role but was adamant about reading for the elderly character. She said it was uncanny how much the woman resembled a relative of hers, and she simply had to give it a shot. Her reading was so incredible that the agency brought her back to meet Wertmuller, who ended up casting her.

Some actors just mesmerize Bowdan. Mary Louise Parker is one. He was casting *Prelude to a Kiss* at Berkeley Repertory Theatre and thought Mary Louise would be a good choice for one of the leads. He had seen her in other regional theaters, but the director was hesitant to cast an unknown commodity. They did feel she was perfect for the part, and after some debate, finally decided to take the chance. Not only did Parker do a superb job at Berkeley, but she went on to New York to capture a Tony nomination for her performance. "It was her very unique qualities: a combination of great skill and technique with an enormous emotional range and a wonderful quirky personality that was very well-suited for this particular role."

Jack Bowdan suggests actors keep in touch by sending him an updated picture and resumé every so often, or a postcard if they're appearing in a showcase or production. (Not too many and not too often.) And a final word of advice: all an actor can do is express who he or she is as an individual. "It may not be what's wanted at the time, but it will leave an impression, and that's really all an actor can do."

*Jay Binder Casting accepts pictures and resumés but discourages video-tapes; they will hold generals when time allows.*

# Ross Brown

## BROWN/WEST CASTING

The hardest thing about being an actor, in the opinion of casting director Ross Brown, is not doing the job but getting the job, and he says most actors haven't been adequately trained in that capacity. Having been in the business for over a quarter of a century, Brown has seen many actors with talent fall by the wayside because of their lack of savvy when it comes to auditioning. "It's all seduction," he believes. An actor should never give his all during a first reading, but only a taste of what he has to offer. "Once you've seen it all, are you going to buy it? It's an art form, and it requires a professional approach."

Ross Brown prides himself on his ability to help prepare an actor to get a job. "I'll basically give them choices as to what we want and different areas to which they can go. I'll even tell them what to wear! They're there to get the job. What I would love is that they would all go in there and *take* the job." The more special an actor is to Ross, the more he tries to help, although he tries to help the actor understand that no matter how good he or she may be, it's not always the best actor who lands the role. There are too many variables in this elusive trade. Aside from talent and presence, Brown believes, the basics for an actor are courtesy, integrity, and a sense of humor. "They're trendsetters.

SPECIALTY:
Feature film,
movies of the week,
and miniseries

CREDITS INCLUDE:
*Texasville*
*Batman*
*The Last Picture Show*
*Planet of the Apes*
*Pennies From Heaven*
*The Burning Bed*
*The Day After*
*North and South, Book Two*
"Shades of L.A."

They're not the pretty girls or handsome boys. They have a uniqueness that makes you not just want to look at them, but see them."

One such individual is Randy Quaid. Brown found him in Houston when he was casting *The Last Picture Show*. It was Randy's first film. And what was so special about Quaid? "You cared about him. If you don't care, my favorite four letter word is *next*."

Another actor made such an impression on Ross that he literally searched the world to find him. This was Rutger Hauer, whom he'd seen in the Dutch film *Soldier of Orange*. Ross was casting the miniseries *Inside the Third Reich*, the story of Albert Speer, and thought Hauer would be perfect for the leading man. "They wanted William Hurt, and while I'm a big fan of Hurt, I was convinced we should track down Hauer, even though he wasn't a big name at the time." After finding the European actor and reading him, the producers agreed. He was the choice.

Brown may be extremely polite to certain actors, but that doesn't mean he respects them. "I'm looking for people you write scripts for. I'm extremely polite to people I never intend to see again, but if there's someone I think has potential and isn't using it, I'll nail them to the bloody wall!" In other words, if you're read the riot act in Brown's office, you've probably landed the role. He doesn't have the time to get angry at those with little talent or those who are what he terms "hungry actors." "You don't give a hungry person filet mignon. You give them Alpo— a whole case of it."

Ross Brown doesn't mince words. He is also a master of expressive analogies. "I feel that all actors are defense attorneys. That's their responsiblity. Their client is their character, and whether they're playing Lizzy Borden or Adolf Hitler, their responsiblity is to make the audience—which is the jury—believe they're innocent. The minute an actor believes his client is guilty, he loses, and so do we." What saddens Ross most about the business are the people who have forgotten to "make believe." That's one of the magical qualities of show business, and he sees it lacking in many individuals.

Another attribute that Ross finds lacking in many actors is the ability to listen. "The most important thing to acting is listening and reacting to what you've heard. You have to listen to what is being said and digest it, spit out what you don't need, but what you hear and like is yours." Ross himself is a good listener. In fact, he prefers to listen to actors rather than hear them read when he first meets them. "I'd rather listen to what they have to say. I'm not really that big on readings." And when he does schedules readings they're usually with the producers and director. "I try to set up as few callbacks as possible."

What exactly is he looking for? "I never know what I want until they come in. I've had many roles written for men and realized a woman would be better." A case in point was *Intimate Agonies*, set in a very WASP environment. In one hospital scene, there was a call for a 55-year-old gruff redneck physician. So whom did Brown call in to read for this character? Two black women, and one of them was cast. "Doctor is number three on my list when it comes to filling a role. Number one is the human being, number two is the human being who's either a male or female, and number three is the human being who's a male or female who's also a doctor."

What's most important to Ross Brown in the casting of a film is the canvas as a whole. "The star is the color red, let's say. Then I'll add different colors that will work with red that will make him look the best. I may find a wonderful blue, but that blue doesn't work on my canvas. That's why an actor shouldn't feel bad when he doesn't get the role. It may just be he's the the wrong match for that particular canvas."

Brown isn't afraid to seek out new or untried actors. In fact, he and his partner, Mary West, have vowed to use a client from a new agency on every project in which they're involved. Not too long ago, Brown found an actor in Dallas with no professional experience. He'd just come along with a friend to a casting session. "He was a real winner, a bigger-than-life character. So I called the William Morris Agency, and they signed him. He wasn't even a member of SAG." Almost immediately after landing an agent, that fine young actor, Thomas Hayden Church, was cast in the TV series "Wings."

Of course, an actor without a union card doesn't necessarily mean that the actor hasn't been well trained. "Training is important," emphasizes Brown. "Smart actors, even when they're doing a series or whatever, will study, because that's where they find their new bags of tricks." He cites the numerous actors who disappear from view soon after their series is dropped from the lineup. He feels it's because they haven't done their homework.

What Ross would like actors to keep in mind is that casting directors are subjective human beings like everyone else. "We're simply buyers. The minute we buy someone, we immediately have to sell him. We can often sell you better than you can yourself." And if he's not buying for one reason or another, it's not because you're not talented or you're not a terrific person. "It's just not our story. It has nothing to do with the story we're currently working on, so I simply have to say, 'Next.'"

*Brown/West Casting accepts photos, resumés and videotapes; no generals.*

# Aleta Chappelle

## INDEPENDENT

Aleta Chappelle started out casting extras for such acclaimed films as *Cotton Club* and *Ironweed*. She loved the work and spent as much time finding the right people for non-speaking roles as many casting directors spend on principals. Her technique? "You get thousands of people in, and you just pick out the really unique ones." She would devote about thirty seconds to each person, accepting the potential actor's picture and resume and asking a few basic questions. "Then, if there were someone who seemed especially nice or serious, someone who just looked right, I put his or her picture in my special box, and later on, as we set up readings, we'd bring them in." In other words, just because someone had always done extra work didn't necessarily mean that the actor wouldn't be considered for a speaking part.

Aleta saw six thousand people during one open call for *Ironweed* and another six thousand for *Cotton Club*. The calls were always announced in the local papers, and anyone was welcome to attend. In Albany, New York, on location for *Iron-weed*, she recalls casting one man who was an alderman; he wound up playing a bum and working four or five weeks. "SAG was really mad at us, because it was such an important part, and we'd given it to a non-pro." She also hired a woman who was head of the arts council in Albany to play a floozy. But one of Aleta's favorite stories was the casting of a homeless family. "There was a scene where Jack Nicholson is supposed to give some food to a husband, wife, and baby who

SPECIALTY:
Feature film

CREDITS INCLUDE:
*Rambling Rose*
*A Rage in Harlem*
*Godfather III*
*New York Stories*
*True Believer*
*Ironweed*
*Tucker*
*Gardens of Stone*
"*Outsiders*" (TV pilot)

are totally indigent, and we got a real family to do this. They were in a situation where they lived above a store with about twenty other people. They didn't even qualify for welfare, and suddenly they became principal weekly players, earning five thousand dollars with a chance to turn their lives around."

Nicholson himself was captivated by one homeless man, and the actor insisted the man be upgraded to a principal. "He was the only person that Jack gave an autograph to during the shoot," remembers Chappelle. Even though Aleta is no longer focusing her efforts on atmosphere casting, she still spends a great deal of time looking for very special faces in a crowd. Even Francis Ford Coppola, she reveals, will meet actors who may not have any dialogue, but whose faces may be on camera for several seconds, or whose action may require more skill than is usual for the average extra.

While casting *A Rage in Harlem*, Chapelle ventured out into the wilds of Cincinnatti to do some location casting. It was there she found an ex-football player at an open call. At two other open calls, she was not only searching for day players, but the female lead to play opposite Forrest Whitaker. Robin Givens ultimately got the role, but two women with no experience were given screen tests. In other words, the motto "Once an extra, always an extra" does not hold true for Aleta Chapelle. "I think it's a good way to learn filmmaking. If it's what you do as a living, then you probably are going to stay an extra because people are going to look at you that way. But if you're a young person or new to the business and really want to get some experience, I don't think it hurts."

Aleta believes casting is eighty to ninety percent based on an actor's looks and attitude, especially in film. "That's why I always like to meet an actor first. My favorite people come out of something in their personality or something they bring in that's real." There are times she won't even read an actor until the callbacks and taping sessions. This is most common when she's familiar with an actor's work, as was the case with John Hurt on *Rambling Rose*. He played a major part in the film and never read. However, Chris Sarandon—whom she'd previously cast in *True Believers*—was auditioned because he wanted to play the part of an older doctor, which was a stretch.

Although Chapelle may prefer hiring an actor who fits the part physically, that's not to say she doesn't respect training. "I really think training is important. It just kind of legitimizes our seriousness. I think it's great to see people coming out of Juilliard. I always give them a break, because they went through more stuff."

And the more you work the better, she believes, even if it's doing student films. "They aren't true filmmaking, but they do give you a lot of experience." She cites the case of actor Robert Burke, who beat out some heavyweight names for a major part in *Rambling Rose*. A friend of his apparently talked him into doing a student project in New York. That piece of film wound up in Aleta's hands, and Burke's career was launched. Aleta also advocates furthering one's general education. "Cultivate writing, cultivate dance. I think some of the people who are most interesting are those who are well-rounded. People should work on being a whole person. That makes you a better actor."

Chapelle cautions actors against unscupulous agents. "There are things like 'Faces International' that I think are a big farce and are really insulting and sad. Every time I go into a small town I see these really corrupt agencies where they make people spend thousands on their stupid classes and photographs, and the actors think they're doing something when it's usually just the agent making money off them."

A better approach, in Aleta's book, is to study, work, and constantly send out pictures to agents. That's one of the things she appreciates about the American casting system. In Europe, she says, actors don't have 8x10s to send to casting directors. In fact, they're insulted if someone calls them in for an audition. "You simply sit and have a cappucino with an actor you're considering for a film in Italy, and if you want his picture you may be presented with a two-foot-by-one-foot portrait!

"8x10s, si! Postcards, no!"—Aleta Chapelle hates picture postcards. Expressing an attitude quite different from the majority of casting directors, she believes that "it really classifies you as an extra." If an actor is not in the players guide, he or she is making a big mistake, according to Chapelle. "I think the actors' books are important. It's very convenient for us. I had many late-night calls on *Godfather*," where I had to use those books literally at the last minute."

Not getting anywhere fast? "Stick with it," advises Chapelle. "I don't think acting is the worst job in the world. I think it's one of the hardest things you can choose, but I think if you work as much as you can, it can only make you better."

---

*Aleta Chappelle accepts photos and resumés but no videotapes; she schedules general interviews as time allows.*

# Brian Chavanne

## CHAVANNE/MOSSBERG CASTING

A warning from Brian Chavanne to actors: he knows when your credits are fabricated, and if they are, beware. "I'm just not going to have time for that person." What he's interested in is people who are serious. "If you send in a picture, and you look like you've gone to a good school and have accumulated good regional credits, I'll take that seriously."

Brian goes to a lot of theater and sees a lot of film. If he's impressed with an actor, he'll track him down. "I've done that a lot," he confesses. "It happens in this business all the time. Casting directors find people's agents and vice versa. It's an incestuous environment." If he believes in someone, he'll go to great lengths to help that individual. "I'll even say to agents I know, 'Look, I just found somebody I think you should meet.'" He's also convinced producers to consider unknown talent in leading roles. A case in point: Brian met an actor at the New York Shakespeare Festival. "He wasn't a name, and the producer wanted to get somebody better known, but I knew my job was to help the script get done as well as to satisfy the producer's needs, so I worked really hard to get him this job. They finally gave in, and his performance was just riveting."

Brian is also open to actors' suggestions. If they're brought in for one role, and they ask to read for another, he often complies. "I did a play at the WPA called *Early One Evening at the Rainbow Bar and Grill.* An actor came in for one role and

SPECIALTY:
Feature film, TV, and theater

CREDITS INCLUDE:
"Tales from the Darkside"
*Navy Seals*
*Toy Soldiers*
*Flight Terminal*
*Steel Magnolias*
(New York casting)
Disney TV movies
WPA Theatre
La Jolla Theatre
American Repertory Theatre

25

asked if he could read for the lead. I really didn't think he was right for it, but we let him do it, and he actually got the part. There was just a side of him I wasn't aware of that he revealed. I didn't think of him as a leading man, and he proved me wrong."

Chavanne finds it challenging to cast against type. When he was casting a film for Paramount, one of the characters he was looking for was a stereotypical Italian bad guy, Spike LaLuna. The producer said he wanted a "really mythical" actor, and as a joke, Chavanne at first suggested the Japanese superstar Toshiro Mifune, "because there's something really powerful and larger-than-life about him. We also thought, why not? All we have to do is change the name of the character. You have to use your imagination as a casting director." Chavanne asserts, "Just because a character's name is Frank doesn't mean that the actor has to be Italian."

Training is important to Chavanne, but so are instincts. "It all depends. There are people in television who are well-known, some of whom trained at Juilliard and others who were models and never trained at all. Some just operate on their own instincts. You either know how to do it or you don't." That's not to say he overlooks impressive credentials, especially if it's theater he's casting. "If they've done Shakespeare at a reputable place, then I can bet they're going to be very skillful."

Brian Chavanne shuns cold readings. If he's met someone he feels is right for a part, he'll read them from that particular script. Once he feels someone fits the bill, he then sees if they've done their homework. "Especially if it's relatively new material to the actor, does this guy think on his feet? Is it clear he knows how to make the kind of decisions about what he's doing in a scene?" What impresses Brian the most are actors who really know how to bring the words to life. "Instead of just acting, they understand that they have to create something that seems like real life: conflict in the middle of the scene, all kinds of things going on at once. Those are the actors I have the most respect for."

To Brian, the purpose of casting is first to satisfy the producer's and director's requirements, but second to stretch the limits a little bit and suggest other possibilities. "If you have a relationship with a producer and director that's trusting, then you can take those kinds of chances."

One thing Chavanne suggests actors never do in front of a producer or director is denigrate themselves or let on how they felt about the reading. "Who cares?" asks Chavanne. "I'm not interested in what you think you did. Just come in and do it, and if you were bad, that happens, but you're not going to help anybody—certainly not yourself—by letting us know how bad you did." You can ask to do it again, but he suggests putting it in a more positive light. "The audition," says Chavanne, "is for the actor. It's not for me."

---

*Chavanne/Mossberg Casting accepts pictures and resumés; videotapes and generals only accepted through agents.*

# Lori Cobe

INDEPENDENT

Lori Cobe enjoys casting low-budget films because she has much more autonomy than she would have if the budgets were over nine million dollars. The same holds true for syndicated television versus network programming. "It's a lot of casting-by-committee there," says Lori of network operations. "If you do a sitcom, and you have someone who has one line, you have to bring in twenty people to a bunch of producers who basically sit there and say, 'He's not funny.'"

Working on smaller-scale productions, Lori pretty much controls the shots. For instance, "Wake, Rattle and Roll" called for a punk genie and, observing that there hadn't been many women on the show, Cobe called the producers and suggested casting a woman. Presto chango! "Now, can you imagine a network altering the script like that?" Lori had much the same power on the feature *Body Shot*, where she was able to cast the two leads. At Paramount or Columbia, the stars are usually set before the casting director is even hired.

It's not so much the power as the challenge that is so attractive to Cobe. "I like having actors come in and read. I'd love to see fifty people for each role if I could." Even after all these years of casting, she never tires of meeting new people and discovering new talent. In fact, Lori has a reputation as being one of the nicest casting directors in town. "I just try to make the actors feel really comfortable, because I figure, if they're comfortable, they're going to be able to give me their best performance."

It's Lori's opinion that at an audition an actor should complete his or her reading before chitchatting with the casting director. "I don't want them to get distracted, so I say, 'Let's read first,

SPECIALTY:
Low-budget features
and syndicated TV

CREDITS INCLUDE:
*Body Shot*
*Night Eyes*
"Wake, Rattle and Roll"
(Hanna-Barbera)
"Divorce Court"

and then we can talk.'" She also encourages actors to ask as many questions about the script or character as necessary. If a scene calls for some kind of business from an actor—making coffee, for instance—she would like the actor to ask if he or she should mime it or simply ignore it. "I don't think there are any stupid questions, I really don't."

Cobe is also one of the few people in her field who believes in telling an actor if he's done well. "And, if I'm sure that I'm going to call someone back, I'll tell them."

Although it's not possible to keep every photo and resumé that comes across her desk, she does go through them all, sorting them by character. When it comes time to cast a specific role, she looks through her files, determining if the look is right and then checking the actor's credits. She won't hesitate to cast an inexperienced actor for a minor role, but she rarely takes chances on a featured character. There are occasional exceptions. Lori saw Scott Thompson Baker on "Star Search"; two and a half years later, Baker's manager pitched him for a role in a film Cobe was casting. Lori assumed that Scott had been working his tail off since his "discovery," and was amazed he hadn't had a real break since "Star Search." But despite his lack of experience, she believed Scott could do the job, and she hired him. Not only did he succeed in that role, he went on to greater success as a regular on "General Hospital."

Lori Cobe feels very strongly about minority casting; it stems from her association with one director in particular, Jag Mundhra. "I've done five or six films with him. He's always really aware of that, and he made me aware of it early on."

Just because Lori casts mainly low-budget features, that doesn't mean it's not necessary to be a member of the guild. "I don't do any non-union because I don't know any non-union actors," she admits. She also believes that an experienced actor has developed a technique that's vital to his or her career. "You have to develop some kind of technique in front of a camera. You can tell when you see someone on TV if he's experienced or not. You can feel it." Even though the budgets she works with aren't monstrous, they are significant, and it's rare that Lori has hired a non-union actor. On "Divorce Court" she occasionally was able to Taft-Hartley* someone if it was necessary. She recalls one episode that called for a wrestler. She didn't know many wrestling actors, and when one

---

* An act passed in 1941 that allows a performer who appears on camera for the first time and has at least one word of dialogue to become eligible to join SAG.

came along who impressed her with his reading, she hired him without a card. If Lori feels someone is really good, despite his lack of experience, she may say to the director, "Listen, he hasn't done a lot, but I think you should take a look at him."

This is not to say that Lori Cobe leads inexperienced actors to believe it's easy to break into the business. She often feels it would be beneficial for an actor to be required to work in a casting office for even one week. "Once they see what the odds are of getting a job, then they should make a decision. If they still want to act, then they deserve to. However, if they say, 'Oh God, how am I ever going to compete?,' that should be the determining factor."

Should an actor opt to pursue the craft, Lori has this piece of advice: relax. "The thing I find most comforting," she relates, "is when someone comes in who's relaxed. Maybe because if they're nervous, it makes me feel uncomfortable for them." She suggests a calm and prepared demeanor. She also likes an actor to take chances. "If it's too big I can always say, 'Bring it down a little,' but if someone comes in and gives this flat, boring reading, you're just going to say 'thank you' and lead him to the door."

Another attribute that impresses Cobe is training. "I'd say number one, you have to study." Her sister learned this lesson the hard way. She had begged Lori for an opportunity to read for a role for which she was sure she was perfect. She had no experience but wanted to be an actress. "I said, 'Fine, come in and read,' and I had the director here. Well, I never heard a word about acting from her since. She just didn't realize it was so hard."

Training and experience are why Lori likes an actor to do as much theater and as many showcases as possible. She even helps actors refine their skills at cold-reading workshops. "I'm a frustrated teacher," she confesses. "I love doing this, but I also realize what teachers earn." At her workshops, she'll meet actors, pair them off, have them read the sides she's selected, critique them or give them direction, and have them do it again. She's even hired actors through these workshops. "Casting directors are desperate to find good talent, and I'll go anywhere I can."

If you're going to be in a showcase or in a theatrical production, Lori Cobe wants to hear from you. Not by phone, but by postcard. It's virtually impossible for her to see every play in town, but if your timing's right, you may luck out!

*Lori Cobe encourages outside submissions, but videotapes accepted only if requested; she will schedule generals.*

# Lou DiGiaimo

**B**oth Barry Levinson and William Friedkin rely on the expertise of Lou DiGiaimo, a truly bicoastal casting director. Although the two directors have very different ways of working, Lou seems to be able to adapt successfully to both styles. Levinson, he says, likes to see a bunch of actors for each role, while Friedkin prefers a narrower selection. Lou himself feels it a casting director's duty to pare down the list of potential candidates. He believes any secretary can accumulate a large group of actors to bring to a director, but only an experienced casting director can separate the wheat from the chaff.

Levinson requires a broader selection only because he works in comedy, which is more difficult to cast. Some actors who appear to be funny at first meeting aren't as funny when presented with the material at hand. Comedy takes a special blend of acting ability and an innate humor. DiGiaimo tries to pepper his theatrical outings with occasional comedy club visits, but he confesses that with all the theater there is in New York, it's difficult to find time to explore other venues.

Lou feels that actors are doing themselves an injustice by not appearing on stage every chance they get. He realizes it's easier in New York because there are more theatrical outlets in that city. "I would advise any actor starting out to spend time in New York. Just living in the city helps you grow." He says most actors in New

SPECIALTY:
Feature film in U.S. and Italy

CREDITS INCLUDE:
*The Brotherhood*
*The French Connection*
*The Godfather*
*The Exorcist*
*The Sorcerer*
*Cruising*
*The Guardian*
*Tin Men*
*Good Morning, Vietnam*
*Rain Man*

York are so dedicated they'll create a project among themselves. "Even if a bunch of them are going to each others' apartments and reading, that's training. That's working at your craft." He admits blame often falls on the casting director. In New York, he says, his colleagues are constantly at the theater, but in L.A. they tend to see more movies and television. Thus the actors feel their efforts may not pay off. Why work for peanuts if you're not even going to be seen?

Lou DiGiaimo tries to see as many actors as he can when he's involved with a project. "I'll see as many as time allows, and I don't care about credits." What he does care about is the reading, and if an actor won't read for a part, he won't get it. If an agent claims his client never had to read for any other casting director, Lou simply states that that's not the way he operates.

If he's impressed with an actor, he'll make every effort to obtain a meeting with the director, even if the director may be reluctant. When he was doing *Good Morning, Vietnam,* he immediately thought of Forrest Whitaker, who had previously made an impression on him in *The Color of Money.* Levinson didn't feel Whitaker was physically right for the part, but Lou insisted. "It was just for me and Barry at first, and he was fabulous, but when he thought he'd be reading with Robin Williams at the callback, he was very nervous, and the reading was not good at all." Fortunately Robin was out of town, and when he did show up for a third audition, Forrest had gotten over his case of the jitters and landed the role.

DiGiaimo spotted talent in John Belushi when Belushi had only been on "Saturday Night Live" one season. He brought him in to read for *The Brink's Job* with Peter Falk. The director, John Frankenheimer, was so mesmerized by this talent that he regretted not being able to hire him for the lead. Meanwhile, there was a falling out between Frankenheimer and producer Dino DeLaurentiis, and by the time the new director agreed to cast Belushi in a supporting role, it was too late—Belushi had already signed on to do *Animal House.*

DiGiaimo respects good actors and isn't bothered, as many casting directors are, by props or costumes. It doesn't even matter to Lou if an actor wants to change a couple of lines if it's appropriate. But he does draw the line when it comes to direction. "So many times they don't listen. I understand that if they've read the script they have their own ideas about it, but what happens when you're shooting? What happens when the director comes up with changes, and the actor won't listen?"

He also feels that a really good actor doesn't need to pester him for a role. If an actor continues to hound him for an audition, it will only irritate Lou. If he's going to be harrassed by anyone, he'd rather it be by an agent he respects. "You've got to get an agent who believes in you, and who is going to work for you. It doesn't have to be a big agent, and agents don't get you the part. You get the part, but the agent does get you through the door."

*Lou DiGiaimo will accept photos and resumés but only keeps those of interest for a particular project; no unsolicited videotapes; generals scheduled only through recommendations.*

# Pam Dixon

P am Dixon doesn't read actors—she meets them. The only time she'll do a reading is when a director is on location and won't be able to meet an actor himself. The readings are usually done at the time an actor meets with the director. And Pam says she's generally able to tell if actors will be able to handle the material without prereading them. "It's instinct; it's different ways to play a role. I don't know that somebody is always right or always wrong. I think you pick qualified actors, and they do the part."

Dixon prefers bringing in three or four choices per role, each providing a totally different way of playing that part. She also enjoys casting against type, and looking for unusual choices. Depending upon the project, she'll even cast non-actors, like author Tom Robbins or musicians Neil Young and Tom Petty, in certain roles.

Dixon usually complies with the director's wishes. But when she was working on *Tremors,* she was certain Kevin Bacon and Fred Ward would be perfect, although the studio wanted bigger names. "In the end the studio was very supportive, but we did fight very hard to have them cast." She's even been responsible for a script change due to an unusual casting choice. For *City Slickers* she was asked to find two dentists. Not only did she find two black actors to portray the dentists, but because of their age difference, they became father and son.

Pam Dixon works primarily with agents, although when it comes to casting children, she'll venture into unknown territory. "I've gone to schools, and for *Baby Boom* we had an open call at the L.A. County Museum." There were fifteen hundred kids

SPECIALTY:
Feature film

CREDITS INCLUDE:
*Music Box*
*Baby Boom*
*The Moderns*
*Career Opportunities*
*City Slickers*

at that particular call. "We advertised it in the newspaper and over the radio, and we did the audition in one day, from 8:30 in the morning till 6:00 at night, and we saw everyone who showed up." She finally found her pair of twins at a subsequent open call she held in New York. Pam enjoys casting kids. "I like finding natural children who don't really have much experience, who have not necessarily gone to acting classes. They just have something special unto themselves. That's fun."

When Pam decides to go to the schools to find her talent, she'll usually call the director and tell him what she's looking for, how big a role it is, and they, in turn, will make recommendations. She also looks at any pictures that may come across her desk. In addition, she attends a great deal of theater. That's where she found Frank Whaley, whom she later cast in *Career Opportunities*. "I think he's really special because he's a young character actor as opposed to a great-looking leading man, and I think he has a great future." Trying to pinpoint the charismatic quality of this actor, she adds, "He's very chameleonlike. He can play many different things, and he has a great sense of humor." Humor is very appealing to Dixon. "It's that ability to relax and laugh every once in a while and not take everything seriously all the time."

When Dixon sees an actor in a play, she's rarely concerned about his ability to make the transition to film. "Most of the actors I've met have not taken any special camera courses, and most of them have made the transition very well." She's also against actors paying a lot of money for workshops. "There's a history of people being payed to attend workshops, therefore I do not, and the actors who pay all this money for these courses are actors who really can ill afford it." She will, however, go to nonequity showcases, and encourages actors to try to get into these or other little theater groups so that casting directors can see their work. "Especially today," she stresses. "Almost all the casting directors really do pay attention to the theater, because it's gotten so good in the past five years that it really is a worthwhile thing."

Actors should be aware that most directors don't want to chat at length at auditions. "They just want to get into it, and I think it's better to wait until after the reading to talk. It saves your concentration. When people start talking and thinking about other things when they go into a reading, their concentration has lessened somewhat." Dixon also warns actors not to apologize for a poor reading. "If they don't think they've done well, they should call the casting director aside and say, 'I really didn't feel good about that. I'd like to come back again, if I may.'" Saying something negative in front of a director, she believes, may hurt an actor's chances because the director may not have felt the reading was that bad.

When it comes to casting, the most important thing to Pam Dixon is instinct. "That's what makes each casting director different from the next—taste and instinct. If you line up five of the top casting directors and have one actor audition, you'll probably get five different opinions."

---

*Pam Dixon encourages outside submissions, excluding videotapes; she will occasionally hold generals when time allows.*

# Carol Dudley

## REUBEN CANNON & ASSOCIATES

If you're wondering which of the many facets of your personality would be best suited to an audition, why not create one just for the occasion? So suggests Carol Dudley, for many years an associate of casting giant Reuben Cannon and now branching out on her own as well as maintaining her relationship with her mentor. Carol advises that an actor who is unsure or awkward about the audition process should create a persona with which to audition. "It's just a device to help people beyond those initial stages. Sometimes they're uncomfortable and nervous, and though they may have a wonderful talent, they can't get to it except through a role." She likens this method to her own use of a "phone voice"—since the age of twelve she's had to overcome a block against speaking on the phone. "It's not a persona to hide behind, simply one to open you up."

Carol tries to make her auditions as comfortable as possible. "We try very hard to give an actor as much information as we can, because if you look good, I look good, and if you look bad, at least you get to leave!" Aside from being on time and being prepared, Dudley also advises the actor to listen to direction and make sure he or she understands a scene before reading. "Often the actor is trying so hard to please that if the director gives him a comment only Albert Einstein and God could understand, the actor

SPECIALTY:
Feature film and TV

CREDITS INCLUDE:
*Josephine Baker*
*Bland Ambition*
*The Unholy*
*Perry Mason*
*Amerika*
"Santa Barbara"
"Matlock"
"Father Dowling"
"Alfred Hitchcock Presents"
"Call to Glory"
"Cutter to Houston"
"Moonlighting" (first season)

goes ahead and makes a stab, even though he doesn't grasp the situation at all." If you don't understand, speak up and say so. This also applies to taking time to go out and work on any adjustment the director has made. "Some actors say, 'That's all right,' and do the scene without spending sufficent time on the revision. It's not all right. It just comes from a desire to please."

If Dudley has one pet peeve, it's that actors who feel uncomfortable with the material often don't say anything until they're in the room ready to read for the director. "If you feel uncomfortable, tell me beforehand. Don't wait until you're in the room to say, 'I don't know why I got called in for this role.' That's like saying you don't know why this idiot over here called me in." She often brings in someone not physically suited for a role on the chance that the director may alter the character if the reading is strong enough. So by asking why he's there, an actor may be thwarting his chances at winning the role.

Carol casts mainly from her own files. She uses agents' submissions when her own sources have been thoroughly searched. "Sometimes it's like shooting darts. Agents don't have ESP. They haven't always read the script, and they try to throw darts in the dark, trying to guess what the character is from the brief description in the breakdown." She prefers her own lists and ideas to start with. Then she'll turn to submissions.

She's very impressed with a theatrical background on an actor's resume. "The actor who's taken the time to go back to theater is someone who's filling up the well as well as emptying it. The camera is a wonderful thing, but it draws from you and doesn't offer anything to put back in. I find that actors who balance their careers between the two end up being more interesting human beings, and therefore more interesting actors." She also says the discipline is different in theater, where a director's guidance may be crucial. It's often not there in television, and an actor will play it safe rather than fleshing out a character. "What you find is that if you do too much TV, you stop taking risks. Television is a land of no surprises."

Reuben Cannon discovered Bruce Willis through the theater. He was doing a Sam Shepard play on Broadway at the time Cannon was casting the pilot for "Moonlighting." NBC, Carol recalls, was not thrilled with the prospect of Willis playing the lead. "The women always responded immediately to Bruce, but the network's main concern was that Bruce wasn't man enough for Cybil Shepherd. In fact, they hired casting directors all over the country to put men on tape for an entire week. They obviously came up empty-handed and settled for Willis. "I mean, Bruce. Can you imagine, when he walks in, and he's got that jaunty air and that wonderful quick wit, and he's so funny and appealing, you can't help but like him. But it was in an era where we were still very much into Tom Selleck."

Carol has also been responsible for several important careers. She was casting *Cutter to Houston* when she met Alec Baldwin. It was his first film job, and she was able to get him his SAG card. What attracted her to Baldwin was what she terms his incredible masculinity and risk. "It was also his walk and bearing and his seriousness as an actor. Alec was always someone who was very focused. He was never accompanied by a set of screaming groupies."

Because Carol gets at least thirty pieces of mail a day, she doesn't advocate actors spending all their money on new pictures and resumés. "A simple postcard telling me what you're up to is just as effective," she suggests. "What I do is stick them on my calendar, and I try to watch the show." But if an actor is going to spend money on photographs, she advises a simple, pearlized 8x10. "I liken an actor's picture to a good passport. You don't spend your entire vacation budget on a passport, but if you don't have a passport, they won't let you into the country." It's important to have your name printed on the pictures, she says, because casting directors are only human, and photos and resumés often get separated. "Actors should also have energy in their eyes. I worry about their eyes more than their expression." In order to find a shot that focuses on an actor's eyes, Dudley suggests blocking off everything on the proof except the eyes, and finding the one that has the most energy and the most life. She also discourages spending hours poring over each shot. Casting directors glance at a photo; so should the actor. If it's got energy, it'll pop out at you immediately.

Carol Dudley understands the actor's plight. "If you tell people you're an actor, they say 'Okay, what do you really do?' It's hard to maintain that courage you had when you initially entered the field, because you don't always get validation from others. And unfortunately," she bemoans, "actors spend a lot of time tearing each other down when they need to be supportive."

---

*Carol Dudley accepts photos and resumés but discourages videocassettes; she conducts generals at which prepared material is presented.*

# Sylvia Fay

INDEPENDENT

Sylvia Fay never works alone. Because of the nature of her casting, she always teams up with a colleague, and enjoys the collaboration. Most recently she's worked with Juliet Taylor, Howard Feuer, and Ellen Lewis. While they cast the primary speaking roles, she casts the one-liners and extras. On some occasions, she'll be called upon to pitch in on other roles if the casting director needs assistance, or she may be asked to give an actor who isn't right for a bigger role in a particular feature an assignment as an extra.

Many an actor has gotten a start from Sylvia Fay. Jimmy Walker was picked up for television after doing a bit part for Fay. Another went on to great success after appearing as a mugger on a train in Woody Allen's *Bananas*—Sylvester Stallone! Fay knew he was destined for a big future. "He had the stamina. He had the initiative. I knew someday he was going to get to where he wanted. He was a nice kid."

Sylvia Fay finds much of her talent through open calls, which she holds three or four times a year. She'll see over fifteen hundred people at a single session. "I give them all my wonderful speech, and then collect their photos and resumés. I have a very good memory," she tells actors. "One girl asked how I'd know if she could act. I told her if she were right for something, I'd be calling her. She asked if I actually read the resumés. I said, 'Certainly. That's how I cast.'"

SPECIALTY:
Extras/bits for feature film and TV

CREDITS INCLUDE:
*Billy Bathgate*
*Another You*
*Ghost*
*Goodfellas*
*She Devil*
*Reversal of Fortune*
*Wall Street*
*Tootsie*
*Taxi Driver*
*Moonstruck*
"Law and Order"
"The Equalizer"
"Kojak"

The biggest difference between principal and extras casting is the quantity of people Fay has to deal with. "We do it in bulk," she explains. "I may need twenty well-dressed people for a party scene or a hundred. I try to get as close to the acting situation as possible. If you were a cop, I'd use you as a cop. I try to get as much realism for a director as possible."

When she's casting bit parts, she'll pre-screen the actors and then send them to the director for what she calls "a look-see." If the director is interested, he or she will read them or sometimes meet them right on the set if they're in the middle of shooting a particular film. Because of the limited size of the part, an actor will rarely get more than a couple of hours, if that, to look over the sides. The readings are mostly cold.

Sylvia rarely reads actors for bit parts; she leaves that up to the director. She'll interview actors, however, and jot down notes to file away for future use. The notes may include the actor's type, be it upscale or hayseed, and will usually list any special abilities the actor may have. Fay needs to know if an actor can sing or dance, do accents, stunts, and so on. "If I need a punk, I'm not going to get a square. I'm not looking for 'actors' as much as real people." As far as training is concerned, it's not as vital to Fay as it might be to a principal casting director. "The training they need is to be on the set and learn the camera angles, and as far as acting lessons, they may or may not be a help. Just because people take lessons doesn't mean they're the greatest."

In Los Angeles, extras belong to the Screen Extras Guild, but in New York, both actors and extras are members of the Screen Actors Guild. Sylvia primarily deals with SAG talent. "But if I can't find someone in SAG, I'll go another way. If I do, I'll simply call the guild and ask them for a waiver."

Open calls and generals aren't the only sources Fay uses to find new faces. She's found kids literally on the street. She recalls needing a bunch of rappers. "I found them at flea markets where they were performing. I went to the park where they worked for money." When they found out they were going to be appearing in a film, they were thrilled. They even hoped they'd be able to make enough money to join SAG.

Another venue for Sylvia is the theater, and she'll attend workshops and showcases once in a while. If someone is really special, she'll often turn them over to a principal casting director. She definitely wants to see her "discoveries" succeed. "I have a great eye," she concedes. "And I enjoy it. It's a big job dealing with the guild and with so many personalities. But I must say I've made a big change in extras casting. I want my people to get the best attention on the set, to have the best places to dress and to wait. It's very important to them and to me."

She's seen too many actors who've made the leap from bit players to feature performers to shrug them off as nonentities. She remembers when Danny Aiello and his sons came to her for work just to keep busy, and now they're having to turn offers down. "Danny had the humility and the warmth. He knew what he wanted. He knew it was a business. Don't think for a minute that acting isn't just like being successful in a restaurant or a boutique. They're exactly the same. It's the attention you give that business that will determine your eventual success."

*Sylvia Fay accepts photos and resumés; she schedules generals once every three months.*

# Mike Fenton

## FENTON AND TAYLOR CASTING

Mike Fenton has been a casting director for more than twenty-five years and has had his own agency since 1971. As well as being responsible for casting many films, he is a consultant to many European producers, helping them not only with casting but with recruiting directors and other primary production personnel. He truly knows the business, and he really knows actors and what they go through pursuing a career in the business. In his opinion, the overwhelming majority of actors who succeed are people who-have been educated. "I don't think there's much place in this business for people who've not at least studied the classics," he postulates. "There are always actors who drop in out of the sky and get a pilot though they've done nothing before, and they can possibly have a career for a while. But when the chips are down and they're asked to walk onto a Broadway stage, I think their lack of training will show."

Mike Fenton has a knack for selecting potential stars. It was he who was responsible for giving Kevin Costner the opportunity to read for Kevin Reynolds when the director was casting *Fandango*. Oddly enough, Fenton was not even casting the project; he was merely consulting on the film and knew they were having difficulty finding their leading man. A friend of his at William Morris happened to show him a videotape of Kevin Costner in a one-minute TV commercial for a computer product. Mike was impressed, and asked if he could show it to Reynolds. Reynolds was as impressed as Fenton, and Costner got

> SPECIALITY:
> Feature film, cable TV film, and pilots
>
> CREDITS INCLUDE:
> *Arachnophobia*
> *ET*
> *One Flew Over the Cuckoo's Nest*
> *Back to the Future*
> *Honey, I Shrunk the Kids*

his big break. "Who knows what it is these stars have?" he puzzles. "You certainly can't bottle it. It's just a charisma. An intelligence."

Mike Fenton doesn't read actors. "I can't. I don't have the time. It's up to the agents to make us really aware of actors with whom we should become familiar." But even though he doesn't read actors, he definitely likes to meet them. "If one of the agents with whom we work closely calls and says, 'I have a girl just in from Broadway, and she's a hit,' I meet her." He prefers leaving the reading to the director. "That's what they get paid for. If an agent calls me and says this individual starred in a particular project, far be it for me to pass judgment on that individual."

Work connotes professionalism in Fenton's estimation. "On a given day, any actor can be wonderful. Any actor can be terrible. Some actors can't read well. Should that preclude their being in a motion picture? Not in my opinion." Unlike most casting directors, Mike believes those in his profession insult actors by making them read. "Agents build careers," he explains. "All a casting director can do is recommend somebody."

Fenton also avoids going out in search of an actor. "There are thousands of character actors. If we can't find one among the people with whom we worked, then we don't know this business." He does, however, try to attend films and theatrical productions as much as possible so that when an agent asks if he's seen his client, he can pass judgment intelligently. As for the actors' guides and directories, he only uses them as a refresher to see who's out there.

Fenton strays from the norm in his use of video testing as well. While many casting directors only use videotape when a director is out of town, Fenton will use video and film when a lead character is under consideration. He cites the casting of *White Fang*. "Randall Kleiser and I put people on tape, then film testing was done, and from that the decision was made." Because it's such a costly process, he admits this procedure isn't utilized unless the actor is a major contender. "It takes a sizeable budget to justify a screen test, but when you're looking for the young lead in a film, you'd be well-served to do it." Another case in point is the casting of Ethan Hawke in *Dead Poets Society*.

Mike Fenton is sensitive to actors, and he tries not to schedule readings for the same part at the same time. This consideration, however, is sometimes is difficult to achieve. "When we're pressed for time it's impossible, but actors should know that when they're reading for a part, they're in competition for the job."

His primary advice to actors: "Remember that if you're called in for a meeting with a director, it's because we believe that you have the necessary skills to do the job. We are the actor's friend, not the actor's adversary."

*Mike Fenton accepts pictures, resumés, and videocassettes; he will hold generals when time allows.*

# Steven Fertig

S teven Fertig has had his base at the Canon Theatre in Beverly Hills since the popular *Love Letters* has been in production. He has been kept very busy casting the highly successful play, with two famous actors needed to fill the bill each week. Although he never actually has to audition these celebrities, he does spend a great deal of time making lists and checking the availability of the stars. It's imperative not only that they have name value, but that the two cast each week are compatible, be it Leslie Nielsen and Carol Burnett or Valerie Bertinelli and Judd Nelson. "Yes, the chemistry between the partners has to be right or else it's disastrous." He admits he's been lucky. "There are actors who literally meet each other the day they open, and by opening night they're famous friends."

Fertig finds little difference between the casting of a play and the casting of a film. The only real difference, he says, is that a theater audition will usually take place on stage to see if an actor has some kind of stage technique and projection. "With theater, it's a little more external. With movies and TV, its more internal." But he rarely differentiates between a theater actor and a film actor. "I think training helps, but I also think there's nothing to it but to do it. You get up on stage, you feel comfortable, and you do it. Yes, there's a difference in technique, but a dedicated actor can get that technique. I mean, there are people who've never been on stage before who do major works. There are people who go on stage for the first time and do great."

Fertig is not afraid to hire an inexperienced actor. He did it in *Stand and*

SPECIALTY:
Theater; occasional film and TV projects

CREDITS:
*Love Letters*
*Stand and Deliver*
*Dakota*
*After the Shock*
*The Kissing Place*
*False Identity*

*Deliver.* "The actress actually wrote us a letter saying she heard about the film and knew there was a part for a valedictorian who's very shy and demure. She said she, too, was a valedictorian, shy and demure, though she'd never been in a movie or on television. We thought, what the heck, let's see her, and she came in and got the role." Not only did she do a good job in that film but she went on to do a play, the first one for which she auditioned. "There are just those naturals."

That's not to say Steven doesn't appreciate a good, solid theatrical background. "I think studying is important. An actor should really be able to find a base through study. For instance, a lot of theater stems from basic Shakespeare and even way back to Greek theater. A lot of the stories are the same. A lot of the characterizations are the same."

Fertig attends both Equity and Equity-waiver theater, showcases, and workshops several times a week, and often finds his actors at these venues. What he doesn't like are actors who display their theatrical training like a peacock displays its tail. "There was this guy who came in to read once," he recalls. "I asked if he was ready, and he kind of put his arms up in the air and started doing this breathing exercise, bending over the back of a chair. Nobody really knew if that was a part of the character or the scene, but it didn't fit. He finally got up after about thirty seconds and said he was ready to go. And one of the producers said 'No, you're finished. You're done.' Producers feel this behavior could cost them all kinds of money on the set." If an actor feels he needs to do some special breathing exercise, fine. Do it before the audition, not during a session.

Steven Fertig is impressed with an actor's sense of security. "A lot of actors come in with a kind of desperation about them. They're so desperate to work, to land a part. I think it would be better for them to treat acting as a business. It would make them a little more relaxed and a little more confident." Steven offers a suggestion that seems to work for a couple of his actor friends. "They have computers and actually have a list of every person in the business they've ever met, where they've met them, when they've met them, what they've auditioned for, what the part was, and so on, so that when they're called in a second time for a certain producer or casting director, they can look them up on their computers and have something specific to talk about at the audition."

While some casting directors are adamantly opposed to the use of props, Fertig believes if it helps an actor get into the part, go right ahead. He recalls casting a play at the Pasadena Playhouse one season and being completely mesmerized by an actress who came in with a whistle around her neck, a curler in her hair and a scarf on her head. "I think she even had a phone," he fondly recalls. "It was a little above and beyond what we thought an actor would do, but this was the character." The actress was Helen Slater, and she landed the part. He warns that props can work to the actors' disadvantage, so it's wise to think it over carefully before taking the risk.

An actor's choice is what the process is all about, according to Steven. "A choice is the one important thing for an actor to make. He should feel secure about the choice he's made for the reading, come in and do his best in the two to five minutes he has, and be flexible enough so that if a director says he'd like to see the scene with more intensity or less intensity, the actor can adapt."

Fertig feels an audition should be a learning process for an actor. "I think a lot of actors go into an audition with the attitude that they have to get the role, when they should really look at it as another stepping stone in their career. They go in, and there are some roles that are going to be right and others that are not. If you've just done an audition and felt it wasn't right, learn from it. You just have to go in and do the best you can, then leave and forget about it."

*Steven Fertig accepts photos and resumés, but videotapes only upon request; he rarely schedules generals.*

# Howard Feuer

When Howard Feuer was a student at Emerson College he wanted to be an actor, but as soon as he began working for a producer and watching hundreds of actors audition, he realized acting wasn't for him. "I just didn't have the drive, let alone the ability," he admits. It's not that he didn't give it a shot. He landed a number of small parts, but he felt he wasn't really getting anywhere. It was then that director Gilbert Cates gave Howard the chance to help him cast one of his plays. "I didn't know what the hell I was doing. How could I? I'd never done it, but I got through it." From there he moved on to an apprenticeship with an established casting agency.

"The most difficult part of being a casting director," he explains, "is having to work with directors you may not see eye-to-eye with." This happened to him on *Stella*. He was doing another project for Disney at the time, and he felt a little short-changed because the schedule for the Disney film was altered, interfering with his new assignment. Instead of understanding his dilemma, the director tried to get Feuer fired from Disney, but Disney wouldn't let him out of his contract. "The main problem was the director was indecisive. He didn't like the actors. He couldn't make up his mind. Instead of firing me, he was abusive and immature. When I'd bring key actors to his attention, he simply picked people he knew." Howard realizes now he should simply have quit. "I always had the philosophy that if you're a professional you'll get through it, but I've changed my mind. If someone treats you badly and they're not smart enough to fire you, you should be smart enough to call it quits."

Fortunately, those situations don't happen very often to Feuer. In fact, he's

SPECIALTY:
Feature film

CREDITS INCLUDE:
*The Fisher King*
*Reversal of Fortune*
*Silence of the Lambs*
*Quick Change*
*Dead Poets Society*
*Mississippi Burning*
*Arthur*
*All That Jazz*

so much in demand, he can pick and choose for whom to work from the highest echelon of filmmakers. He has solid working relationships with Alan Parker, Peter Yates, Peter Weir, and Norman Jewison. Working with Jewison on *Moonstruck*, for instance, was especially satisfying; Howard was allowed a great deal of flexibility in the casting of that film. "I thought of Olympia Dukakis. She was a first-rate stage actress at the time. We all knew her in New York. When I met with Jewison, he expressed dismay at the fact that they didn't have enough money to hire Anne Bancroft or Maureen Stapleton for the part, and I thought of Olympia immediately. In fact, I was able to use all these New York character actors I'd known for years." The film, incidentally, was cast in just three-and-a-half weeks, and Dukakis went on to win an Academy Award for her performance.

Feuer has helped a great many actors with their careers. "I was the first to use Meg Ryan in a feature film," he recalls with much pride. "She was a student at NYU, and I was doing the East Coast casting for *Rich and Famous*. We were looking for someone to play Candy Bergen's daughter, and Meg was perfect." And when he cast *Married to the Mob*, he campaigned heartily for Alec Baldwin as Michelle Pfeiffer's husband, despite the director's preliminary reluctance to use this "newcomer."

Despite his ability, Howard Feuer says he would never want a director to leave the casting entirely to him. "Even the tiniest role should be seen by the director. I wouldn't be comfortable with it. A terrific filmmaker has a very specific vision. Even if it means putting an actor on tape and getting it to the director, I like the director to say, 'Yes, this is what I want.'"

Peter Weir knew exactly what he wanted for *Dead Poets Society*. He had taken over the reins from another director, and by the time Feuer was brought aboard, many of the actors had already been set. But it took three months to find Charly, the young student who brings the girls to the cave. Weir wanted all the students about the same age—eighteen. "After seeing hundreds and hundreds of kids, we just couldn't find Charly," recalls Feuer. "We hired people all over the country to put kids on tape for us. None of them wound up in the movie. We had open calls. We went to prep schools; we talked to numerous agents." Then Howard came across Gale Hanson. "His resume said he'd played a waiter in *Zelig*. Well, that was in '83. He said he was only twenty-one. I told him it was okay if he had lied to get in to see me, but now it was time to be honest. He insisted, so I called Juliet Taylor, who cast *Zelig*, and she figured out he must be closer to thirty. So I called him and he confessed, saying he had lied because his agent told him to." Weir was devastated. Although he wanted to cast Gale, he was concerned that someone who blatantly lied about his age might not be worth getting involved with. Hanson was eventually set, but only after Weir spent an entire day with him on location to make sure he was the genuine article. "I don't mind someone lying to get in the door, says Feuer. "But then, be brave enough to admit it."

Since Feuer has a great deal of acting training, he wouldn't dream of hiring anyone else to read with the actors at auditions. In rare instances, however, a director will insist on reading the actors. One such director is Alan Parker. "Alan likes to read with actors in private. I'll bring an actor to him, and he'll insist on being alone with that actor. He then videotapes the reading, so I will eventually get to see the audition, but I'm not allowed to sit in on it. He'll hold the camera and tape while he reads the scene. I think it's because he wants the most intimate feeling he can get with the least amount of pressure on the actor to perform."

Any actor who won't read for a director gets a demerit in Feuer's book. "In New York, most actors have no qualms about reading for a director, no matter how successful they are. Actors there are used to having to hustle for a part. In California, however, actors are often pampered. They never have to do it, and so they don't. They have superlative agents who are very good at protecting them."

Needless to say, Howard was very impressed when Jeff Bridges agreed to read for director Terry Gilliam on *The Fisher King*. "The character on paper reads like a very aggressive New Yorker, so we thought in more ethnic terms. That didn't seem right, so we sought out Bruce Willis or Michael Keaton. They weren't available. Then we thought of a middle-America male to make it more of a Prince Charming fairy tale, and I immediately suggested Jeff." Gilliam's problem with Bridges was that he hadn't worked with American actors very much, and he felt he needed a little more confirmation. "And obligingly, Jeff agreed to read for the part, since he really wanted it. It was so different from what he'd ever done." Even successful actors may have to please the powers that be.

It's very common to find Howard Feuer jetting between New York and L.A. Many of his projects are bicoastal, and instead of splitting the work with another casting director, Feuer would rather endure the jet lag and do the job himself. That's one of the reasons he isn't as accessible to newcomers as many other casting directors are—he just doesn't have the time. He finds himself relying on agents he trusts and on referrals from friends and colleagues. Working on several films a year, he realizes the day may come when he has to face the dreaded job burnout. But so far he doesn't mind putting up with the long hours and tedious cross-country hops. Don't be surprised, however, if you soon see Howard Feuer's name featured more prominently in the credits. He's admittedly on the lookout for a good property to produce.

*Howard Feuer accepts photos and resumés; he does not hold generals.*

# Leonard Finger

Leonard Finger is considered the King of Horror in the casting community. "The business is nothing but associations, and it just so happened that I had clients who were working in the horror field, and I simply kept doing it and kept getting referrals." Does it bother him that he's been "type-cast?" Not at all. "The one thing about it is that it gives me the opportunity to provide work for new actors, to discover people, and that's enjoyable."

Some people might think that horror films require exotic or unusual-looking actors, but Finger is seeking exactly the same people other casting directors are searching for, people with great comic timing and wonderful dramatic ability, and as far as their looks are concerned, he wants pretty faces and interesting character types just as his colleagues do.

There are special skills, however, for which he's always on the lookout. When Leonard is scanning a resume he'll make a note of an actor who can speak an unusual language or perform an unusual feat such as rolling his eyes in separate directions or wiggling his ears. He also has a file of impersonators and actors who are good at creating interesting sound effects. Finger enjoys the flexibility he has with his genre. He can almost always cast against type and create fascinating characters. When he was doing "Tales from the Darkside" one season, he happened to meet an East Indian actor who had a beautiful Kensington accent. "It had a marvelous sort of urbane decadence to it that I thought was really great. I'd brought him in for another project, but I thought what a wonderful twist to cast him as a vampire on 'Darkside.'"

He's not afraid to take chances. "I

SPECIALTY:
Feature film and TV;
occasional theater

CREDITS INCLUDE:
*Monsters*
*Creepshow Two*
*Mixed Blood*
*Forty-Deuce*
*Spike of Bensonhurst*
"Tales from the Darkside"
"Friday the 13th" (TV)

think most people want somebody else to take the first chance. They want to know that somebody else hired an actor, and that the actor didn't get drunk or disappear. To me, if it weren't for the enjoyment of discovery, I'd be doing something else. The enjoyment to me, the fulfilling part of it, is that sense of constantly finding talent and nurturing it, and allowing it to be rewarded. That's what I like most about casting. If I stop taking chances, I might as well get out of the business and open up a store or something."

Leonard Finger sees his role in casting as someone who provides the intervention of reality. He feels that many actors are blind when it comes to seeing who they really are. "When you ask an actor how he felt about an audition, he'll say, 'I felt really good about it.' That's absolutely ridiculous. It's not what the actor feels; it's what the audience feels. It's what the people watching the actor perform feel. It's evocative; it's not self-congratulatory." If an actor is going to judge a performance, he believes it should always be through the responses of others. "What I'm saying is almost in direct conflict with what is a sanctioned narcissism with acting teachers, a kind of acting that I really think is destructive."

As a matter of fact, Leonard is not a proponent of acting classes. Although he admires a well-trained actor, he thinks that many young actors are wasting their money on the majority of classes that are out there. "To me, the best thing you can buy is a directory of all the people working in the industry. Actors should be well-informed and know who's working in the industry, learn the vocabulary of names, because at this point, it's all associations. Training is not nearly as important so long as you can deliver the lines. If you have real ability, it will be cultivated. If someone really has talent, teachers will come to him, whether he has money or not. I've seen that happen time and time again." He also suggests that actors pay attention to what's on TV, in films, and on stage. "See who is like you, who is getting cast, seeing who's doing the casting and what the shows are about. Know what you're selling," he advises, "and learn to market it."

Finger gets a sense of an actor in the first thirty seconds of a meeting. "I think you also get a sense of whether they have ability in the first minute and a half." Therefore, he keeps his auditions short and to the point. "I get the actors to come in, I treat them nicely and don't engage in too much chitchat, because all that does is heighten their anxiety, and I just want them in and out."

During a reading, Leonard expects an actor to be in character, but before the reading, he's looking to see the person behind the mask. He discourages costumes or props. "An actor should convey his character with his acting, not with superficial or external things."

"I'm really a student of the old theater," confesses Finger. He loves plays set in the nineteenth and early twentieth centuries, and he also loves finding actors from the past. "I think that we're a society of fashions, and actors are a fashion too, with people having a moment of popularity and then falling from view. I like to rediscover them." And he did just that with one actress in particular, who was the original Effie in *You Can't Take it With You* on Broadway. He cast Paula Truman in one of his TV series, and she's been busy ever since. Other stars with more familiar names, whose careers were on the slide but who've re-emerged thanks to Finger, include Abe Vigoda, Darren McGavin, Debbie Harry, and Carol Lynley.

He's also made some promising discoveries on the streets of New York. When he was casting *Forty-Deuce* for Paul Morrissey, they found Rodney Harvey literally on the street. "We started talking to this kid and brought him up to my office. We found out he was interested in acting, talked to his mother and got her permission to put him in the film." From there, Harvey got a recurring role on the series "The Outsiders."

While discovering untrained actors may be fun and challenging, Leonard admits he gets most of his actors from the stage. "I like to get people from the theater with training and a real awareness of training. I can't begin to tell you how many people I've gotten into SAG." Finger considers himself a businessman first, and an artist second. "To me, we are accomplices to the director. We are serving out someone else's vision, and I look at it most definitely as a business." And that's exactly how he sees acting. "There are a few artists who manage to struggle through and survive, but there's very little art in what's done today. There are a lot of actors I tremendously respect, but very few are tremendous artists."

Should an actor give himself a time limit in which to succeed? "Of course," recommends Finger. "There's an old Talmudic saying: when three men say you're drunk, lie down." He thinks that actors have to have a cut-off point when they realize their lives aren't going anywhere, and they're not getting what they want out of it. "Because the first and foremost thing is to enjoy one's life, to be functioning, and if that's not happening, it's time to move on to something else."

---

*Leonard Finger accepts photos, resumés, and videocassettes (half-inch only); he conducts generals.*

# Jerold Franks

## ONORATO/FRANKS CASTING

Jerold Franks has just written a book that's an invaluable source for actors. *So You Want to Be an Actor? Act Like One* explains his philosophy of casting and exactly what actors should avoid when trying to get their careers in gear. He has a genuine respect for actors, and paints a more optimistic picture for the 1990s. "Actors have a much better shot today, because instead of going just for the Ken and Barbie look, we're going for all kinds of faces, real faces—interesting, everyday faces." He feels that's what contributed to the success of *Bagdad Café*. "Every face in that picture was a real face." Even Jack Palance was cast in a role originally written for an artistic, romantic type. "The producer and director could not visualize him at all because he usually plays more menacing roles. But we fought and fought and finally got the producer to have lunch with Jack, and the minute they met, he signed him right on the spot!"

Frank really enjoys trying to bring in actors who may not be the obvious first choice. When he was doing an episodic TV show, he recalls having to cast the part of a pimp who was to be a Mafia type. "I changed it to a black actor who looked like an attorney, and wardrobe even dressed him like an attorney, and it worked much better because it was a surprise element at the end of the script."

That is one of the things Jerold finds most challenging about casting. "There's nothing more exciting than having an actor walk in and you can tell by instinct that there's something there. It's extremely exciting, and I think

SPECIALTY:
Feature film, movies of the week, and TV series

CREDITS INCLUDE:
*Bagdad Café*
"From Here to Eternity"
*Fallen Angel*
"Jake Spanner, Private Eye"
*The Sword and the Sorcerer*
"Blind Vision"
"Fame"
"Freddie's Nightmares"
"Vietnam War Stories" (pilot)

that's what casting is all about, always looking for the interesting." He says he found that quality in Mickey Rourke when he was casting a project for Columbia back in 1980. "His agent brought him in. He had never done anything in his life except theater. He didn't even have a union card, but the minute he walked in, there was a sense of incredible energy. I thought he was perfect for the role, so I took him to the producer and director the next day, and while the reading was wonderful, they didn't feel that physically he was the right type. They went, instead, with Robert Ricardo, simply because of his coloring." It was shortly after that episode that Mickey Rourke made a hit in his first feature.

Franks prides himself on his ability to look beyond the facade to the inner actor. He knew there were the makings of a star when he first auditioned Emma Samms. He introduced her to producer Gloria Monty, who was looking for one of the regulars on "General Hospital" and was quite impressed with her reading. She did feel, however, that Emma was too young for the part. Franks felt differently and suggested that with makeup and a new hairdo she could fit the role to a tee. "Gloria said if you feel that strongly, bring her back, and sure enough we brought her back for a second test, dressed totally older, and New York flipped over her."

Franks feels just as adamant about his casting of pilots. "That's why casting directors see so many people for pilots, because someone is the 'perfect' person. You look at any given hit, and you think, 'I can't think of anybody who would have been in that role who could have done any better.'" He cites "The Golden Girls" as a case in point.

His desire for precision has led Franks to cast a variety of disabled actors in roles both for the disabled and the able-bodied. An illustration of the former was casting James Stacey in the role of a Vietnam vet opposite Jane Seymour in *A Matter of Trust*. Stacey, a big star in the 1960s, unfortunately lost two limbs in a motorcycle accident, but thanks to casting directors like Franks, he has had an opportunity to continue his career. Another example was the casting of "Superior Court". "There was a wonderful actress who happens to be blind, and I brought her in to read for a character who was already seated in the witness chair. The reading was so good, the director never knew until the end of the day that she was blind. When he expressed his concern, I explained that she didn't even have to walk into the room. And if you look at the tape of the show, you'd never know. The point is," he adds, "she was a very competent actress. It's the same thing as hiring someone in a wheelchair who sits behind a desk. What's the difference if he can't stand up?"

When Jerold Franks meets an actor, he prefers a general interview to a cold reading. "I'd rather know who they are, and what their goals are, and if they're newcomers just starting out." He also never asks an actor to read at generals. "I don't believe in monologues. I think that somebody could study a monologue for three years, and that's all they know. It's not going to show me anything." He prefers reading someone for an appropriate role, and that's what he does when he calls an actor back for an audition.

Franks frowns on an actor smoking at an audition. "Even though I smoke, I think it's inappropriate." The other thing he cautions actors about is their dress. "I treat this business like a profession because it is, and I don't think an actor should walk in in shorts and a T-shirt. They don't need to go out and buy a new wardrobe. They just need to be clean and neat." Actors should also avoid trying to impress a casting director. "I don't like a cocky attitude. I think it shows a lot of insecurity when someone comes in and pretends to be something he's not. I think the most important thing in a general interview is being who you are. That's what I'm looking for. I want to see who the person is rather than the actor."

He tries to impart to actors that they're perfect the way they are, and there's no need to look around the reception area to see who the competition is. "An actor cannot sit and compare. It's a waste of energy, and they need to put that energy into themselves and the role. Period. That's it!"

---

*Jerold Franks accepts photos and resumés and will look at videocassettes as long as actors pick them up after they've been viewed; he holds fifteen generals a week when not in production.*

# Jan Glaser

O ne of the tools that that many other casting directors seldom utilize but frequently comes in handy for Jan Glaser is videotape. She videotapes actors being considered for both "Heat of the Night" and "Dark Shadows." Taping auditions is vital for "Heat of the Night" because the show is shot on location in Georgia, and the producers and director need to see the choices Jan has provided them. "We like this tape process," she confides, "because you can always refer back to the tapes and ask the producer if he remembers the person he saw last week, and would she be right in this next episode? It provides a reference."

Glaser also relies heavily on the players guides, thumbing through them to find faces that are right for specific parts. Agents are another source of actors, and although she prefers dealing with agents with whom she's had success, she's open to suggestions from any reputable representative. And while SAG actors are her usual choice, she says she will consider anyone who may be right for the role.

At an audition, Jan expects an actor to stick to the script without improvising. "A lot of our writers are very sensitive," she explains. "They don't like their words played around with." She is also against an actor memorizing his lines, preferring him to have the scene in his hands.

Intelligent questions from an actor are appreciated, and Jan in turn will ask actors about themselves and what else they do with their time besides acting. "I'm interested in knowing if they've taken a cooking class or traveled or gone scuba diving. I may need someone with those skills down the line, and it'll stick with me."

What really catches Jan's attention is

SPECIALTY:
TV series and feature film

CREDITS INCLUDE:
"Heat of the Night"
"Dark Shadows"
*Scissors*
*Karen's Song*
*Crazy People*

a sense of humor. That's one of the things that she first noticed about Kirstie Alley, whom she met early on in her career. "There was just something really special about her, a natural, funny quality." It's not beauty that's important to Glaser, it's more of an offbeat quality that captivates her.

What she doesn't like is gum chewing or cigarette smoking, even if it might be appropriate for the character. "It's just annoying to watch," she imparts. She also despises anyone in her office rearranging her desk or asking to borrow a stapler. "I can't tell you how often people come in and ask to borrow a pen to write down their latest credits. Do that," she insists, "in the waiting area or at home." And don't harrass her assistant even if you've been waiting a long time. She realizes it's often frustrating to be kept waiting, but she insists she does the best that she can under the circumstances, and that it certainly isn't her assistant's fault.

Another tip: Make sure your name appears on the front of your 8x10 as well as on your resumé, and keep your pictures up to date in the players guides. Jan discourages phone calls asking for her address or directions to her office; she prefers that you ask your agent for that information or check a directory. If you need to inform her that you're appearing in a play, send her a flyer instead of phoning. Postcards with a photo are appropriate reminders of an actor's whereabouts, while another way to keep in touch . . . well, it may not be quite orthodox, but Jan admits she has an awfully sweet tooth and occasionally succumbs to a favorite dessert.

---

*Jan Glaser accepts photos and resumés but no videocassettes; she attends showcases and conducts seminars when time allows, and schedules generals April to June.*

# Pat Golden

## GOLDEN CASTING COMPANY

P at Golden has a specific method of conducting general auditions. She asks an actor to prepare two contrasting monologues (each two to four minutes long) that should be delivered for the camera as opposed to the stage. To obtain a general with Pat, send in a picture and resumé; if it interests her, she'll try to set up an audition when her schedule isn't unduly hectic.

Golden suggests that when auditioning, an actor should make sure the material selected is within his or her age range. "I get a lot of people who are forty or fifty and pick a twenty-year-old character. That's fine for the stage, but for the camera it just doesn't work."

If an actor makes a good impression at the first screening, Pat will set up a second audition or callback and supply a script to work on. The third stage is a reading with the director. She doesn't expect an actor to memorize the scene. "What's most important," she states, "is that the emotional content of a scene comes across, whatever that is, and that it is conveyed convincingly."

Pat says she tends to cast temperamentally. "So what I want them to do is take the scene, look at it, think about it, and do the best job in the most concentrated way they possibly can." She appreciates intelligent questions from actors prior to a reading. "I'd like to know from their questions that they've read the scene, and the questions are not something obviously on the page."

Sometimes Pat utilizes videotape at the second or third audition, depending on the director. "For instance, I tend to work with Europeans," explains Pat. "I'll work with an actor, spending

SPECIALTY:
Feature film; occasional TV
and theater

CREDITS INCLUDE:
*The Killing Fields*
*The Handmaid's Tale*
*Platoon*
*Blue Velvet* (New York casting)
*Waiting for the Moon*
(American Playhouse)

whatever time it takes, within reason, to get the best tape." She'll then send the tape on to the director to decide who to meet when he or she is next in town.

Due to the changing technological nature of the audition process, Golden suggests an actor take a course in acting for the camera. "It's a matter of delivery," she believes. "If you have a video camera six or seven feet from the actor, you don't need them to shout because the mike is right in their face. It's a different process."

When Pat sits down to cast a movie, she looks through the wealth of pictures that are either submitted through agents or sent by unrepresented actors. "I read those pictures. I can't explain it, but I try to read past the airbrushing, past the touch-up, and into the eyes and temperament of the photograph." The resumé is also important to Golden: what they've done, what characters they've played, where they've performed, what they've studied, where and with whom. "Not that somebody's going to be eliminated if they haven't studied. Karen Young is a perfect example of that. I cast her in something a long time ago when her picture came across my desk. No agent. Literally almost nothing on her resumé. But she looked right. I read that photograph, and I said if she looks like this picture when she comes in, she's probably got the part, and that's exactly what happened."

Looking like the character on the page isn't always the criterion for Pat. When she was casting *The Handmaid's Tale* she immediately thought of Elizabeth McGovern for the part of a woman who, on paper, came across as a strong, no-nonsense, probably quite plain character. Having worked with McGovern on *Ragtime*, she knew this skilled actress could handle the role, and McGovern really wanted to do it.

Pat Golden finds actors in all sorts of atypical situations. She recalls having attended a wedding in Oxnard when she met Haing Ngor of Cambodia. Since she'd brought her Polaroid along to photograph the bride and groom as a wedding present, she decided to take Ngor's picture and see if he was as photogenic as he was interesting in person. "And the photograph jumped. I don't know how to explain it." He had no acting experience, and when she asked him to come in for an audition, he didn't. "I had to track him down twice. I was just too curious to let him slip by. When I finally did persuade him to come in, it was just like the photograph. I'd met thousands of Cambodians who'd walked to the Thai border to escape, but none could translate it into the words of the script the way he could. He just had a gift for it."

It's obvious Pat Golden gets a kick out of her work. "I think of casting as detective work most of the time, and other times—because I believe in leaving no stone unturned—I think of it as fishing." In fact, the logo on her checks is a fisherman. "You cast out the rod to *Back Stage* or Breakdown Services, you see who bites, and you reel it in. I also believe in casting with a wide net. I put the net out as wide as I can and see who gets caught in it, just because you never know what you'll find."

*Pat Golden accepts photos and resumés, but no videocassettes; she will schedule generals as time permits.*

# Peter Golden

## VICE PRESIDENT OF TALENT AND CASTING, CANNELL PRODUCTIONS

"Part of what got me into this business," confesses Peter Golden, "is my awe of actors. I think there's something magic about them. I don't know how they do what they do." Golden does know one thing about successful actors, and that's their commitment to their profession. "The one thing I see about actors who come in and don't ever seem to really make it is their lack of commitment to acting. They'd love to be a star and make a lot of money, but when it comes down to going to the Ashland Shakespeare Festival or going to Louisville or taking classes, forget it."

Golden conducts his interviews in his office at Cannell Productions. He tries to get audition material to actors at least one day before they're scheduled to come in to give them a chance to read the script with someone else. "So the first time they come in, it's not the first time the words have come out of their mouths with another person there." As for the material utilized at an audition, Peter prefers selecting the script. He often opts for cold readings to judge whether an actor is able to listen and respond, especially at a general.

Golden sometimes spends a good deal of time with an actor to find out about his or her background, but if he's short on time he'll merely read the actor, jot down a few notes, and move on. Actors seen by Golden are recruited from agents, files, and the *Academy Players Directory*. "I go through that guide constantly," he explains, "so I always recommend that people somehow get into that book." He also says he goes through all his mail and looks at every picture that comes in. So if an actor wants to submit a new 8x10 or drop a line to let him know he's appearing in town, the timing may just be perfect to be brought in for an audition.

SPECIALTY:
TV series

CREDITS INCLUDE:
"Wise Guy"
"Dream Coast"
*Seize the Day*
"WIOU"

Even if he's pressed for time at an audition, Peter appreciates an actor asking questions about the character or material. "I wonder sometimes if people come in and don't ask a question, how they could possibly have any sense of what's going on. It makes me crazy," he adds, "when someone reads a scene and says to me later, 'By the way, is this a comedy or drama?'"

What the actor wears is unimportant to this casting director, but Golden does appreciate some modicum of respect. An actor's attitude is vital, too. "I don't like seeing people who come in desperately trying to please me, because what I'm looking for are people with a very strong sense of themselves, a sense of confidence. If they're desperate, it often comes out in their performance."

But Golden stresses that an actor should take every audition seriously. That, he says, is the hard work, and the payoff is often unrewarding, but it's a primary part of an actor's life. He recalls actor John Rubenstein telling him that he loves what he does so much that he'd perform free; his salary really goes to pay for the grueling work of the audition.

If you audition for Peter Golden, you may be one of four reading for the part—or four hundred! He sets up two or three people every fifteen minutes, and he hopes that after seeing about seventy actors, he'll hit the jackpot. "Sometimes I'm lucky and it's less, and sometimes it's a lot more." Golden recalls a casting session he did for "The Dick Van Dyke Show." "We were looking for the wife of Barry Van Dyke, and we had 750 actresses read for the part. There were a lot of good readings, but no one really clicked until finally, it was the last person who came in."

Golden seeks to cast minorities in roles that are not necessarily written for any specific ethnic type. His concern dates back to his days on "The Bill Cosby Show," when Cosby asked him to bring in a mix of people simply to talk about their acting careers. "He sat down and asked them what roles they were used to playing, and they all, without exception, mentioned gang leaders and hookers and such. Cosby said, 'We're not going to do that here.' If there was a role for a pregnant woman, a doctor, any part like that, we'd instantly think, 'How can we get an Asian or Native American for this?' It was a real challenge." And that's the way Peter Golden operates today.

*Peter Golden accepts photos, resumés, and videocassettes; he schedules generals when time allows.*

# Jeff Greenberg

**INDEPENDENT**

Jeff Greenberg advises actors to do their homework before coming in for an audition. He's not impressed by an actor who comes in to read for "Cheers" and asks, "What kind of a show is this?" He appreciates questions that are integral to the script at hand, and doesn't like questions that have already been answered by the text.

Jeff suggests that actors look as much like the character for which they're auditioning as possible without actually dressing in costume. If you're reading for a nurse, for instance, a uniform is unnecessary, but a starched outfit would be appropriate. Attitude is much more critical to him. "I like them to be themselves. Whatever energy they bring into the room is their own energy. That's very helpful to me."

When Greenberg sets up an audition at Paramount, the actor is requested to pick up the material prior to the reading. The actor then either reads with Greenberg or with one of his associates. Jeff may provide some adjustments, or he may simply thank the actor, make some notes, and bring in the next candidate. He tries very hard not to keep actors waiting interminably, and schedules his readings far enough apart in hopes of preventing that.

Greenberg doesn't use Breakdown Services very often. He puts out a breakdown for one out of about thirty parts, and many of those are for children. The fact is, Jeff knows so many actors from his many years in the business that it's not necessary for him to recruit talent. "For example, if I need someone to play a doctor on 'Cheers,' I know a lot of people, and I don't need to put out a breakdown to get people in." He adds, however, "If I need an Elvis imitator who can also speak Spanish, I need to put out a break-

SPECIALTY:
Feature film, TV series, and theater

CREDITS INCLUDE:
Look Who's Talking
Top Gun
"Cheers"
"Wings"

down because I obviously don't know enough of those."

Jeff does appreciate getting ideas from agents. "We're in constant communication," he acknowledges. "A lot of them call to see what's coming up, and as I talk to them about one project, I might mention, 'Oh, by the way, there's another part coming up on this show on this date, if you have any ideas.'" Jeff also utilizes the players guides, checking them daily. "An actor is foolish," he believes, "if he's not in those guides." He doesn't discover new talent leafing through the pages, however. He says he mainly uses them as a reference when an agent mentions an actor with whom he isn't familiar.

When Greenberg is casting a role, he may not read any actors at all until he's ready to bring them in to meet the producer or director. That, again, is due to his knowledge of a vast array of actors. But there are times, he admits, where he's had to audition hundreds of actors for a particular role. "We just added a new character to 'Down Home,'" he cites. "It's a sixteen-year-old kid, and I read about 250 till I found the best ones to bring to the producers."

Casting against type is often part of Greenberg's method. "If you cast too much on the nose, there are no surprises. You know what that character's going to do. It's like hiring Tony Perkins to play the killer. There's nothing fresh about that." If it's hiring a minority actor to fill a role, Jeff is adamant against stereotypical or quota casting. "I want to make it really mean something," he stresses. "I want to give the actor a part that has some meat to it as opposed to a one-liner. That smacks of tokenism to me."

What makes an actor right for the role to Jeff Greenberg is his connection with the material. "He enhances the material in a way that seems to be coming from him viscerally as opposed to off a page." He is impressed when an actor can create a person rather than a written character. Kirstie Alley is a prime example. When he saw her read, he knew she was right for "Cheers." "I knew there were very big shoes to fill when Shelley Long left the show, and it needed to be an actress of power." Alley was it. It was a combination of her looks, her humor, and her reading. "I just knew her to be an actress to take big chances, and it was a very big chance."

"Star" quality to Greenberg is a combination of talent and a sense of danger. "It's who they are in life, and when they translate it into the role they're playing, they bring an aliveness to it that makes it special, unique, and riveting."

---

*Jeff Greenberg accepts outside submissions including videotapes; he will schedule generals when time permits. He uses union and non-union actors.*

# Karen Hendel

## DIRECTOR OF CASTING, HBO/NONEXCLUSIVE

Karen Hendel was responsible for several prominent actors getting their SAG cards, including John Malkovich, Amy Madigan, and Julia Roberts. Talent and confidence are primary considerations to this casting director; it doesn't matter whether or not the talent is union—she'll Taft-Hartley them.

The single most important piece of advice Karen would like to impart to actors is to avoid setting themselves up as victims. "If you come in as a victim," she explains, "I can tell, and so can most casting directors. If you come in so scared you don't have any freedom, you can't possibly act." She feels that the basic problem most actors have is thinking "this" job will save their lives or change their lives. "Don't come in desperate," she stresses, "and don't come in with a chip on your shoulder because you don't like auditions."

Hendel is convinced that about 70 percent of the job is the audition. She believes that an actor looking for validation is simply missing the mark. "This is not a business for personal validation, because most of the time you're going to be rejected. That's just the nature of the business." Hendel hopes an actor can get involved with outside activities so that the audition isn't the most important thing in his or her life. "There are too many variables," she says. "We do not make personal judgments at an audition. It's a choice the director makes. Maybe there are already three blondes in the film, and I cannot go with another blonde, or maybe it's something in the script where you have to look Italian or be forty years old, or you have to look like the woman who's already set to play your mother. There are so many things to take into consideration, and an actor has to understand that."

SPECIALTY:
Feature film and TV movies

CREDITS INCLUDE:
Turner and Hooch
Dead Man Walking
Fatal Vision
The Last Innocent Man

Hendel hopes that actors will ask questions at an audition so that she can get a sense of who they are and make them feel more comfortable prior to their reading. "I often find it rather shocking when someone doesn't have any questions. The actor who comes in and says no, he has no questions, nine times out of ten doesn't know what he's doing."

Karen Hendel relies mainly on agent submissions, and she says she looks through every one that comes in, "which, I would say, for a two-hour movie is probably about 3,000-4,000 pictures." What she looks for on a resumé are credits and training. Karen has taught acting at UCLA, so training to her is a vital part of an actor's duty. Doing as much theater as possible also shows her just how devoted actors are to their craft.

If an actor refuses to pre-read for Hendel, she'll refuse to bring him in to read for the director or producer. "What most actors don't seem to understand," she says, "is that every time I bring an actor in to see a director I'm saying I think this person is viable for the job. I'm not going to put my reputation on the line by bringing in somebody whose work I don't know." And if an agent says his client doesn't pre-read, Hendel simply responds, "Then your actor doesn't see the director."

Hendel's auditions often take longer than ten minutes, because she feels it her duty to get what she needs out of an actor. As for the number of people per role, she tries to limit it to eight. And she does not expect actors to memorize the audition material. In fact, she prefers that they don't: "You're giving the wrong message to the director and the producer, that it's a finished performance." She suggests, instead, that an actor be very familiar with the material, but always hold that piece of paper in his hand. "You may forget the lines—why give yourself that added pressure?"

The Hendel dress code is strictly untheatrical. "I take it as a personal insult if somebody comes in wearing a costume. That's telling me they don't think I have any imagination. If you're playing a lawyer, I don't need to see you in a suit. I've had people who have read for me for army roles who've come in in full camouflage. It turns me off!"

Another thing that turns Karen off are cold reading workshops. "I don't think cold readings have anything to do with acting," she postulates. "If an actor has some problems auditioning and goes to cold reading classes thinking he's studying acting, he's fooling himself. He's not. He's studying how to audition, which has nothing to do with acting. They're separate issues."

Karen Hendel finds casting against type a wonderful challenge. She was responsible for casting Ruben Blades and Danny Glover in *Dead Man Walking*, which was originally conceived for two white actors. She also suggested Lou Gossett as the cowboy in *El Diablo* instead of a Ben Johnson or Richard Farnsworth clone.

If you want to reach Hendel, there's no better place than on stage. That's where she expects dedicated actors to be, practicing their skills. "Would you expect Perlman to get on stage without having done his scales for the last six months?" she asks. "An actor, too, has an instrument, a physical, emotional body, and you have to take care of it like you would a Stradavarius."

---

*Karen Hendel usually does not accept outside submissions; she will view videocassettes, but she rarely grants generals.*

# Marc Hirschfeld

## LIBERMAN/HIRSCHFELD CASTING

It's not important to Marc Hirschfeld if actors have an agent. "If they're right for the part, I'll hunt them down and find them." A case in point: Wayne Kennedy, a stand-up comic from Chicago. "I called him up and said, 'You don't know me, but I hear you're really funny. I hear you might be right for a series regular on '227.' If you're interested, would you put yourself on tape?' I sent him the script. He taped it and sent it to us. We ended up flying him to Los Angeles for a test option." While he didn't get the part, he did get an overall deal with Columbia for his own show. "It's an emotional and financial investment for some actors, but I think if you seriously want to be considered for the Los Angeles market, you have to be willing to take risks. Otherwise, you might languish in Boston or Cleveland for a long time."

What Marc is looking for from an actor is confidence, intelligence, and a well-rounded character. He's also always on the prowl for an inventive and original actor. Taking direction is a prime requisite as well. There have been instances where a producer has changed a role to suit the script, and an actor who can't be flexible will simply wind up being replaced by a more accomodating talent. Hirschfeld believes most actors want direction, but some who are more insecure take it personally. "If you take it personally, then become a director, not an actor."

He also cautions actors against changing lines during a reading. "Usually the producers you're auditioning for are writers, and writers

SPECIALTY:
Feature film and TV

CREDITS INCLUDE:
*Phone Calls*
*Pulse*
"Fame"
"The Wonder Years"
"Alien Nation"
"The Seinfeld Chronicles"
"Alf"
"It's Gary Shandling's Show"
"The Days and Nights of Molly Dodd"

are very sensitive about their words. Each word is individually placed, just so, and actors who come in and rewrite it get comments like 'If I wanted a writer, I would have hired one.' " He does admit, however, there was one instance where a producer was so impressed by an alteration an actor made in the dialogue, he asked, 'If we don't hire you, can we buy that?'"

Marc also feels an actor should make decisions before coming into the room, and not ask the director whether to sit or stand or move around. It's part of an actor's choice, just as his or her interpretation of the character is his or her own choice. Hirschfeld will consider an individual with raw talent, but he prefers dealing with a trained actor. "You can see raw talent, but it's either going to take experience, outright auditioning time after time, or some serious study to fine-tune and hone that talent."

When he cast the original "Married With Children," several cast members had little television experience but were trained in the theater. He spotted Katie Sagal in a play at the Pasadena Playhouse, and when Sam Kinison turned down the role of Al Bundy, Marc thought of Ed O'Neil, whom he'd seen at the Hartford Stage in Connecticut doing Lenny in *Of Mice and Men*. O'Neil was the complete antithesis of Kinison, but his "gentle giant" quality really intrigued Marc, and when he brought him in to read, "He just kicked butt!"

Not only does Hirschfeld frequent the theater in New York and L.A., but he visits San Francisco, Chicago, and Dallas to scout talent. He also attends the League Auditions in New York featuring the graduating classes of Yale and Juilliard, and is invited to Northwestern for its graduating class performances.

While Marc has little time for phone chats with actors, he does appreciate them sending in a postcard letting him know if they're appearing on TV or stage. And despite the frustrations actors may feel facing one rejection after another, Marc advises them to leave it all behind at an audition. "Just go in there and win the part. Don't second-guess yourself or say, 'Oh my God, I'm one of ten people sitting out in the hallway.' Producers aren't thinking like that. They want to cast the role. They have better things to do than sit there and read actors. You just have to go in there with the attitude, 'Well, I'm the one!.'"

*Marc Hirschfeld accepts pictures, resumés, and videocassettes; he rarely schedules generals.*

# Judith Holstra

**INDEPENDENT**

J udith Holstra's advice to actors at an audition is simple: be professional and try not to impress her with personal quirks. "Some people," she relates, "come in and want to let me know who they are in all aspects of their lives, and that's just not fitting to the situation." It's not that she doesn't care, she says, but she doesn't need that kind of information. "What I need to see them do is the character they have in their hands." She respects intelligent questions pertaining to the script, "but I don't like it when people come in and say, 'Who is this person, tell me about him.' It's the actor's job to decide who that person is. If they don't have enough information, they can read the script."

Judith always tries to provide actors with the material before their audition. Scripts may be picked up ahead of time so that the actor can work on it and feel as comfortable with the material as possible. She believes it's vital for actors to see how they fit into the entire scenario. "I like them to be totally prepared. It's also time-saving."

Holstra will often see hundreds of actors for a project, even if there aren't many characters to be cast. "I think we saw thousands of people for 'thirtysomething' between L.A. and New York, and there were only about six roles." When it comes down to reading for the producers she limits the selection to about five for a TV movie, perhaps a few more for a pilot.

Casting against type is another Holstra trademark. On *Streets of Fire*, Amy Madigan was brought in to read for one part and wound up playing what was origi-

SPECIALTY:
TV pilots, cable movies, and feature film

CREDITS INCLUDE:
"thirtysomething" (first year)
"Capital News" (pilot)
*Cold Sassy Tree*
*Baja Oklahoma*
"My Life and Times" (pilot)
*Pump Up the Volume*
*Great Balls of Fire*
*48 Hours*

nally written for a Hispanic man. "The character was Mendez," recalls Holstra, "but I couldn't find anybody, and I knew Amy would ask to read for the role. They loved her, so they changed the character's name so that she could play it."

When it comes to hiring minorities, Holstra tries to bring in as many ethnic types as possible, although she says it's often an uphill battle when dealing with certain agents pushing their Caucasian clientele. Working with Michael Apted on "My Life and Times" was a treat for Judith, since he truly encouraged minority casting.

Holstra takes agents to task when it comes to submitting her casting list to Breakdown Services. "I sometimes wonder why I do it, because I find that the agents don't always think high enough in terms of who they represent. I have to call them up and talk them into the people that I want. They send me their hopes and wishes as opposed to *my* hopes and wishes." Fortunately, she has her own lists that she works from, and more often than not, it's from those lists that she casts.

What Judith Holstra is looking for is someone who has real, solid technique and who brings something more to the role than is what is on the page. "I see hundreds of readings that are fine, but there's nothing special about them, and I'm always looking for that something special." She found it with little Samantha Mathis, who came in to read for *Baja Oklahoma*. Julia Roberts wound up with the part because Samantha was just too young at the time. "But she stayed in my mind, and every time I'd read a script, I'd think of her." She was brought in to read for *Great Balls of Fire*, and then came *Pump Up the Volume*. "Samantha was in Europe," Holstra relates. "But I knew she was the part. We saw everybody, and I kept saying, 'There's this one girl, maybe you'll like her.' She finally came in, not knowing anything about the part. I practically got her right off the plane, and she was it! Everyone thought she had read the script."

What is it about these particular actors that makes them unforgettable? "There's almost a different light about them," muses Holstra. "It's as though their skin literally glows. They radiate an energy, an aura, if you will. I think it's what people call star quality." She adds that if an actor has that particular quality and learns to act on top of it, they're set.

The most unstarlike quality an actor can have, in Judith's opinion, is a neediness. "I think that's the thing that turns me off the most. It's a need for approval and attention. It upsets me because I

74

feel that I should be doing something for them other than what I'm doing, but it also detracts from what they're doing. We want to see a professional, confident, prepared actor." Of course, there are exceptions. Holstra fondly remembers an actor who desperately wanted to be seen, and though he overstepped his boundaries, he landed the part. "He jumped over my secretary's desk and ran into my office. He had very few credits at the time and really wanted to read. I wasn't there, but when I returned and heard about how desperately he wanted the opportunity to audition, I called him in. It just so happens it was exactly in keeping with the character, and so he got the part." That was Allen Autrey, now a regular on "Heat of the Night."

A better way to attract Judith Holstra's attention is to do theater or SAG showcases. She attends these events as often as she can, and hires a lot of talent from them. To keep in touch, a postcard is always well-received, but please, no phone calls. "I really keep good records," Holstra assures actors. "If you want to say hi, just drop me a card."

---

*Judith Holstra accepts pictures, resumés, and videocassettes; she conducts generals occasionally.*

# Billy Hopkins

## LINCOLN CENTER THEATER

Billy Hopkins has been casting long enough to know whether an actor is talented the moment he or she walks into the room. "I just know, believe me. I've only been wrong once. The actress was great at callbacks, but once we got into rehearsals, she couldn't handle it. That's not to say there haven't been actors I've cast who weren't good, but I was aware at the time that I was taking a risk."

It's because of Billy's insight that he prefers to meet with actors rather than have them read for him right away, and he never asks actors to come into his office with a prepared monologue. "I don't need to see that. I consider myself different from other casting directors in that I much prefer talking to people about their families and where they grew up than about acting."

Hopkins will set up a meeting with an actor if the picture catches his eye or if an agent suggests the actor for a particular part. If the person seems right for a specific role, Billy will then set up an audition. If he's impressed with an actor but there's no appropriate role at the moment, he'll keep him in mind for the future. Although he says he doesn't discriminate between film and television actors, he admits there are some who have a hard time auditioning for one medium if they're used to reading for another. "A theater actor can act in any medium if he's a good actor, but there are some film actors who couldn't act on stage if their lives depended on it, because they don't have the technique or the training." He laments the fact that there are so many good theater actors who

SPECIALTY:
Theater and feature film

CREDITS INCLUDE:
Jacob's Ladder
Desperately Seeking Susan
Fatal Attraction
Wall Street
Born on the 4th of July
The Mambo Kings Play Songs of Love
Speed-the-Plow
The Cherry Orchard

don't get nearly enough work in film because of their looks. "They're not considered pretty in the Hollywood sense."

Hopkins will hire actors he's seen on stage even though they may not be "pretty" or may have little camera experience. He loves New York stage actors and has helped many a career blossom, including that of Laurie Metcalf. "We saw her in the theater and then we cast her in *Desperately Seeking Susan*, as well as a number of films since then." Another actress who owes her start to Hopkins is Ellen Barkin, whom he hired for an Off-Broadway play over ten years ago.

Billy usually reads with the actors at auditions. If the production will pay for a reader he won't object, since he admits he is not an actor. "I do think an actor should be able to read against anybody, though I often think that we can be more helpful than a reader, who may sometimes throw an actor off." Actors will usually read only once for Hopkins, followed by a callback for the director. If Hopkins knows an actor's work, he'll probably skip the first reading and send the actor on to the director right away. "I work differently with everybody. Some directors like to see everything on tape first. I know, for example, that Clint Eastwood never sees anybody in person. I don't cast for him, but he supposedly does it all by tape."

Hopkins isn't against the use of videotape for audition purposes, but he does think that not all directors are equally adept at using it. "I worked with one director recently who hardly read anyone. He just had me film the meetings with the actors, and he would simply call in the actors he was interested in and do an improv with them based on a situation that had nothing to do with the script. I think it is possible to cast that way, but only if you trust your instincts. I mean, that's what casting really is."

Hopkins feels he has more autonomy on a film than he has with a theatrical project. "Many times, with the smaller parts, the stage director will simply trust you, but when it comes to the bigger roles, they'll often use the same people over and over. At Lincoln Center, we have a whole company of actors we use time and again. When I'm doing a film, the director usually wants new faces, and you have to keep looking until you find the right ones."

But Hopkins enjoys researching his films. He does it all the time when working for director Oliver Stone. "I knew nothing about Jim Morrison or the Doors before I started working on the Morrison project. I never listened to music as a child, but within a couple of weeks, I knew everything there was to know about them. You do your homework." Billy made sure he studied the Stock Exchange before tackling *Wall Street*, and he made frequent trips to a veteran's hospital while researching *Born on the 4th of July*.

Authenticity is important to Hopkins. He will often cast real people in certain roles, such as attorney William Kunstler in *The Doors*, Abbie Hoffman in *4th of July*, and several financial people in *Wall Street*. "You have to balance it, though, with experienced actors, because you cannot cast a movie with only real people and expect it to be professional."

When Madonna was cast in *Desperately Seeking Susan* she had never acted before, and when she did *Speed-the-Plow* it was her first time on the theatrical stage. "She loved David Mamet's work, and her audition was just as good as anybody's. In fact, the girl who took over the role was equally good, and she was an unknown actress named Felicity Huffman."

Casting someone based on ethnic suitability is somethink Hopkins finds disagreeable. Kevin Kline portrays a Cuban in *Mambo Kings*. "I think Kline is brilliant in the role," says Hopkins, "and you ultimately go with the best actor, no matter what nationality he is. The whole controversy over Jonathan Pryce in *Miss Saigon* was ridiculous. I was a little disappointed in Brad Wong, who put up all the fuss. I brought Brad in for a movie that wasn't written for an Asian, and I never thought twice about it." For *Jacob's Ladder*, Hopkins brought in Elizabeth Pena to play the lead, even though the part was not originally intended for a Hispanic. "The other major contenders included Julia Roberts and Madonna. It was actually considered a risk when we cast Pena in the role."

Billy Hopkins likes to think of himself as a man who takes risks, and he's well-respected for the risks he takes. He, in turn, respects actors and encourages them to take chances too. If there's one thing he appreciates most, however, it's tact. "I always remember an actor who says thank you."

---

*Billy Hopkins accepts pictures and resumés; he schedules generals as time allows.*

# Phyllis Huffman

## VICE PRESIDENT, WARNER BROS. TELEVISION CASTING

**P**hyllis Huffman has a very definite feeling about casting. "I think that the really important thing about casting is creating a place for the actors when they come in to audition. The actor should know that he or she is the most important person here, and that the atmosphere is created from the minute he or she steps off the elevator and comes into my reception area." She makes every effort to let actors know that her office is a welcoming, tranquil place, and that she wants them to get the part. "When someone comes into the inner office to meet the director and producer, it's my job to make it as nonthreatening as possible so they can see whatever it is that they have to see in a very short amount of time."

It's not that she feels superior to other casting directors, but Huffman is aware that it's a very powerful position, and that some casting directors tend to take advantage of that. "I think that the people who don't really give a lot of thought or understanding to the idea that it's really about producers and directors get sort of carried away with this power." She admits that the casting process can be a terribly hectic, nerve-racking business with a lot at stake, but after being in the business for so long, she's learned to take the frenzy in stride to a certain extent.

Phyllis Huffman makes sure an actor has sides in hand before the audition is scheduled. "Then he'll come

SPECIALTY:
Feature film, movies of the week, and pilots

CREDITS INCLUDE:
*White Hunter/Black Heart*
(New York casting)
*Ratboy*
*National Lampoon's Vacation*
*Xanadu*
*The Betty Ford Story*
*North and South, Book One*
"China Beach" (pilot)
"Murphy Brown" (pilot)
*Triptych* (Mark Taper Forum)

in, and if I don't know him, like at a general audition, if I haven't seen him work or haven't read him before, I'll have him read for me before meeting the producer or director. We would just read the scene together, and then I would decide if I thought he should come in and read for the others."

Because she lets actors know the script is available ahead of time, she expects them to be well-prepared. "I think that's the best thing an actor can do for himself. The competition is fierce. The volume of actors is staggering. As an actor, you get one shot when you walk in the door." The rest of the impression an actor gives is about who that person is. "There's a sense of confidence that comes in the door with an actor, and that comes from an actor who's been studying, who's been up on his feet in a class or in different situations—somebody who takes it quite seriously and works at it, even when he's not at an audition or professional situation. That brings a confidence to an actor."

Huffman finds her actors through the usual channels: pictures, directories, and agents. But she also makes use of her invaluable assistant, who scours the New York theater. "She has this gift. You could line up maybe ten people whom nobody knows, and she could always pick out the good one. She's at the theater every night." That's how they discovered John Finn. "Olivia had brought him to me a year before he got cast as the Irish drill sergeant in *Glory*. We used him for a bit part on "Hawk," after seeing him do some little play Off-Broadway." Of course, there are times when Phyllis will think she's discovered a winner, only to find she's been gravely mistaken. "It was my first pilot at Warner Brothers in 1982. I had just been made vice president, and I went over to CBS with five fabulous actors to play the third lead in 'Murphy Brown.' It was an enormous part. This one fellow was wonderful at the auditions, better than all the others. I don't know what it was, but when we saw the dailies, he was terrible, and the worst thing about it, it was a comedy!" That experience taught Phyllis a valuable lesson about comedy, something Juliet Taylor keeps in mind all the time when she's casting with Woody Allen. An actor must make you laugh without even opening his mouth or he's not really funny. "This one particular actor could be funny, but the script didn't call for people who could be funny—it needed funny people."

Authenticity is a big plus with Huffman. "If you go back to the people who just sort of knock you out, in every case they're the genuine article." She cites Marg Heldenberger of "China Beach" as an example. "Her agent really kept after me and after me to see her. I always liked her, but she wasn't number one on my list. When I finally brought her in, at the persuasion of her agent, I was wowed and immediately brought her to the producers, and they hired her right on the spot." It wasn't just her authenticity, although that quality was there, but it was what Phyllis calls her "grit" and her amazing versatility. There are some actors Huffman would never think twice about bringing in for either a pilot or feature film. But there are others whom she feels are right for either one medium or the other, not both. "I think their persona may not be big enough for film. They're just not good enough. You've seen many people who've tried to make that crossover from television to movies, and for some reason they just don't hold up on the big screen." That doesn't mean they're not good enough for smaller roles on TV. "That's the nature of television. You do settle a lot. The way television eats people, you can't always get quality."

Working with Clint Eastwood on most of his films has made up for the occasional disappointments of TV casting. "We've worked together for so long. A couple of times, I've just shown him one actor, and he has such terrific casting sense, he's said, 'That's it!'" To Eastwood, film is a very visual medium, and Phyllis says many times he'll opt for just a feel or a look about an actor as opposed to a great intellectual, accomplished, technical actor. He's very much aware of what the camera picks up, and even if he's casting a number of "bad guys," he'll insist that each has a distinctive, dramatic look about him. "So that they don't get confused. He's very conscious of that, and it's really fun, going out of our way, often sacrificing a great actor to hire someone with this terrific look. As soon as the camera's on him, you know what's going on."

Phyllis Huffman appears to have the best of both worlds: major film projects and quality television pilots. Does she prefer one medium over the other? "No. I know a lot of people who form a pecking order: feature films and then television. A lot of people disregard television, but I like it. It's fast, it's very diverse, and there's an enormous amount of energy that goes into it."

*Phyllis Huffman accepts photos, resumés, and videocassettes; she conducts general interviews.*

# Jane Jenkins
# & Janet Hirshenson

## THE CASTING COMPANY

It's likely that if Rob Reiner is directing a film, he'll be calling on Jane and Janet to cast it. They've cast every single movie he's done since *The Real Thing* except *Spinal Tap*, which he cast himself. The Casting Company is also the first choice of directors Francis Ford Coppola and Ron Howard. As you might imagine, they're a very busy office, casting at least five major films a year.

When Jane Jenkins admires an actor, she remembers him and is not reluctant to use him time and again, provided he's right for the role. Patrick Swayze is a prime example of her loyalty: she has cast him in *Skatetown U.S.A.*, *The Outsiders*, *Red Dawn*, *Grandview U.S.A.*, and most recently in *Ghost*. *Ghost* was a different vehicle for Swayze, but she considered him because he was "passionate for the part. After a great deal of persuasion, Jane was finally able to convince the producers to give him a shot. "They'd thought of him as a jock with no intellect whatsover. I kept saying, 'I've known Patrick for a long time, and there's a sweet, gentle soul there.'" The producers ultimately agreed.

Jane and Janet were also

> SPECIALTY:
> Feature film, TV movies, and pilots
>
> CREDITS INCLUDE:
> *Curly Sue*
> *Only the Lonely*
> *Ghost*
> *Air America*
> *Godfather III*
> *Parenthood* (film and TV series)
> *When Harry Met Sally*
> *Mystic Pizza*
> *Willow*
> *Tucker*
> *Beetlejuice*
> *The Princess Bride*
> *A View to a Kill*

responsible for casting Whoopi Goldberg in the same film. "I auditioned 105 women," recalls Jane. "Whoopi seemed an obvious
choice from the day I read the script, but the producers wanted to
see if maybe there was somebody else out there. So I tried to fulfill
the possibility of finding the perfect person, and granted, though I
discovered some very interesting actresses in the process, ultimately it was Whoopi."

The Casting Company has very specific ways of handling the
auditioning process. For starters, Jane and Janet don't like cold
readings and make sure an actor has his sides at least one day
before the meeting. They'll generally chat with the actor for a few
minutes before a reading, although they admit there are times an
actor is so into character it's better to simply proceed with the
audition and chat later. They do hope, however, that actors will ask
questions before commencing a scene, especially if they haven't
had a chance to see the script. "They may not even know if it's a
film or a sitcom or what," states Janet. "They have to know the
medium they're dealing with, so it's vital to ask." If an actor is
afraid to ask the casting director, they suggest inquiring with the
receptionist, who usually has the answer.

Jane's pet peeve at auditions is the prop. "I hate props. I had a
kid in recently," she reflects, " who brought in a bottle of Pepsi and
a bag of potato chips and opened the bottle, spritzing it all over
everybody. Then he opened up the chips. They went flying. There
was no way to recover, and everybody just sat there mopping up
the Pepsi and feeling like idiots." This was a callback for a lead on
a network TV show, and this incident certainly destroyed any
chance for this young man.

Jane and Janet also recommend that actors keep their pictures up
to date in the players guides. "It seems people aren't putting their
pictures in the directories lately," bemoans Jane. "Every time I try
to look somebody up, they're not there. I think actors should get
their pictures in, especially if they're up and coming." The Casting
Company not only uses the guides to check on specific actors, they
also use them to come across new and interesting faces for upcoming projects.

They also rely a lot on videotape. "Working with Ron Howard,"
explains Jane, "there's no other way. He lives in Connecticut, so we
audition everybody on videotape, and he looks at it. When he
comes to L.A., he lets me know which ones he wants to meet."
They'll occasionally even resort to expensive screen tests when the
role is important enough. "We used it on *Ghost* for Tony Goldwyn,

the actor opposite Swayze and Demi Moore, because it was the biggest part he'd ever done, and we thought we needed to see what he was really going to look like on the big screen."

Although it's not necessary to dress for the part at an audition, Jane and Janet prefer an actor who's neat and professional. Jane recalls her first meeting with Julia Roberts during casting for *Mystic Pizza*.. "She really didn't understand the part. She looked like a slob. I told her to go home, read the script, and come back the next day and try it again." Fortunately for Julia, she was given that second chance and aced it. It was her first feature film. What impressed Jane and Janet about Julia Roberts and other young actors they've discovered, including Michael Keaton, is their apparent training. "Talent is something from God," Jane believes. "But then actors who've been well-trained to channel that talent become indispensable."

"Be yourself," advises Janet. "It is an intimidating process, but it's often your only shot." Jane's and Janet's philosophy, borrowed from friend Ron Howard, is that 90 percent of the actor's work is getting the job. They feel that the audition is the work process and getting the job is the reward. "So you come in and do the best you can do," suggests Janet. "You do your best work right there at the audition in an environment that's hopefully conducive to bringing out your best work." And you might as well get used to it, because, adds Janet, "I don't think you ever stop auditioning."

---

*The Casting Company accepts pictures, resumés, and videocassettes; they will schedule generals when a picture "really grabs them."*

# Caro Jones

**INDEPENDENT**

Caro Jones has been gainfully employed in Hollywood for the last thirty years. She started her career in television, casting such classic shows as "Love American Style," "Petticoat Junction," and "The Beverly Hillbillies." Today she's as busy as ever, concentrating on feature films with such notable directors as Dan Petrie, Jr., John Avildsen, and Joe Sargent.

Things have changed a lot over the three decades Caro's been in the business, but the biggest change was the institution of Breakdown Services. "It's changed casting drastically, especially here in Hollywood. It's opened it up to a lot of unqualified people." Whereas, in the old days, casting directors had to create their own breakdowns, today, she believes, virtually anyone can submit a script to Breakdown and simply wait for agents to engulf them with photos and resumés. Jones, however, still prefers making her own lists and scouting for talent. "I still think there's no substitute for going around and seeing actors work."

Not only has the system changed immensely, but the technical aspect of casting has also evolved over the years. "The electronic world we live in has changed a great deal. We put 99 percent of the actors on tape today. We tape our interviews rather than bring actors back four or five times to read for us." Of course, not all casting directors use videotape to the extent Caro Jones does. She tapes everything. "I do it for all the roles I cast, both in town and on location. Eventually the director meets with those actors he's seen on tape and is considering for a role. It saves

SPECIALTY:
Feature film and TV

CREDITS INCLUDE:
*Toy Soldiers*
*The Promise*
*Rocky* (I and V)
*Karate Kid* (I, II, and III)
*King*
*The Martian Chronicles*
*I Know Why the Caged Bird Sings*

them the tedious process of elimination: I do it for them."

While most casting directors discourage actors from memorizing their sides, Jones thinks it's in their best interest to do so. "First of all, it's impressive to the director. It shows that you think enough about the part and enough about your work to spend that extra bit of time and energy on the material. Also, if you don't have a script in front of you, you're going to do a better job. There's just no substitute for it." Caro makes sure an actor has access to the sides or script hours before the audition. "That's one of the rules of the Screen Actors Guild, but people don't take advantage of it. An actor can ask, and if a casting director won't deliver it to you, you can always go to their office and read it."

When it comes to a substantial part in a film, Caro insists on actors reading the entire script before an audition. "How can you possibly do a motion picture without seeing how your character fits into the whole story, and how can you expect to fully understand the character unless you've read through to the end of the script? A good film actor has to know where he's going, otherwise he can't do his job." Jones always employs a reader at her auditions. She expects actors to relate to that reader as they would to the actor to whom they're playing on camera. If there's action involved, the actor may be required to display his skills. Since Jones casts many features focusing on physical dexterity, such as *Rocky* and *Karate Kid*, she expects an actor to be prepared to show off muscles or physical agility.

"I think a lot of actors suffer dreadfully from nerves when they get to a really big audition, and that's something they have to learn to cope with," Jones emphasizes. "It's important to try to get as calm as you can without losing your energy." Energy, she feels, is vital to an actor's performance. Without it, the performance is dead.

If an actor feels he's gotten off on the wrong track during an audition, Caro suggests he or she ask to start over. "My camera person will be glad to run the tape back and start again. A lot of people feel they have to go through the audition to the bitter end, even if they're unhappy with their performance. You have to use your time to your best advantage, not try to be all things to all people."

Jones is most impressed by actors who constantly try to improve their readings. She recalls Patrick Dempsey's audition for *Can't Buy Me Love*. "We were pretty well down to the wire, and I think we had him back five times, and put him on tape every one of those times, but I'll tell you that each time he came in, he brought something new to the role. He never just settled. He added more.

A lot of actors," she says, "figure if they did something right the first time they better do it exactly that way again. But if the audition was absolutely perfect, then why would I have to call you back? We've got to see something more. You've got to go back into that part and find out what you can add to that character."

While Caro Jones truly believes talent is an inborn quality, she definitely feels camera training is a must. "An actor has to learn how the different media work. You've got to keep up your technique, and when you're not working, classes are vital." If an actor doesn't know where to turn, she suggests asking other actors, or finding out with which coaches the actors they admire studied. For young actors starting out, she encourages training, along with auditioning for as many good agents as they can find. "Just call them and say you'd like to audition for them. Agents usually hold auditions once a month. You have to get an agent. It's almost impossible to function without one."

Jones casts a lot of young talent for her films, and they are the toughest challenge she faces. She'll often hold open calls to give actors a chance to display their merits. When she was working on the film *Gladiators* she held two open calls, one in New York and one in Chicago. From the nearly one thousand hopefuls, she put 215 on tape. "We had a huge staff, two cameras, twenty-five Guardian Angels, four readers, and several people showing the actors where to go and giving them their sides." Out of the hundreds seen, about 75 percent were eventually cast in the film. "It's the joy of discovery that thrills me the most," she confesses. "I love finding a real talent and helping to nurture it. I think that's why most of us are in this business, because we get excited by it, by contributing to the artistic process that goes into making a film."

There are times Caro may make a suggestion to a director, and the director will turn it down. It can be frustrating to a casting director, but then again, it can be quite satisfying when that actor goes on to stardom. Such was the case many years ago when Jones was casting for television and tried several times to get Warren Beatty considered by the producers. To no avail. "They kept turning him down, and he gave brilliant readings and everything." She ran into similar roadblocks with George C. Scott and Alan Alda. "You can't let it get you down, because all those people have been turned down. I think it's just a fact of life. If you want to be an actor," advises Jones, "you have to work extremely hard to learn your craft, to learn every aspect of it. Hopefully you have a natural talent to go on with it, but if you don't, you just have to work harder. You must be prepared for a lot of rejection along the way, and the rewards have to mean so much to you that you want to take that risk. Because that's what it is—it's a risk every day."

*Caro Jones accepts photos and resumés but no unsolicited videotapes; she rarely schedules generals.*

# Lynn Kressel

Lynn Kressel has the distinction of being the first casting director to win an Emmy. The award was presented to her for her work on *Lonesome Dove*, a miniseries that entailed a cast of some ninety actors, of which Lynn was responsible for about eighty or so. As with most films, the major stars were set before the casting director was even brought aboard. But it was the supporting cast that caught the attention of the Academy of Television Arts and Sciences. It was one of those perfect blends that contributed to the overall success of the production.

Kressel recalls her work on *Lonesome Dove* with deep affection, and is proud of her "discoveries" such as Chris Cooper who played July Johnson. "He was an actor who came out of New York. That was one of the reasons I was hired, to make it a bicoastal cast, and bring in some unknown actors. Glenne Headley was another unknown who's now on her way to a successful career." But Lynn refuses to accept all the credit. "It's clearly the director's vision. Ideally there's a good relationship and process that happens between a casting director and a director, and what a casting director does is try to make the director aware of the possibilities." That was indeed the case with *Anastasia*. The producers were thinking of hiring Nastassia Kinski for the title role, but Kinski apparently wasn't well, and they needed an alternate choice. That's when Kressel suggested Amy Irving, who wound up portraying the romantic heroine.

Kressel got her start working for Andy Warhol in New York.

SPECIALTY:
Feature film and TV

CREDITS INCLUDE:
*Drop Dead Fred*
*Twins*
*Teenage Mutant Ninja Turtles*
*Lonesome Dove*
*Anastasia*
*Playing for Time*
"Law and Order"
"Kate and Allie"

She helped him cast *Bad*. "I cast that film out of an ad agency I was working for at the time. I loved casting interesting and offbeat faces and personalities. Negotiating the deals was amazing," she recalls. "I'd call up Andy and say, 'This actor wants this credit, and that one wants that.' He'd say, 'Well, what do you think?' I'd say, 'Well, I think that would look peculiar,' and he would say, 'If it's peculiar, I like it.'"

Lynn has worked for directors who like to be surprised as well as those who are extremely rigid. "The most interesting directors to work for are those whose minds are open, who can see possibilities in different actors." After talking with the director, she'll start showing him or her three to four people for each part, trying to correspond to what the director has asked for. Then she'll bring in another couple of actors who are not quite to the director's specifications, as a contrast. Sometimes they'll buy the offbeat approach, other times they'll stick with their original intent.

The only difference Lynn finds between casting for features and casting for television is the availability of actors. She says it's easier to get talent for theatrical releases than for movies made for TV. There's simply more money in features, and it's still considered more prestigious. "It's the availability of actors, convincing the agents the script is good that's the hardest part of my job. I have to make sure it's the kind of atmosphere that's conducive to the actor in terms of meeting with the director, and then making sure they'll be available for the shoot."

But as far as the actors are concerned, Kressel feels any actor she would hire for a TV project, she would feel equally comfortable bringing in for a feature film. "I consider the actors I use of the same caliber in both media. Absolutely. They're just interesting characters. There's a complete crossover."

Lynn feels it's often easier to convince a director to go with an unknown name for a feature than for a television project. "Oftentimes feature directors will take greater chances with unknown talent—they don't have to play it so safe, since TV executives aren't involved."

She's been able to get many undiscovered actors their first credits through her inexhaustible search of capable talent across the country. She put Matthew Modine in his first film, *Private School*, back in '83. "There was no doubt in my mind that he had star quality. There are just people you know who are destined: stars waiting to happen." Julia Roberts came in to read for Diane Lane's part in *Lonesome Dove* before her first feature was released. Why didn't she get the role? "It wasn't my decision. I think she would have been wonderful."

Casting against type is a common Kressel practice. When she was casting the pilot for "Law and Order," she remembers seeing the part of a mayor's assistant in New York written for a white preppie. She decided to bring in Courtney Vance, who transformed the white preppie into a black preppie, and that's how it eventually wound up on the air.

Lynn Kressel is rather flexible when it comes to auditions. What actors wear, how they behave, whether or not they memorize their sides are not her concern. She does feel that asking too many questions of a director may frighten him or her into not hiring the actor, and that a positive frame of mind is preferable to a negative one, but she would rather not place any restrictions on an actor. There is one thing, however, that leaves a sour taste in her mouth, and that is an actor who refuses to read for a director. "Any actor who really wants the part will read for it," she believes. She heard that Glenn Close agreed to read for *Fatal Attraction*. Lynn will sometimes have to convince an actor to read, which she doesn't enjoy. "It means the actor doesn't really want the part." She recalls an audition she attended on Broadway for *Once in a Lifetime*. Meryl Streep was there. "It wasn't her best audition, but she was hired, because the director could see behind the reading. The most important thing about the process of casting is keeping one's mind open. Consider the possibilities you have, and be willing to talk about stupid ideas. You begin to arrive at the ones that might be really interesting and wonderful, to find the surprises that make things special. That's what it's about—possibilities, exploring. It's about having the confidence and wisdom to look at anything."

---

*Lynn Kressel accepts photos and resumés but no videotapes; she schedules five or six generals every week.*

# Elizabeth Leustig

Elizabeth Leustig has learned much from actors, and is sensitive enough to their plight that she follows their lead in her casting methods. She used to try to break the ice with actors by chatting with them before the audition, until one outspoken actress informed her that their little discussion had completely blown her concentration and she couldn't easily get back into character. From that day on, Leustig decided to save the getting-to-know-you routine until after the reading.

But chitchatting is important to Leustig. "I talk with actors about anything that comes up. I just want to learn what each person is about: energy, personal tastes, what makes them tick." This communication goes on not only at the audition itself, but also during the general interview she'll set up if she hasn't met an actor before.

Elizabeth goes through all of her submissions, looking carefully at the pictures and resumés to decide which actors to bring in either for an interview or an audition. She also frequents the theater and sees most of the films that have achieved some degree of recognition in the industry.

Leustig is sensitive to actors who need to do several takes before delivering their best reading. She even encourages talent to try again if they're not comfortable with the first delivery. "I like them to do it their way with no input from me first, just to see what they come up with, their own ideas. Then, if they deviate from what I want or need from the script, I tell them and we redo it. As long as the actor commits to whatever he or she is doing, even if it's not the right choice, I'm interested. I

SPECIALTY:
Feature film

CREDITS INCLUDE:
Dances with Wolves
Shag
Frances
A Night in the Life of Jimmy Reardon
Scenes from a Class Struggle
in Beverly Hills
The Bear
China Moon

usually find that if the person is interesting, he or she is going to do an interesting reading, even if it's not the one I need." Through this method, Leustig hopes to discover the actor's ability to take direction.

As for memorization, Elizabeth leaves that decision up to the actor. "If the actor is going to end up looking at the sides and never glancing up from the page, then that person should really learn the lines, because he or she has to communicate, and we need to see the face. But other actors can give a good performance even with a piece of paper in hand. So it's up to them."

At callback time, Leustig usually winds up reading with the actor for the director or producer. In the case of *Dances with Wolves,* however, director Kevin Costner preferred reading with each actor. "He was great," she recalls with admiration. "He'd get down on the floor with the actor when the scene called for them to be sitting. That's unusual. It's more common at a reading to sit in a chair or walk around. A director doesn't usually get as involved as Kevin did, which I think is fun for the actors." Costner, she adds, was as concerned about the one-liners as he was about the more extensive roles, and he read with the day players as well. Sometimes he would see several actors for a specific part and hire someone immediately. At other times, he would ask Leustig to keep looking, after he'd seen a number of faces that didn't quite fit the bill.

The only time Elizabeth Leustig didn't get involved with the total casting of a picture was when she was hired by Paul Bartel for *Scenes from a Class Struggle in Beverly Hills.* Bartel had already decided on the majority of his cast by the time Leustig was brought aboard. That arrangement didn't bother her, though, since it wasn't a reflection of the quality of her work.

What does mean a lot to this casting director is the ability to find the perfect person for the part, which she did so admirably when she brought River Phoenix to the attention of the director of *A Night in the Life of Jimmy Reardon.* "It's difficult to find that internal quality in children. There are so many children who can act but who can't be genuine, and then when you have to add more complicated emotions, as in *Jimmy Reardon,* it's a momentous task."

River Phoenix was one actor Leustig can say had "star quality" when she met him. But what exactly is star quality in her book? "It's several things: a presence and a commitment. It's important for me that people dare to make their own choices and go with them, expressing who they are. I like intelligence and a sort of presence. You have to want to watch them." Physical attributes are not part of her definition of a star. "You have people like Dustin Hoffman who are powerful. To me, it's a matter of the inner personality and a fantastic skill."

She definitely encourages actors to hone their skills on stage. "That's where you get to work on material, rehearse, and be in front of an audience. It's a training ground and also a place where you can explore another way of working. It's not chopped up like a movie. You can also have access to other kinds of characters. That's the number one attraction, another way to express yourself. It's also a place you may get to be seen by a casting director, and that's obviously helpful, but I think the main point is that the theater is another avenue in which the actor can exist."

It's not that Leustig won't hire an actor without extensive training. There are times, as in *Dances with Wolves*, where training is irrelevant. In fact, she and another casting director, who was handling the extras, were sent to South Dakota to scout real people, not actors, for the film. "It was like going on an adventure. It meant going to a sweat lodge and taking part in some of the Indian ceremonies, trying to understand their culture and how they function." They found it fascinating, but also a bit intimidating. "One night we were on top of a hill and we discovered we were the only people for miles around. We'd just started learning from our Indian friends about the ghosts, and we kind of freaked out. It's not a situation you usually encounter when you're casting!"

Even when Leustig isn't specifically asked to find minority actors to play certain roles, she's always hoping to steer away from typecasting. She cites *China Moon* as an example. "I changed a couple of parts that were written for men. I told the director there was no reason these parts couldn't be done by women. So we hired women to portray a gun salesperson and a hotel clerk—roles originally intended for men." She doesn't blame the director, but feels it's merely an oversight. "They're usually very open. It's just that they haven't thought about it. But if you put it in front of their eyes and show them the lack of balance in the script, they're more than willing to comply."

To the actor, Elizabeth Leustig advises, "Be yourself." She despises actor who try to ingratiate themselves. "That's not where your energy should go," she warns. "Your energy should go into your work, and if you do a good job, that's what's going to impress me."

---

*Elizabeth Leustig accepts photos and resumés; videotapes accepted only upon request. She schedules generals as time allows.*

# John Levey

## DIRECTOR OF CASTING AND TALENT, WARNER BROS. TELEVISION

**J**ohn Levey likes actors, and he's known to have given many actors their first roles. "Upstairs, here at the casting administration," he explains, "they sometimes call me John 'Taft-Hartley' Levey." That's because John often hires non-union talent, first-timers he discovers from his extensive file of pictures and resumés, local theater, and his dealings in the community. Because "China Beach" required young people in their late teens and early twenties, John could not always rely on established actors. And many minority actors, including Vietnamese, were sought by Levey for "China Beach." He says he established a working relationship with the Vietnamese community in Los Angeles, which assisted him in his talent search.

John Levey not only hires minorities for minority roles, but he enjoys casting women, ethnics, and the disabled in parts not necessarily written for those specific types. Levey prides himself on being more than a "list-maker." "I hate the concept of type," he says. "I try to find a human being, who embodies the qualities that the scene and the character require, and I try to go as far in it as the material will let me. I want rich people in my stories." John cites as an example his casting of Dana Delaney as Colleen McMurphy in "China Beach." "The character was written for a flaxen-haired midwestern beauty, but Dana got the job because of her heart and her eyes. She certain-

SPECIALTY:
TV series, miniseries, and TV movies

CREDITS INCLUDE:
"China Beach"
"O'Hara"
"Head of the Class"
"Witches of Eastwick" (TV series)

ly wasn't what anybody was looking for, but she was the first person I thought of."

John Levey conducts his casting sessions in a fairly routine way. He expects actors to conduct themselves in a professional manner: to be on time and prepared. That is not to say he expects them to have the material memorized. That's up to the actors, he says. He does expect them to ask any questions pertinent to the part, and he'll ask them questions to try to get a sense of their personality and their sense of humor. "I try to play with them a little to see if they come back at me with anything. I might challenge them, or I might flirt with them or whatever to try to get a sense of them." Levey may also ask about their previous experience or training.

As for dress, John is pretty flexible, although he counsels, "If you're playing a district attorney, it's probably not a good idea to come in in a bathing suit!" But, he adds, it's really not necessary to dress in a nurse's uniform to read for a nurse. It's not what you wear that impresses John Levey—it's that elusive attribute called charisma. He recalls the time he and his associate, Patricia Noland, were looking for a love interest for Dana. It was a very demanding part that took weeks to cast. They had seen nearly seventy young men before Tom Sizemore walked in; he had been sent over by his manager. "I had been at a meeting, and when I came back he was leaning up against Patricia's desk with a cigarette dangling from his mouth, sort of blowing the smoke in her face, which she hates normally, and she was looking at him like he was the cat's meow." He wasn't handsome, he explains, "but he was using his sense of humor, his audaciousness, and his confidence to take control of the room, and I knew he had the qualities that we were looking for."

Levey believes acting is about accessibility, identification, and sexuality. An audience, he posits, wants to be able to feel what the actors are feeling. "It takes a kind of openness and also a kind of enthusiasm for being a human being. I think you've got to love people to represent them in stories," he adds. "And I think if you do, it comes through, even if you're playing horrible killers or people in conflict. If you can embrace and express the humanness of the person, then you're likely to be very exciting to watch."

If you want to reach John Levey, don't phone him. "I hate phone calls—I don't have time for them," he insists. If an actor has something professional to communicate, such as his latest theatrical gig or a change of agents, he'd prefer a note. Will candy help? No way! "If I have a bribery point," quips John, "it's quite higher than a piece of candy!"

John Levey is most proud of his work on "China Beach." "It was instrumental in making my reputation and the reputations of lots of people in lots of areas." He's grateful to John Young, the executive producer, for giving him the opportunity to cast the critically acclaimed series. "I was happy as hell to work for him. Every day."

*John Levey accepts pictures and resumés but no unsolicited videotapes; he rarely schedules generals. He does not attend casting workshops, but prefers to attend theater.*

# Meg Liberman

Meg Liberman is a product of show business. She grew up in a family of show people. Her father was a press agent who at one time handled the career of the young Patty Duke; her mother, Pat Harris, was a well-known casting director; and her aunt Radie Harris was a columnist for the *Hollywood Reporter*. But while she was firmly planted in the middle of Hollywood, Meg never really understood actors or acting. When she finally chose casting as her career, she decided she'd better do something about this gap in her education. The necessity became all the more clear when she was interviewing a young man prior to his audition. "He sat down, and I started having a conversation with him. I wanted to chat with him and get a sense of who he was before he started reading, but after our conversation, he basically lost his entire preparation for the scene. That's when I realized maybe I should study acting, because I didn't have a clue as to why he found it difficult to get back into character." Liberman immediately enrolled in acting school. "I studied every Monday and Saturday evenings for two years." It never became a livelihood she herself was interested in, but the classes greatly improved her understanding of what actors go through in their quest for gainful employment.

She's especialy interested in young actors, since the shows she casts call primarily for children and young adults. What bothers Meg the most are the "stage mothers" who often push their youngsters into

SPECIALTY:
TV series

CREDITS INCLUDE:
"The Days and Nights of Molly Dodd"
"The Slap Maxwell Story"
"Fame"
"The Wonder Years"
"Parker Lewis Can't Lose"
"It's Gary Shandling's Show"
"Good Sports"
"Alien Nation"

show business careers even when the kids themselves aren't very enthusiastic. "I've seen children dragged to auditions simply because their parents wanted to be actors," laments Liberman, who recalls her casting days on "Little House on the Prairie." "I saw hundreds of mothers all the time and thought I was going to lose my mind!" That's not to say some kids aren't ideally suited to the profession. There are the exceptions, the Fred Savages of the world, who Meg feels are gifted actors, and whose parents are instilling the proper values. "I don't think Fred Savage has a clue as to how much money he's making." She only hopes those youngsters who pursue acting get out when they don't want to do it anymore.

"The Wonder Years" is a real challenge for Liberman. Having a star such as Savage poses a dilemma—anyone hired to play opposite him must be special, too. "It's especially hard to find young girls. Fred is such an amazingly in-tune kid, to find girls who can interract with him on his level is an incredible task." Liberman has done quite a few talent searches to find her youthful casts. "I've done open calls. I always look under every rock. What has been most disappointing lately are the schools. I haven't been as successful finding talent there as I have in the past."

The major stumbling block is the high quality of the shows she casts. "The level of work that I need is really strong on 'The Wonder Years.' It was different on 'Fame.' If we found a fabulous dancer or singer, then we could just sort of walk them through the acting, and if they were really honest with themselves, they'd listen and take direction." Liberman is quite capable of coaching children through auditions. "That's not necessarily what my job is, but a lot of it comes down to that. You've really got to break it down for them and take the time, which is a lot of what was done on 'Fame.'"

Meg remembers one of the open calls she conducted in Los Angeles for "Fame." There were five thousand actors who showed up. One of them was Jesse Borrego, an actor she feels should be doing the roles that have recently gone to Lou Diamond Phillips. "He was one of the first people to read, but he failed to put down a number where we could reach him, and there was no way to contact him. So we put an all-points bulletin out on the radio to find him. Luckily, someone heard it and found him. He happened to be a student at Cal Arts." Out of the five thousand people, he's the only one she hired for the show. Borrego has since gone on to do "Fresh Prince of Bel Air" and to land a development deal with NBC. Madonna, who also auditioned at that open call back in '83, did not get cast, nor did Paula Abdul.

A good lesson to those who have been on the receiving end of numerous rejections: don't give up if you feel strongly about your profession. Persistence is the key, or at least one of the main keys to success. "When I was a casting assistant," Liberman recalls, "this kid used to come in all the time, and he would annoy me to death. He was so persistant. It was Steve Guttenberg! He was always showing up, dropping off a picture, trying to get in to see people. He never got in to see anyone in our office, but he was kind of charming, and I gave his pictures to the people for whom I was working."

In her earlier days of casting, Meg and her sister enjoyed scouting for talent. "We used to get together and hang out. We would find people in restaurants, and we would go up to them and offer them an audition if they seemed interesting." There may not be as much time to make the restaurant rounds today, but Meg is still on the lookout for interesting faces, especially for "Parker Lewis Can't Lose." It's a very visual show and requires highly unusual-looking actors. For instance, Liberman had to come up with a six-foot-eight-inch football player for one episode. "We're always looking for nerdy kids, head-banger, heavy-metal kids and the strangest teachers you could ever imagine."

Despite the complexity of her chore, Liberman refuses to rely on the players directories because she feels "it's sort of cheating." She will go through them as a last resort, especially if she's seeking out an agent for a particular actor. Fortunately, the directors with whom she's worked rely on her knowledge of who's out there. "I have long-standing relationships with people that have gone on over seven years, and that's where the love of the job comes in for me, when you really connect artistically with someone else, and they trust you, and you can bring whoever you feel is right, and it all comes together."

Distance is no deterrent to Liberman: she recently sought out an actor she'd seen in London for Rob Reiner's film *Partners in Life.* And there should be no deterrent to an actor who really wants to act, in the opinion of this casting director. "You've got to really want it. There are so many ups and downs, but ultimately it will pay off. But you can't just be good. You've got to be great, because there are a million people out there who are just okay, and okay is simply not good enough."

---

*Meg Liberman accepts photos and resumés but no unsolicited videotapes; she will schedule generals when time allows.*

# John Lyons

INDEPENDENT

John Lyons prides himself on being a perfectionist in a very unperfect business. With all the capriciousness that's part and parcel of casting a film, Lyons feels he's able to be at least somewhat objective as he screens the hundreds of actors who come through his door.

Lyons has been in the business over ten years, having started in television, working up to East Coast casting director for Warner Bros., and currently casting some of Hollywood's most acclaimed feature films. Although John spends weeks at a time in Los Angeles when involved in a Hollywood-based project, he's definitely more comfortable with the East Coast system. "There is a difference," he insists. "Everybody knows everybody else in New York, which isn't true in L.A. Out here, I find it's a much bigger business, and consequently, it's more all-encompassing." He feels it comes down to a New York sensibility and a Los Angeles sensibility. "In L.A., I've found that a lot of the theater comes from the showcase mentality. In New York, there's still a sense of the theater being an end in itself. You work hard. You do a good job in a play, and that's the only reason for it to exist." To find an actor in New York, John has simply to frequent the Manhattan Theatre Club, Circle Rep, or the Ensemble Studio theater and voilà! In L.A., however, it's the obligatory agent route that Lyons employs.

Although he feels that New York theater is a lot richer than its West

SPECIALTY:
Feature film and theater;
occasional TV

CREDITS INCLUDE:
*Lame Ducks*
*Henry and June*
*Miller's Crossing*
*Raising Arizona*
*Dirty Rotten Scoundrels*
*The Believers*
"Spenser For Hire"
*Playwright's Horizons*
*Manhattan Theatre Club*

Coast counterpart, Lyons will attend theater in L.A. He believes it behooves an actor on either coast to find a good company and showcase his or her talents on the stage rather than through showcasing. "I don't think people really rise to the top through these situations. I think people rise to the top through doing their best work under the best circumstances, and showcases, in my experience, are just the nadir. There's often no director, they're not put together properly, people just choose bizarre scenes that indicate they don't really have a handle on what they're presenting in terms of themselves as actors. You need a great director. You need good writing to look good, and I think that showcases frequently lack that."

Another difference that John Lyons encounters as a casting director is the distinction he draws between the film and theater actor. "When I'm doing theater, I'll see a lot of people, because I think that in theater, craft and technique often overcome whether somebody's dead-on for a part. In film, however, it's really about an essence, who the actor is. The camera's going to do a lot of the work for you in a way, but the camera doesn't lie, and you can't be someone you're not. So when I'm working on a movie, there's a certain process of elimination that is done for me." John will spend much more time talking with an actor being considered for a screen role. In fact, his generals are almost always just meetings, not auditions. The auditions are only set up when an actor is being considered for a specific project.

Lyons admits there are actors who can cross over and do both film and theater with no trouble. "But some, I think, are destined to do stage work, which, I realize, is the kiss of death economically." There are other actors, however, who John feels are solely movie material. "People with film background alone are often completely lost when confronted with a stage. They're used to having that camera coming to them, picking up everything they do. All of a sudden, when they're on stage and have to create a characterization and throw it across the footlights—it's a mystery." The most prolific actor, according to Lyons, is the well-trained stage actor who can cross over 99 percent of the time.

Training is something Lyons feels is vital to the stage actor, but often unnecessary to the film or television actor. "If you've got that 'thing,' nothing is going to stop you on film, nothing. And unfortunately, I think there's now a whole generation of television acting that's coming to the fore, which is really appalling, and makes film actors regret they've been at the Royal Shakespeare Company for ten years." He's talking specifically about the run-of-the-mill formatted sitcoms, which he feels are often damaging to the actor. "I think great acting is rooted in life, in observing life, and those TV shows are so artificial and so far around the bend. It's like doing commercials without balancing it with something else. You get this sell, sell edge to everything you do. It's plastic." In fact, if an actor should ask John whether or not to take a role on one of these shows, he'd say no, don't do it. "In general, if you've gone to a casting session you'll hear, nine times out of ten, a director turning thumbs down on an actor because he's a 'television actor.' If you're working on a good feature, it's the kiss of death."

What Lyons expects from an actor at an interview is a clear sense of who he really is. "I don't want him to impress me. I don't want him to perform for me. I just want to see that persona and what's interesting about it, what's compelling." He's most intrigued by an actor who is subtle. "I always find the really interesting people make you come to them. It's not like a game or anything, but it's an actor with a strong personality who doesn't need to perform or be 'on.' He wants to cut through all the superficiality and get to the nitty gritty. "If an actor doesn't make you see that, then you're stuck. You have to have a good handle on who the actor is after an interview."

An actor will usually get the opportunity to read more than once when auditioning for Lyons: "I think it's almost impossible to do it right on the first try." Another reason for a second reading is for Lyons to determine if an actor can take direction. "If an actor says he understands the adjustment and proceeds to do the scene the same way he did it the first time, that's pretty instructive."

Casting against type is another ingredient of the Lyons technique. When casting *Lame Ducks* he must have seen six hundred actors for the part of a comedian in the vein of a Groucho Marx— fast, sarcastic, and articulate. John Turturro may not be the first person you'd think of for a role of that complexity, but he was the first to come to Lyons's mind, and it took a great deal of persuading from Lyons for the producers to consider him. Turturro had never played a comic; he's usually cast as a crazed psychotic as he was in *Miller's Crossing*. But there was something about the actor that kept him on the top of John's list, and so they went to New York and put him on tape. "He was just fantastic. I will never forget sitting in that room and thinking, this is it! I get goosebumps just thinking about it."

But many actors don't get the parts they feel they deserve, even with John Lyons behind them. "It's capricious and it's arbitrary, and the thing that actors have to remember is that 90 percent of the time, it's not about them. It's a committee process involving a director, a producer, and a casting director, and frequently a studio. You simply have to be at the top of your form every time you audition, and you've then got to kiss it goodbye when you walk out that door."

*John Lyons accepts photos, resumés, and videotapes; he schedules generals as time allows.*

# Mindy Marin

## CASTING ARTISTS, INC.

**M**indy Marin made her move into casting in 1978, working with talent in the TV division at Paramount. From there she headed to Warner Bros. Television and eventually managed the talent and casting department, putting together numerous pilots and series, including "Head of the Class."

In early 1987, Marin moved to Warner's to concentrate on feature film. She continues to bring the same drive and creativity to this medium as she did with television, enjoying the challenge of finding new talent as well as selecting the right actors for the right roles. "There are times," she says, "when a person will walk in, and you know he's the character. And then there are times when after two or three meetings, an actor will build and grow with the role and emerge as the right person for that role."

Mindy Marin enjoys the opportunity to read unknowns for prominent roles. She feels there's a great deal of subjectivity involved in that pursuit. "It's exciting to find a newcomer who hasn't been given a chance to show what he or she can do. It often lends authenticity to the film. For instance, when we had a film set in the baseball world, we needed an actor who could pitch or a ballplayer who could act. Through the casting search, along came a guy who was struggling to make it as an actor. He was a good actor, and he also played ball. He was a perfect match for the script. So instead of, 'Oh, there's so and so you've seen so many times before,' there was some mystery, which I think is refreshing."

But Marin is also quick to point out that a casting director

SPECIALTY:
Feature film

CREDITS INCLUDE:
*The Naked Gun 2½*
*Talent for the Game*
*L.A. Story*
*Flight of the Intruder*
*Chattahoochee*
*Miss Firecracker*
*Betrayed*

doesn't always have that luxury, often having to bring in studio choices for a particular film. "For another sports movie, it was important for the studio and the producers to have name recognition for the film, which meant that the actor had to learn the specific sports skill. That can work just as well."

To find actors for a film, Marin will go through her extensive files as well as magazines and newspapers, keeping her eye out at restaurants, comedy clubs, theaters, and even supermarket checkout lines. "Anywhere life is. It's an exhausting but necessary process. Casting can be such a chance thing. You never know when or where a person will appear. It can be magical." There are also times when a person is right under her nose but up for a different role. "When I'm involved with a project," says Mindy, "I try to stay tuned to the film as a whole. When someone talented is reading for you and not clicking with the part they've come in for, I envision them in another role—it's instinctual." Marin will also carry ideas to her next project and finds herself bringing back familiar faces. "I want to see the people I bring in get the part, and if it's not this project, it may be the next."

When conducting meetings with actors, Mindy follows the basics. She expects thorough preparation and professionalism. Dressing for the role isn't crucial, but "looking your best within the framework of the character can be useful, as long as it's not full costume."

She also believes that an actor needs to do what's necessary to be a contender for a role. "If the people behind you aren't enthusiastic about sending you out for something, then you've got to do it yourself. If you're passionate about a role, you need to let people know." That includes asking questions about the character and the material and listening to the suggestions of the casting director. An example of that came for Marin when casting *Naked Gun 2½*, a comedy for Paramount. "The director didn't want anyone to read the material with a smile; the more serious the better. But when actors saw the material, they wanted to play into the comedy. I had to explain—sometimes three or four times—that they had to bring it down, straighten it out. It didn't seem natural to do it that way, but for this particular film it was what was needed."

Knowing the relationship between the character and the story is critical, and questioning that relationship is expected. "It helps the casting process if I can help the actor clarify the picture. I'm representing the director's and producer's views to the best of my ability, and I want to convey those views to the actors."

Marin also finds it important to cast against type. It's the person behind the face that she finds interesting. "I always look behind the physical framework, to glimpse inside the vehicle and minimize the exterior limitations." When casting Steve Martin's *L.A. Story*, for instance, there were several roles that called for stereotypical Angelinos. Marin went the other way. "There were actors available who didn't fit the roles in a traditional sense but gave it a slant. They were people with a real history in this town. As it turns out, they worked great." Sometimes, however, it can be difficult to persuade the powers-that-be to see it her way.

Of course, there are times when someone's physical appearance just isn't right for a role, a fact that Mindy believes all actors must accept to persevere in the business. "It's a fact that isn't going to change. I try to do my best to limit its effect, but sometimes it's not possible."

Marin feels that an actor's commitment and persistence will win out in both the short and the long term. "It can be quite obvious in a reading if an actor is not committed to the profession, and that will kill it for me. You've got to be in it for the long haul, and that takes patience."

Mindy Marin gives much credit for her style of casting to the directors with whom she's worked. "I've really been fortunate to have directors who are willing to take chances. It allows me to be creative with the process and keep things interesting. I'm always grateful for that."

---

*Mindy Marin accepts photos and resumés, but videotapes only upon request; she schedules generals as time allows.*

# Ellen Meyer

## WITT/THOMAS/HARRIS PRODUCTIONS

Ellen Meyer is both blessed and burdened by her success as a casting director. She's blessed with business associates who are top-notch in the television industry, such as Witt/Thomas/Harris, with whom she's had a fruitful relationship for the last several years. She's also burdened with the task of finding the best in the available talent pool. She can't settle for good when her producers are used to, and demand, the best. "They refuse to settle for someone who is just okay at a reading. They want somebody who is special, and they have a right to, because it really does make a difference in the quality of the show. A guest star who isn't funny or doesn't have the right rhythm or pacing can really hurt a scene."

Every script is a challenge to Ellen. "Not every script is special," she admits. "Some are more exciting to cast than others. Some are easier, with the actors just falling into place, but others require more effort to find the right people." The way Ellen goes about finding the right people is through her extensive files and the agents with whom she's established a relationship. She'll use Breakdown Services, but not as frequently as many of her colleagues. "When I'm doing half-hour comedies that I do from week to week, I often get a script a day in advance, and there's really no time to send out a breakdown. You have to know these people off the top of your head, depend upon your knowledge, and occasionally find time to read a few other actors to see if they're worth adding to the pool." Meyer

SPECIALTY:
Sitcoms, movies of the week, and miniseries

CREDITS INCLUDE:
"Golden Girls"
"Blossom"
"Empty Nest"
Love Among Thieves
Sins
Passions
Wanted: Dead or Alive

says when she's casting a miniseries or pilot, however, she has more time to submit to Breakdown Services.

No matter what the source, the actors she brings in to read are ones who have a certain energy and interest. She never looks for pretty faces without talent and personality behind those handsome exteriors. "If they're sort of on one level, and there's nothing going on aside from that, you know an audience is going to get bored."

While training is a positive item on any actor's resumé, Meyer believes that training alone does not an actor make. "I think there are a lot of talented actresses in town who've had no training. They just have a special spark to them, and they bring it to the role, and they're wonderful. And then again, I think there are some actors who've had a wide range of training, and they're just not special. I do think, however, if an artist is special and trains with somebody who's special, then it can only enhance whatever talent he or she has."

When casting a show like "Golden Girls," it might seem that Ellen seeks only those actors with plenty of sitcom experience under their belts. Not necessarily. "I always try to be open to people without comedy experience, because it's always a challenge to find somebody new, fresh, and different." But while she feels that most good comedic actors can do drama without much of a stretch, she doesn't feel it necessarily works the other way. Good dramatic actors often cannot make the transition to comedy. It may call for several more callbacks to make sure the actor can handle the material.

One of her biggest challenges is children. She casts a lot of teenagers, and she often has to rely on her instincts when a young actor hasn't proven himself through years of on-camera experience. But, so far, Ellen has proven herself able to pick the winners. When she was casting "The Lynn Redgrave Show" several years ago, she recalls being impressed with a young man named Michael J. Fox. He'd done very little TV at the time, and what he had done hadn't been comedy, but he was real and interesting, and she decided to give him a shot. "I remember it was a complicated process, too, because he was Canadian, and there was a lot of legal work needed to get him on the show, and I remember an attorney saying to me, 'Couldn't you get someone else to do this role? Wouldn't it be easier?'" Easier, perhaps, but the uppermost factor to Meyer was the quality of the show, and she felt Michael was a quality performer.

Some youngsters, she feels, have been overly trained, and have lost that spontaneity and naturalness. "If you make every sentence bigger than life, you lose the character. You can't make everything bigger than life, and you can't force a child who doesn't have self-confidence to go into a reading and land the part."

One of the reasons Ellen prefers not to use videotape at an audition is because she wants to see actors at least a couple of times before casting them. "I think actors are human beings, and if you bring them in for a callback and they can surprise you with how much they've improved and how terrific they've become with the role, it can be of great value. On the other hand, if you bring them back, and you see that they just don't have the tools to sustain the first reading, and their level has dropped way down, it's obvious I'll have to look elsewhere." If she's put an actor on videotape and merely reruns the audition two or three times, she has no way of judging if that performance can be enhanced or if the actor can even maintain the quality of that first audition.

"Every actor should know his strengths and weaknesses," states Meyer. "Some actors can take a couple of minutes to study the sides and go in to a reading and do fine. Others need more time with the material." Meyer feels it's up to the actors to know what works best for them. "If you're an actor who doesn't feel comfortable without some preparation, then you should say, "In order to do my best reading and put my best foot forward, I'm going to pick up the material the night before or come in two hours ahead of time, go get a cup of coffee and run it through a few times." This does not mean an actor must memorize the scene. "This is not a test to see whether or not they can memorize the material. That's not my job. My job is to see if they have any talent, and if it helps them to memorize the scene, then they should do it, but if they feel it helps their rhythm and continuity to look at the page, that's equally fine. I just want to hear how you read."

Ellen Meyer doesn't expect up-and-coming actors to spend a lot of money on fancy photography or a designer wardrobe, but she does encourage them to find a good acting coach to whom they can relate, and to invest in some videotape on which to capture their best on-camera moments. "I think, as an actor, if you've been in a film or television show, you should get that piece of film and make sure to put it on tape, because not every casting director can see everything that's out there." She also considers it worthwhile to take out an ad in the trades (if you can afford it) when you're going to be on TV, to let casting directors and producers know you're alive and productive. If you can't afford an ad, a little note or postcard will suffice.

"I think actors should be aware of reality," she adds. "There's an enormous pool of actors out there, and the proportion is not level with the amount of material that's available. Therefore, when you choose your profession, you should give it all you have, and if it's a positive thing in your life, stay with it, but if it turns negative, as it does with many artists, you should move on to something that can be a positive force in your life."

*Ellen Meyer accepts photos, resumés, and videotapes; she schedules generals as time permits.*

# Bob Morones

## INDEPENDENT

The only way for an actor to meet Bob Morones is when he's casting a particular project you may be suited for. He's adamantly opposed to general interviews or auditions. "I avoid them like the plague," he insists. He'd much prefer to see someone on the screen or to look at a videocassette of an actor's work. The only favor he asks is to please pick the tapes up after a month or so. "I must have about five hundred of them sitting here. I just keep them until they come and pick them up. I have some that've been here three or four years. From major stars, too."

What Morones wants to see in an actor is pure, unadulterated talent, whether it's natural or developed. "If an actor can suck you into his world and into the character's world, then he's done his job. He's made you forget about everything. You suspend time. He gives you a new sense of time and really plays with your emotions." One such actor who had a riviting effect on Morones was Nick Nolte, whom he spotted in a performance at the Contempo Theatre during his days at Universal Television. "I tried to get the producers of 'Rich Man Poor Man' to see him, but nobody knew who he was, and so they refused to bring him in for a reading." But Bob believed in Nolte and insisted that the director see his performance. He did, and Nolte got the job. "I think that series launched his career and showed the world that he was an excellent actor."

To Morones, the number one thing that can ruin a potentially good performance is nerves. When he's conducting an audition, he sees actors destroy their chances by failing to overcome the jitters. "Actors who get nervous get

SPECIALTY:
Feature film and TV

CREDITS INCLUDE:
*Angeltown*
*Romero*
*Platoon*
*Salvador*
*Scarface*
*El Norte*
"Columbo"
"McCloud"
"Night Stalker"
"Night Gallery"

uptight, the words don't flow properly, and their timing is off. It's usually because they're not very confident. They've stopped training or working out." Training is vital in Morones's view. "Training gives you confidence, and once you have that, you can release the restraints you put upon yourself and be honest to the character you're portraying. People believe an honest performance. If they see you 'acting' they're put off."

Training alone isn't the answer, however. It's a combination of honing your craft and living life. "It's being an observer of life. It's education. The more educated you are, the easier it's going to be to grasp things and see things others wouldn't see, because what happens in life is that you can become prejudiced and closed to the richness of other cultures and ideas. Education opens you up."

Morones is known for his color blindness when it comes to casting. When he was working on *Wolfjudge*, he was called upon to find someone to portray a forensics specialist. Typically, Orientals have been cast in those roles, but Bob decided to change that stereotype and cast a Hispanic. Another case in point was the casting of *Platoon*. Although Willem Dafoe was eventually given the role, Morones searched the entire state of Arizona for an Apache to portray the character. The script specifically called for an Apache, but when Dafoe was called in to read for another character, which ultimately went to Tom Beringer, he asked one of the producers if he could read for the role of the Indian; he did so well that he wound up getting the part.

Working for Oliver Stone is a challenge for any casting director. He's apparently quite a perfectionist. "Oliver is extremely demanding," reveals Morones. "Actors have to learn to be very resilient. The ones we ended up hiring had to come back for eight to ten callbacks before Oliver made his decision. He just kept mixing and matching, and that would tick a lot of actors off. But the ones who hung in there were the ones it paid off for."

Unlike many casting directors, Morones recommends an actor memorize his material prior to an audition, especially an audition for a producer or director. "It helps. If an actor's really worked on a scene and has it memorized, he usually doesn't have to worry about holding a piece of paper, and he can work, instead, on embellishing the character."

An actor who at one time helped Morones read other actors at auditions was Charlie Sheen, and Bob felt that Charlie would be terrific in *Platoon*. "But Oliver didn't even want to meet him, because I guess he'd met him before and didn't feel he was right for this film. But I knew that he had grown as an actor, and so I showed Oliver a clip of another young actor that also featured Charlie. Oliver was sure the other actor was Charlie's brother, Emilio, and I asked him if he thought we should bring the kid in. He said yeah, but 'you know Emilio isn't available.' When I told him the actor was Sheen, he was stunned." And the rest is history. Stone used Charlie in *Platoon* and cast him in *Wall Street* as well.

Bob Morones has not only given a boost to the careers of many adult actors, but he was a major factor in the meteoric explosion of a younger performer's career. When he was searching the country for a new Alfalfa for "The New Little Rascals," he discovered a five-and-a-half-year-old little boy at an open call in Chicago. "I just thought he was an exceptional kid, and I wanted to bring him in to meet with the producers in Hollywood. The director, however, felt he was a little strange." As luck would have it, the youngster's manager was bringing his client to town, and asked Bob if he wouldn't mind introducing him to the show's executive producer, Norman Lear. "I didn't think there'd be any harm in asking his secretary if Norman could meet with this kid for a few minutes, and he happened to be in his office at the time and invited the kid in." Well, when the precocious little tyke asked Lear to pose as a producer for him, with his feet on his desk and a cigar in his mouth, he was just enchanted. "He immediately called the producer and said, 'This is one of our new Little Rascals, isn't it?' And of course he was signed for the show." The program never made it on the air, but Gary Coleman sure made it as a TV superstar!

Morones advises any actor aiming for the top to plot his career wisely, "actually designing a career as if he were going to college, with checkmarks along the way, either quarterly or triannually. An actor should carefully budget his time. After four months, he should have accomplished so much, and after a year, so much. Just as if he'd completed a year of college. If he does that, then by the time he gets to his third year, he can see that he's getting somewhere." Of course, Bob realizes it's not always easy to do it on one's own, and he suggests an actor seek out a good manager or coach to ease the way. "They need some kind of guide, be it a spiritual leader or even a grandmother, someone who's going to keep them honest. Because if they're not, the years are going to come and go, and nothing's going to happen."

---

*Bob Morones accepts photos, resumés, and videotapes; he never schedules generals.*

# Barry Moss

## HUGHES MOSS CASTING

**T**he Hughes Moss philosophy is to maintain an open-door policy to actors. "Anybody can walk into our office and leave a picture and resumé," says Barry Moss. "We'll even try to talk to people when they come in if we have the time. We're always looking for actors. We really feel that actors are a product, and to cut ourselves off from actors is really cutting off your nose to spite your face." Barry never knows what talent may walk through his door. It's happened time and again. "We were casting the pilot for 'Bay City Blues,'" he recalls, "and in walks this guy who said he loves baseball. We told him everybody in the room had an appointment, so he just waited. Three hours! Well, I was running around the office and kept seeing him sitting there, so finally I brought him in, and he got the part."

Moss always tells actors that if there's a role they think they're right for, stop at nothing to get it. But just be sure you're selective. "I mean, don't just decide you're right for every role that comes along, because after a while, if you're constantly persistent and obnoxious, a director will think that's the way you'll be on the job and won't want to hire you." But if an actor truly believes he's right for the role, Moss encourages persistence. He remembers the time when he was casting "Rags to Riches" and was looking for a dancer. "I saw a girl in a class. She

SPECIALTY:
Theater, feature film, and TV

CREDITS INCLUDE:
*Grand Hotel*
*My One and Only*
*Woman of the Year*
*Nine*
*Torch Song Trilogy*
*42nd Street*
*Children of a Lesser God*
*The Little Foxes*
*Triple Play*
*Missing Pieces*
*Ghost Dad*
*Dominick and Eugene*
*Heart of Dixie*
"The Cosby Show"
"A Different World"
"Liza Minnelli Special"

was a twenty-five-year-old Hispanic with a wonderful voice and fifteen years of dance. I asked her why she hadn't auditioned for *A Chorus Line*. She said, 'I sent a picture, but you didn't call me.' I said, 'That's a once-in-a-lifetime part, the part of Morales, and you would have been ideal. You should have been sleeping on my doorstep. You should have sent a carrier pigeon with your phone number, anything to get my attention!'"

Another thing that Barry feels stands in the way of an actor getting a part is a lack of confidence. "They often come in with their heads slumped down instead of their chins held high. They're not there to help us with our job, they're there to be judged. Well, it's not about being judged. It's about coming and solving our problem." That's why Barry feels there are so few actors who get the jobs, and the ones who do get them believe in themselves.

If actors are unsure how to present themselves in the best possible light at an audition, Moss suggests Gordon Hunt's *How to Audition*. He believes it's the greatest aid actors can have, besides an understanding of their strengths and weaknesses. It's also imperative that actors read a script before an audition, and he suggests finding out as much as you can about a director for whom you're reading. "Talk to other actors who have worked with him. Find out what the director has done before." And when you're into the audition, take your time. "If you feel things aren't going right, you can excuse yourself, and ask to start again. Nine times out of ten, they'll say it's okay."

If an actor is auditioning for a musical, selecting the right song is very important. "What you should do is find an audition piece that fits your voice beautifully, just like a dress should fit you beautifully." He also stresses the importance of acting the material, not simply singing it. "You should be telling a story. It has lyrics. Think about what you're singing. Pretend you're Scarlett O'Hara singing to Rhett Butler. It doesn't matter, as long as you can put yourself in an acting frame and really communicate."

Because Barry Moss casts a lot of theater, he's a stickler for training. "How can you do a job unless you've been trained for it?" he asks. He concedes that in film an actor can occasionally get away with little training, but he says it can never happen on stage or even in weekly television, where time is of the essence, and professionalism is a must. He encourages actors to do scene study to keep their muscles flexed. He does, however, advise actors to audit any class they're considering to see how they respond to the teacher. If the teacher believes in tearing apart an actor's psyche only to build it up again, he believes it's harmful to the actor. "If you want your psyche ripped up, you should go to a qualified psychiatrist, not to an acting coach." He's adamant about this and cautions actors to be wary of certain teachers.

Moss is also frustrated with certain actors—those who profess to want to do theater, but when the time comes and an out-of-town role is offered to an L.A. actor, they make excuses. "They don't seem to understand that it's a job with a steady income for a length of time. Some of them just want to sit around and wait for a TV show or a movie." And although he won't say he'll never consider that actor for any other role that might come along, "I'm not gonna be real happy about bringing them in." It's the duplicity that bothers him most. "If only they were upfront about the subject. But when they profess to want theater and then won't come in, that angers me."

There are few "don'ts" in Moss' vocabulary. He likes to encourage actors to do what they feel is necessary. "The casting director is on your side as your kind of little cheerleader." He likens himself to a sort of surrogate agent at times. "There's always someone you can count on. We'll remember someone from an audition two or three years later and bring them in. So it's never over. Every time you audition, you put a little deposit in our safe deposit box of actors."

---

*Barry Moss accepts photos and resumés but no videocassettes; he doesn't usually do generals.*

# Meryl O'Laughlin

## IMAGINE ENTERTAINMENT

**M**eryl O'Laughlin has had a prestigious background in casting. Prior to her stint at Imagine Entertainment, she was executive in charge of talent at MTM, where she supervised the casting of all series, pilots, and movies of the week. She was also responsible for developing new talent, and has since conducted classes for actors in the art of auditioning. The first thing she tells actors is the good news: there's a lot of work in Los Angeles. "The bad news is that you can't do anything to experiment in front of a professional," meaning that if you're not really ready for the major leagues, don't try to learn your craft in Hollywood. "If I were a young actor," O'Laughlin advises, "I'd get out of L.A. You can't go to Melrose Avenue and play a part you're wrong for, just to learn, because you're going to be seen by professionals." Do your experimenting in a small town or in New York, she suggests, where there are hundreds of little theater groups from which to choose.

If you are a professional, there are a couple of pointers that may come in handy, pointers that she often reiterated to her students. Never memorize the script. "Never put that script down. Even if you have it memorized, never let me know, because if you put the script down, something more is expected of you, a much more professional, finished performance." She also advises against idle chatter at an audition. "Don't make jokes. Even if

---

SPECIALTY:
TV movies, miniseries, and pilots

CREDITS INCLUDE:
*Lucky*
"Alf"
*The Blue and the Gray*
*The Hunchback of Notre Dame*
*Malibu*
*RFK*
*Sadat*
*Alice in Wonderland*
*Gidget's Summer Reunion*
"Blue Thunder"
"Crazy Like a Fox"
"T.J. Hooker"
"Fantasy Island"
"Hart to Hart"

you know the people, don't start talking about your personal life unless they ask. Just do your work and get out." A thank you is sufficient, but be sure to say your name to make sure they know who it is who's just read. Resumés often get mixed up, and you could be a victim of that possibility. Dress to indicate the part, but never come dressed in costume. If you're reading for the role of a cowboy and come in wearing an Armani suit, she says, you probably won't get it unless you're a star. On the other hand, cowboy boots and a lariat aren't necessary, either.

O'Laughlin stresses the importance of being on time for an audition, and if you happen to be early, don't sign in unless you're prepared to be seen right away. "The minute you sign in they'll probably take you, because it's no longer what time your appointment is, it's who was there first."

One point that may not occur to many actors but is critical to Meryl is what an actor says upon leaving an audition. "Never say to a casting director, 'Glad to have met you,' because you never must indicate that you don't know me. It's psychologically very bad for a producer and director to think we've never met." And never leave an audition, she cautions, until the next actor comes in, "because what happens a lot of times is that you'll have given a good reading, but you weren't doing it exactly the way they wanted it, and by the time they say, 'Gee, she was good, but maybe she could have done it this way,' and I say, 'Well, why don't you direct her,' if you've already left, you've missed your chance. So wait at least until the next person goes in. It can mean the difference between getting a job and not getting the job."

Study, study, study is the other key ingredient to being a successful actor. "Take dance classes, voice classes, movement classes, acting classes. That's where your money should go," recommends O'Laughlin. Before signing up for a class, however, she suggests auditing it to make sure it meets your criteria. An actor should also invest in a couple of outfits for auditions and a decent 8x10 with a professionally written resume.

Although Meryl discourages actors from sending in unsolicited videotapes, she does like to see an actor's work once he or she has read for her. "I love to see cassettes because they're usually an actor's best work, stuff they've really, really done." A good videocassette can sometimes land an actor a job. Case in point: the casting of *Shattered Innocence*. The script centered on a young porno star, Shauna Grant. "It was such a hard part to cast. She had to be beautiful, sexy, and a wonderful actress because she was on every page of the script, starting out at seventeen and ending with her death at twenty one. We saw so many actors. One had the looks, another the talent, but nobody had it all." It was at that vulnerable time she happened across a videocassette on her desk. It belonged to an actress name Jona Lee. "I had nothing to do at that moment, so I put the cassette in, and it was so good. There was nothing on it but episodic television, but she had some good roles, and someone professional had obviously put the tape together. That's the beauty of having a well-edited, well-done cassette."

If you're called in to read for Meryl O'Laughlin, be prepared for several callbacks if she's impressed with your audition. For a movie of the week there may be only one or two callbacks, but for pilots there may be three or four, since the networks are involved. She'll usually see thirty people a day when she's casting a television project and time is of the essence. Her assistant will read with the actor while Meryl listens and takes notes. She shuns monologues, and although she realizes that cold readings are not the perfect way of determining talent, she feels they're the lesser of two evils. "Monologues are very hard to do. You have to be very good to do a monologue well." She's also concerned that an actor may have spent a year working on the monologue, which wouldn't show her how he could perform given a shorter rehearsal time.

O'Laughlin doesn't think talent alone is always responsible for success. "There are a lot of mediocre actors out there who are more successful than some very good ones, but because they're persistent and professional and don't get their feeings hurt and keep plodding, they make it. The bottom line," she says, "is to learn how to act and learn how to become a professional. They are two totally different skills. You can be a wonderful actor, but if you do not learn how to be a professional in Los Angeles, you will not work."

---

*Meryl O'Laughlin accepts photos, resumés, and videotapes; she rarely schedules generals.*

# Richard Pagano

## PAGANO/BIALY CASTING

"**I**'m known as the bad guy," admits Richard Pagano with a devilish grin, comparing himself to his partner, Sharon Bialy. While Sharon might stifle her anger at agents whose clients fail to show up for auditions, Richard will let them know in no uncertain terms how he feels about an actor's lack of responsiblity. "When somebody cancels at the last minute, and I've got a director flying in from New York, I don't simply let it go—I call the agent and rail at them." In the old days, when Richard was just starting out, he admits he lost his temper at the drop of a hat, but now, "while I lose my temper more often than Sharon, I always do it strategically. I only lose my temper now when it's to my professional advantage to lose my temper."

Pagano didn't start out as a casting director. In fact, he taught literature. Yet he always wanted to get into show business, "and someone said to me: just knock on doors!" Others, of course, told him knocking on doors was a crazy idea, but he felt he ought to try the aggressive approach. "I got a job the first day," he beams, "and every single person I met was just great." And he suggests actors follow his example. "If I were an actor, I'd start going to casting offices and knocking on doors, and if the only person who wanted to talk to me was the receptionist, that's the person I'd talk to. I'd give my picture and resumé to her, because the receptionist of today is next year's agent."

Richard Pagano doesn't like

SPECIALTY:
Feature film, theater, and TV

CREDITS INCLUDE:
*Rules of the Game*
*Point Break*
*Drugstore Cowboy*
*Say Anything*
*Extremities*
*Tamara* (L.A. production)
La Jolla Playhouse
Old Globe Theater
"Heat"
"El Diablo"
"Crime Story"

actors to harass him with phone calls, but he does appreciate a note from an actor who's appearing in a play. While he admits he doesn't attend as much theater as he did when he was younger, he does send his assistants, who report back to him if there's someone in the cast who is a "must-see." And every new season, Pagano and Bialy hold generals that are open to anyone who wants to audition. At these generals, Pagano likes an actor to prepare a monologue rather than deliver a cold reading. "I wish more actors would prepare something," he laments. "Most people don't, and even when we request a monologue, many aren't even willing to prepare one." The only warning Pagano issues actors is not to select outdated or overly popular material. "A lot of it is just horrible. It shows that the actor has no imagination." What does impress this particular casting director is an actor who can take the text of a scene and manage to figure out all the information and make choices based on an intelligent appraisal of the scene.

Questions prior to a reading are always respected, unless they show that an actor hasn't done his homework. When they were casting *Tokyo Diamond*, which is set in Japan, Pagano and Bialy were looking for a Japanese reporter who speaks English, and one actor asked Richard if he needed a Japanese accent. Well, that really made a negative impression. "Most of the time," he says, "that lack of perception is fulfilled in the reading. It gives me a signal that they're probably not very good, and when I see the reading, that's exactly what happens."

A poor reading is the last thing Richard is looking for. "I want to get the role cast so I can move on to something else. I don't want people to be bad. The most important thing that any casting director can say is that none of us wants actors to come in and be stupid or underprepared. It's a waste of our time." Richard was very impressed with the system in Japan, when he was over there casting *Tokyo Diamond*. "The actors are much better prepared, and you don't have to tell them what to do. They work all the time."

The reading isn't the only thing that tells Pagano if an actor meets his qualifications. "We also get them to improvise to give us a sense of the actors. You get them on a baseball field, throwing a ball, or, in the case of *Point Break*, you get them out there on a surfboard to make sure they can handle those waves."

Pagano's thrill is casting against type. "I've never been very good at television for that reason; I don't know how to cast right on. Sharon's much better at that than I am. I'm sort of a quirky guy. Offbeat casting has never been something I'm conscious of. I've just always been doing it, and that's why I gravitate to theater and the more unusual films." A good example of Richard's casting technique is *Fatal Beauty*. For the role of Rita Rizzoli, he thought of casting Whoopi Goldberg, someone whom no one else had in mind for the part. The selection of Kelly Lynch for *Drugstore Cowboy* was another case of Pagano versus the mainstream.

While actors tend to be an angry lot, at times, depending on how their careers are going, Pagano cautions them not to direct that anger at anyone in a casting office or at an audition. It's the kiss of death. And while almost any kind of attire is fine with Richard, from blue jeans to business suits, he doesn't want to see an actor in costume. "It's very boring and predictable. You're creating a one-to-one correspondence between the role and you, which leaves nothing to the imagination."

If you're wondering whether to be a little more aggressive in your approach to this business, Pagano likes to tell a story passed along to him by his neighbor down the hall, Sylvester Stallone. When he was a struggling actor in New York, Stallone decided to go through the Yellow Pages to find all the agents and casting directors who were listed. Then he painstakingly called each one. There were twelve hundred of them, but he'd make a point to do ten each day. Then, when he got to the bottom of the list, he'd go back and start all over again. Each round would take about six months, but he refused to give up. He'd call and say he'd just gotten back from Europe and was checking in to say hello. "I'm sure that's what did it for him," declares Pagano. "It might not have been the actual phone calls, but it's the attitude that you develop from steeling yourself to the business. It's not that you want to be constantly looking for work, but that's what you've chosen to do. You have to just put yourself in the way of a Mack truck that's speeding along at sixty miles an hour, and grab on. If you've choosen to be in this business, then goddamn it, do it!"

*Richard Pagano accepts photos and resumés; he schedules generals every new season.*

# Jennifer Part

## UNIVERSAL STUDIOS

J ennifer Part has a compassionate view of casting. "My attitude is that everybody who walks in for a role is the right one for the job, as opposed to 'Oh God, here comes another one.'" Of course there are days when she sees fifty actor, and none of them gets cast, but she does try to maintain her optimism.

Although Part prefers seeing actors only when she's casting a specific project, she will look through all her mail. "I'm one of those people who saves stuff for the future." That's not to say that every single photo that comes across her desk will be filed away, but if an actor sends in a postcard or a note, and it makes an impression, an actor may get a call in the near future. Jennifer strongly impresses on actors the importance of being listed in the players directories, which she uses constantly. "Even if it's just with a service number. You don't have to have an agent." She relies on the directories for finding people who might be right for a role when she's not sure exactly what she's looking for, and she turns to them when she's compiling her numerous lists for herself and her clients. Part says she tries to bring in at least ten actors she's not familiar with for each of the smaller roles, to build up her inventory.

When actors are brought in, Jennifer tries not to keep them waiting more than five minutes. She'll schedule three actors every fifteen minutes for smaller parts and two every fifteen minutes for more substantial roles. She discourages memorization. "I find it a hindrance, because they're so worried about whether or not they

SPECIALTY:
TV series, movies of the week, and pilots

CREDITS INCLUDE:
"Golden Girls"
North and South, Book One
The Case of the Hillside Strangler
"Growing Pains" (pilot)
"Webster"
"Taxi"

know their lines that they completely leave behind the consistency of the character they're attempting to create." Even when it comes down to the screen test, she often advises against committing the material to memory. An actor may not have enough time, and he'll make a better impression if he's not under pressure to learn the lines on top of everything else.

Part hopes an actor will ask her any questions about a role before the reading. "I hate when they or their agent call to say they'd like to come in again because they didn't feel they gave a good reading. They didn't feel they had enough information. I think it's their responsibility to make sure they feel as comfortable as they can with the material." She finds that a surprising number of actors who come in for series leads don't have the right attitude and are unprepared. "It makes the casting director look like a fool. It's as if the casting director didn't provide the actor with sufficient information, when indeed it's the actor who didn't go to the trouble to find out what he or she needed to know."

Another taboo in Part's book: asking about a callback at the end of an audition. "Don't put me on the spot," she asks of the actor. "We're all very nice, and we'll say 'Thank you, that was wonderful.' We don't say 'That was really bad.' What are we going to tell you?" And don't bring props to an audition. "When I was on the staff at Columbia TV we did scene studies, and somebody did *On The Waterfront*. He actually brought out a gun, and everybody was sort of nervous, and my boss said to him, 'I don't think you need the fake gun.' He responded, 'It's not fake. It's real.' You just never know. Better to leave the props at home."

Another memorable episode in Jennifer Part's career was during her casting stint on "Taxi." It was the episode when Latka was about to marry Simka. "That was a real interesting bit of casting because we had no dialogue. We had this fake language. So I was reading actors who could make something of it. I needed the man who was going to perform the ceremony in this fake language and his interpreter." She brought in two of her favorite actors, Vincent Schiavelli and a British gent, Peter Elbling. "I just thought about the funny peope I knew, and they handed it perfectly. They put everyone away, and it was great."

Jennifer also fondly recalls her part in furthering Ted Danson's career. She says the producers of "Cheers" became aware of him through a minor role on "Taxi." "He played this very flamboyant hairdresser who completely ruined Marilu Henner's hair." Jennifer was so desperate to find someone for the part, she even read somebody's facialist. Fortunately, Danson was available, and she personally delivered the script to his door, a service she hasn't performed since.

Part is particularly fond of casting children. Having worked on "Webster," she's quite familiar with the difficulties of finding young talent, but she enjoys the challenge. "I sort of troll for kids. My girlfriend cast a pilot and needed a really tall girl, and they were really bombing out. It turned out that someone's secretary had a daughter. She got the part." That's one way she'll come across a candidate. Then, of course, there are the more traditional channels: agents and schools.

If Jennifer Part can impart one major piece of advice to actors, it's never to touch a casting director during a reading. She squirms as she relates the uncomfortable tale of a "Growing Pains" audition. There was a scene between a man and his wife. They were getting ready for bed, and he was trying to get her to wear a sexy pair of pyjamas. " And this guy came in to read with me, and he pulls out this black G-string and kind of threw it at me. Well, I was so taken aback I had to stop the reading! I was embarrassed and flustered." It's interesting to know that it's not just actors who often feel out of place at an audition.

_Jennifer Part accepts photos and resumés but no unsolicited videocassettes; she rarely conducts generals._

# Johanna Ray

**INDEPENDENT**

I t's the essence of the person that is of primary concern to Johanna Ray, who's perhaps best known for her work with director David Lynch. She'll overlook acting experience at times, if the person has a certain special quality. She did it with Grace Jones, and she did it with Wilt Chamberlain. As far as Jones was concerned, "I felt pretty sure she could pull it off since there wasn't a tremendous amount of dialogue, and as for the physical specifications of the part, she fit them to a T." She cast Chamberlain in the same movie, *Conan the Destroyer*, and as far as she knew, neither had any acting experience.

Of course, she would like to be able to find the ideal combination of looks and talent, but it's not always possible. Working for David Lynch has made her finely attuned to character. "David is the kind of director who will sit down and talk to a person and immediately tune into certain qualities and be able to make them work. I've always said to David that he could pick people off the street and get a performance out of them."

Ray says Lynch just has a knack for making actors feel comfortable. "He's very patient and painstaking, and he really directs actors much more so than most directors." He's also quite open to any suggestions Ray might present. When they were casting *Wild at Heart*, for instance, Johanna wanted to bring in David Patrick Kelly because she remembered his reading for *Blue Velvet* and liked him a lot. "He ended up writing a part especially for Kelly because he was so intrigued by him." Another example is with the TV phenomenon "Twin Peaks." They were searching for an

SPECIALTY:
Feature film and
special TV projects

CREDITS INCLUDE:
*Wild At Heart*
*Blue Velvet*
*Gaby: A True Story*
*Satisfaction*
*Firestarter*
*Conan the Destroyer*
"Twin Peaks"
"Amazing Stories"

127

actor to portray the sheriff and were thinking along the standard macho male lines until Johanna suggested Michael Ontkean. Again, Lynch made script adjustments to hire him.

Lynch rarely reads actors. It's usually enough for him to meet with them and talk. "The interview just takes a life of its own. Its uncanny," explains Johanna. "I've spent afternoons with him, where he has this ability to draw out strange and interesting information. I remember one actor talking about beekeeping. It's rarely about the film or the part." The actors often don't even know what they're reading for, she confesses.

When Ray is working on a project, she always uses Breakdown Services and casts mostly from agents' submissions. "I know that they are submitting to the best of their ability who they think are right for a specific part. When actors send in their own pictures, they're sending them with the hope they'll be right for something, so basically, it takes up a lot of my time going through all those submissions that aren't even remotely close to anything I'm looking for."

When Ray is meeting actors, she prefers they come in exactly as they are. The one thing that impresses her is not *trying* to impress her. "I like to make the meeting as social as possible, so that I'm getting the essence of the person. That way, when I bring them in to read, they make more of an impression as they show me how different they can be in character." Ray is even empathetic to a painfully shy actor who may not know how to conduct himself in an interview, who mutters or is monosyllabic. "That's fine with me. It just says that the person is a shy and sensitive and insecure person—it doesn't mean he can't act." And she won't even take that into consideration when it comes to the type of role she may have him read for. "A perfect example is Will Patton. When he came into my office, he was very shy and said how he hated interviews. He'd much rather I see his work. His discomfort in the interview situation sort of endeared him to me." Patton had just taken over from Ed Harris in *Fool for Love* in New York, and that night Johanna went to see him. "He was absolutely magnificent. He was electric!"

There are no absolutes in Johanna Ray's methods. Although she prefers actors not to rely on props at auditions, there are exceptions. When she was casting *Gaby: A Love Story*, Lawrence Monoson came in to read for the part of a cerebral palsy victim in a wheelchair, having researched the part to the point where everyone thought he was a true CP patient. "He pulled it off, though it could have backfired. We saw a lot of actors for that part, but he was always the first choice."

Johanna Ray's sensitivity and flexible thinking is commendable. Perhaps it's because, as she admits, she is a basically shy person who had to make a long, hard climb herself. She was doing low-budget films for years, until she was "discovered." To actors wanting to be "discovered," she offers encouragement to do as much acting as possible, no matter how unprestigious it may seem. "When you're first starting out, you may think this is not the kind of film you want to be in. But my advice is to take it, because that's just the kind of film you want to make your mistakes in."

---

*Johanna Ray discourages outside submissions; she conducts generals for specific situations.*

# Robbi Reed

**I**f you're wondering where Spike Lee finds all his unusual characters for his films, much of the credit belongs to Robbi Reed. She's been casting Spike's movies since *She's Gotta Have It*, which she confesses Spike cast himself. Although Robbi is based in Los Angeles, she frequently heads East to work with Lee, since he prefers shooting his films in New York.

Reed has been casting for about seven years, having started in television as an assistant to Diane Demeo. She says the biggest difference between casting for TV and film is the number of people who have a say in the final decision. "In television you have your network as well as your producers and director, whereas in film it's usually just you, the director, and producer. You have a little more creative room with feature casting."

One of the few black casting directors in the business, Robbi Reed is very aware of the recent improvement in job opportunities for minorities in film. "The projects have always been around, but now there seems to be an interest from the studios and networks, because they realize there's a market for black films and television shows." She says much of the change in attitude is due to the success of such directors as Spike Lee and Robert Townsend. She also feels that black actors are getting more work because of their ability to hone their skills, something she says was difficult a few years ago. "So, by the time an opportunity opened up, you weren't as prepared. You need on-the-job training much more than just acting classes." That's not to say that Reed is against an actor studying his craft. "It's just that when you're in a play and actually doing it and living

SPECIALTY:
Feature film and TV

CREDITS INCLUDE:
*Jungle Fever*
*Do the Right Thing*
*School Daze*
*Harlem Nights*
*Sweet Dreams*
"A Different World"
"Cagney and Lacy"

it, it's very different, unless of course you're at Yale or Juilliard."

Robbi is a fan of the theater. She attends a great deal of Off-Broadway and Off-Off-Broadway when she's back East. In Los Angeles she'll see plays as well, but she doesn't feel they merit the same attention, with the exception of a few L.A. theater companies.

Many of the actors that Robbi has hired have extensive theater credits but have done little film work. For those actors, she advises taking on-camera classes. "It helps, because the stage is bigger than life. I've noticed that theater actors seem too large and over-the-top, and it's simply because they're used to doing it that way for the stage. I wouldn't spend a great deal of money on classes—just enough to get the idea of bringing it down and containing it." She also believes in cold-reading classes for all actors, be they stage or film performers, "because that's what you're called on to do most of the time."

Reed not only lists the roles she's casting with Breakdown Services, she also submits her list to *Back Stage* magazine in New York. "A lot of the actors in New York share information, so usually within a couple of days, those actors who have no representation will find out about the project and drop in," which she doesn't mind in the least. "I like to find new faces. That's what I've kind of been known for, discovering people."

One of the people she's discovered is Cynda Williams, who appeared in *Mo' Better Blues*. Williams had only done a couple of community productions in Indiana, but she had what Robbi calls "the right look." In this case, the right look meant it suited what Spike Lee was searching for at that moment: a young, attractive actress. She also had the talent, despite her lack of experience. She sang beautifully at her first audition, although her reading had a somewhat nervous quality to it. Robbi had her read again when she was more relaxed, and it was much improved. With each reading, it got better and better until she knew she was ready to read for Spike. Cynda was lucky. If she had just sent in her photo and resumé, she probably wouldn't even have been called in for an audition: her picture was just horrible, recalls Reed. But because she was sitting just outside her office, Robbi decided to have a look-see, and she was delighted to find a much more attractive person than she'd expected. "The picture is very important. It's your calling card," explains Reed. "Actors try to save money, but they have to think about pictures as an investment in their career, their livelihood. A bad picture can prevent you from getting a job."

A neat resumé, carefully and accurately typed, is another requisite for an actor, and a personal note to the casting director is much appreciated. Some actors may feel a form letter with the casting director's name penciled in should suffice, but Robbi doesn't agree. "It just takes a couple of minutes more, and it's so much more personal." A note after an interview is another suggestion. Not only does it refresh the casting director's memory, but it's polite.

One thing that Reed suggests actors not do is telephone her. "Calling on the phone and leaving messages for me to call back is ridiculous. A simple note saying hi, just to keep in touch or to keep me abreast of what they're doing, is much more appropriate." She recalls an unpleasant incident where an actor tracked down Robbi's home number and called her after hours, and another irksome situation where an actor found out which car she was driving and kept leaving pictures on her windshield. "When I did *School Daze*, someone even showed up at my mother's house!" She was not amused.

*School Daze* had other memorable moments for Robbi. It was a lengthy project requiring several open calls, including one in Atlanta at which she saw four hundred actors. "I would see sometimes a hundred people a day in my office. I'd start at 8:00 in the morning and end up at about 10:00 at night." The auditions consisted of a prepared monologue and a song. One young actor made an excellent impression during his monologue and was doing quite well belting out his song when suddenly, in the middle of the tune, he raised his arms and his pants fell down. "I froze. He froze, and we just sort of stared at each other. To this day, I don't know whether it was planned or not, but it's stayed in my mind, and whenever I run into him, we just look at each other and laugh." He didn't get the part.

Very seldom will Robbi Reed ask an actor to come in to read for her a second time. If an actor is called back, it's usually to read for the director and producers. She also gives actors a second chance if they think they can improve on their reading during their audition. "I don't say okay, thanks, goodbye, after one shot. I think that's rude, and actors are subject to enough rejection. I try not to add to it. I think I still have a heart."

---

*Robbi Reed accepts photos, resumés, and videotapes; she schedules generals as time allows.*

# Shirley Rich

**INDEPENDENT**

**S**hirley Rich began her casting career with Richard Rodgers and Oscar Hammerstein and has worked with such theatrical geniuses as Hal Prince and Michael Bennett. She currently works independently, moving from place to place depending on the project with which she is involved.

To Shirley, the most important thing on an actor's resumé is training. "I believe in studying. I feel you can study all your life, and that any education an actor has, whether it's psychology or drama, I want to know about it. I want to know how you learned to be who you are." She also feels it imperative that an actor continue to study. "Can you imagine walking onto a stage without having done a workshop or taken a class for a year?" Keeping one's craft finely tuned is a must in Rich's book. She also encourages actors to find a job that still allows a career. "You have to have another profession, whether it be in a restaurant or building cabinets. You must pay your rent."

When Shirley Rich calls an actor in for a part, he or she will audition by reading from the script she has been hired to cast. "I've never done readings except for the thing I'm working on," she explains. "I guess it's because I'm theater-trained. I need to see an actor actually perform either on stage or on screen, not in my office." And she'll go to showcases a great deal to find good talent. "I feel that theater training is the secret to acting, even though you may change to another medium.

SPECIALTY:
Feature film, TV features, and theater

CREDITS INCLUDE:
*Fiddler on the Roof*
*Cabaret*
*Rachel Rachel*
*Serpico*
*Saturday Night Fever*
*Three Days of the Condor*
*Kramer vs. Kramer*
*Taps*
*Tender Mercies*
*The Ballad of the Sad Cafe*
*Diary of a Mad Housewife*
*Ballroom*

133

If you look at all the actors today who have become names, like DeNiro, Hoffman, Duvall, Hackman, and Streep, they were all theater-trained, and it's shown in their technique and diversity of their talent."

Rich also feels strongly about preparation. She'll always provide as much material to an actor before a reading as possible. "I have never had an actor read cold," she stresses. "Maybe lukewarm, but never cold. If I cannot get the material to them ahead of time, they at least must have time to look at it earlier that day." She'll also sit down and explain everything leading up to what they're doing. "They cannot," she adds "do justice to the script when they only have two pages of dialogue. They can't possibly know the character's history, and what's going to follow. It must be explained."

Rich will also make sure all the actors who have read are notified as to whether they've gotten the role or not. "I feel strongly about that. It's the worst business in the world, right? What you've got to do at least is give them the chance to forget it and move on. And if an agent calls, I'll give any input I've gotten from the director to pass on to the actor. I will tell them what I felt happened at the audition, because if it's something constructive, it can only help."

Shirley's favorite moments come when actors surprise her with their talent and charisma. While casting *Taps*, she was looking for an actor to play Tim Hutton's roommate. The script called for an upper-middle-class, sophisticated type. "And in comes a kid that you would have thought had come out of Oklahoma's dust bowl," Rich recalls. "Gorgeous, Sean Penn was not. Sophisticated, he was not. But he did a reading for me that totally blew my mind. It was one of the most inspiring I ever heard." Because she was so dazzled by his performance, Shirley rushed him into the producer's office and did her utmost to convince them of his ability. He got the part. "Sean Penn is really a brilliant young character actor. And he was eighteen at the time."

She also admires an actor who can display a range. "Someone takes a reading you give them and explores it, maybe providing something no one else saw when reading for the part. If the director is secure, he's going to see it and give that actor an opportunity to explore the part."

Shirley tries to convince actors of the importance of making choices. "You cannot decide what all those people in that room have in their heads for a part. You simply have to make a decision and go with it. Sink or swim."

An actor should also remember to take time with the material. "Don't rush," she advises. "Take a deep breath, and don't start until you're ready." She also suggests an actor keep the chatting to a minimum. "To talk just because you're nervous doesn't do you well." And try to avoid carrying a chip on your shoulder. "If you don't like the way your career has gone, keep it to yourself."

A final piece of advice from Shirley Rich: don't be afraid to ask questions of the director about the interpretation before a reading. "I think that those two or three minutes may be your life for the next year or ten years. Make the most of it."

---

*Shirley Rich does not accept unsolicited photos, resumés, or videocassettes; she does not schedule generals.*

# Marcia Ross

VICE PRESIDENT OF TALENT,
WARNER BROS. TV

Marcia Ross has been a casting director for twelve years, two of which have been at Warner Bros. Television, where she is currently a vice president in charge of television casting. Prior to her position with the studio, Marcia was partnered with Judith Holstra, and together they were responsible for casting prominent feature films and several acclaimed television projects, including the pilot for "thirtysomething."

Despite stories attributing the casting of several of the series's major stars to the show's executives, Marcia claims it was she and Judith who brought Mel Harris and Ken Olin aboard. "I had met Mel on a feature film about a year before, and though the producers really wanted a star, I told them they really had to meet this woman. So she came in and read for me, and though her reading wasn't the best, I felt this actress could be a television star." Ross finds it difficult to pinpoint exactly what quality made Harris stand out from the rest, but whatever it was, Marcia was convinced she was the right choice. "So I kept bringing her back for more readings, and each time she got better and better. Three or four other people had been reading for the same part, but they kind of began to fade away, while Mel kept improving." They had her do a test, and she won it hands down.

As for Ken Olin, Marcia says she's known the actor

SPECIALTY:
Series, pilots, and movies of the week

CREDITS INCLUDE:
Crossroads
Heartbreakers
48 Hours
Murder in Mississippi
My Name is Bill W.
Baja Oklahoma
"thirtysomething" (pilot)
LBJ
Bitter Harvest
Cocaine: One Man's Seduction

since the two were in their early twenties. "He was dating my best friend, and I started sending him out when I was a secretary at a talent agency. Then I became his first agent and kind of followed his career over the years. In fact, he was on my list for 'thirtysomething' from the first day." Ross says the producers were hoping Ron Silver would accept the role, but when he didn't materialize, they turned to Marcia's protégé, who of course landed the role.

To Marcia Ross, casting is a threefold process that requires both passion and a good memory. The first part is a thorough knowledge of actors: a casting director must know who's out there and continually explore that vast pool of talent until he or she retires from the profession. "I used to go to the theater in New York four or five nights a week. The minute you stop being interested in meeting actors, it's over." In addition to attending the theater, Ross reads magazines and newspapers voraciously, always on the lookout for articles on interesting new actors. She's open to any suggestions from agents regarding new clients, and will set up general meetings with any talent who comes highly recommended.

Step two is negotiation, the nuts-and-bolts portion of Marcia's job. "It's really just a skill like any other, something you have to embrace rather than be afraid of. It's not that hard if you take the time to learn it, and it doesn't take an incredible amount of talent. But it doesn't happen overnight; it takes time to develop. The secret to negotiating is learning to develop long-term relationships with the people you work with, like agents, and understanding how to make the best possible deals with them. If you can't make a deal for an actor, then you don't have that actor."

And the final stage is the politics of casting, perhaps the most difficult to deal with. "It's taking a process from the very beginning and getting it down to the end. It's getting a roomful of people to agree on one actor. You can find the greatest actor in the world, but if you can't get everyone to agree on him, you haven't cast the show." Although Marcia has been casting for over a decade, she feels she is just now beginning to master that aspect of the business.

The most important thing about an actor to Marcia Ross is the true nature of that individual. "It's very simple. I want the actor to be real. Whether that comes from rigorous training at the Strasberg School or whether it's innate, it doesn't matter to me. I simply look for the person to come in and appear real. Whatever it takes." That's not to say training isn't a valued commodity to Ross. Learning one's craft, she admits, is vital for an actor. "Being a movie star is a different skill from being a day player. A day player with only a couple of lines really needs to know how to act, or else how can he be consistent each time? An actor needs to understand how to get to the point where he can come in, take somebody's material, read it, and make it believable." That's why Marcia feels it so important to meet actors. In fact, she goes through every single picture that crosses her desk, and after narrowing the stack down to a workable size, she'll try to see as many new and interesting faces as she can make time for. Looking at people in pictures and on tape is not the same as meeting people face to face. Although she is often asked to audition certain actors on videotape for certain directors, Marcia feels this can do an actor an injustice, because "something else comes through when you're in the room with somebody."

Now that Ross has made the transition to executive, she no longer handles the day-to-day casting that was so much a part of her previous routine. Instead of reading actors for every episode or every movie of the week, she now casts only four films a year and concentrates on selecting new faces for the company's pilots. "I think pilot casting is the hardest form of casting, although a casting director has more say so in terms of who gets seen. We're always needing new people—nonstars—whereas in feature films the producers tend to gravitate toward bigger names. I mean, no one but a Bertolucci or a Scorcese is going to make a forty-million-dollar movie with an unknown." So even though it's the toughest part of her job, Ross enjoys finding the casts for her pilots. "Everyone knows stars. Where our work as casting directors comes into play is in all those other parts."

"Casting is a very positive experience," she maintains. My job is to get the project done. I represent and serve the producer. I'm not here to serve myself. I don't have that much power. Though I can be influential in helping the situation, it's finally up to the actor to get the job. For me, the joy of casting is seeing people get the job. It's not keeping them from it. The power I have, if any, is being supportive of the creative environment."

---

*Marcia Ross accepts pictures and resumés; she schedules generals as time permits.*

# David Rubin

**DAVID RUBIN CASTING**

It's a vagabond lifestyle for David Rubin. He doesn't maintain a permanent home, but moves from place to place depending on the project on which he's working at the time. Before making the transition to independent casting director, David worked for Mary Goldberg in New York and Lynn Stalmaster in Los Angeles. The training and experience he received were invaluable. He learned about the collaborative aspect of casting, the importance of understanding the director with whom you're involved. "There are some inexperienced actors," he notes, "who you would more readily introduce to the 'actors' director, but would be reticent to leave in the hands of a director less equipped to elicit a performance." In *Days of Thunder*, for instance, the role of Rowdy Burns was always slated for a well-known actor to play opposite Tom Cruise, but Rubin felt that Michael Rooker would be best suited to the role. While Michael had previously only appeared in supporting roles, it was up to Rubin to convince the director that he could pass muster. "My taking a strong stand resulted in his getting the role."

With so many capable actors from which to choose, it's David's belief that it's his job to suggest those who would illuminate the nuances of a role in unexpected ways. "This usually involves winnowing down the thousands of possibilities to a very short list of varied but stimulating choices." In casting the housekeeper in *The War of the Roses*, for instance, many of the finest young comedic character actresses were passed over in favor of Marianne Sägebrecht, who Rubin says brought a cross-cultural twist and a unique sensibility to the role. In smaller roles, he

SPECIALTY:
Feature film

CREDITS INCLUDE:
*Days of Thunder*
*After Dark My Sweet*
*The War of the Roses*
*Men Don't Leave*
*The Big Easy*
*The Name of the Rose*
*The Addams Family*

adds, the inclination is even greater to experiment with new faces or oblique approaches to casting. "The number of possibilities we can explore is usually limited only by time constraints and other casting priorities."

The basics expected of every actor reading for David Rubin are as complete a knowledge of the script, character, and production elements as possible, and enough preparation that you're not tied to the page and can have sufficient contact with the person with whom you're reading. Whenever the script is not available, actors should ask their agents or the casting assistant for information, and if details are still sketchy, make their own choices based on the material they do have. Rubin believes that an actor need not memorize a scene for a first reading, since most directors acknowledge the audition process is exploratory in nature. Memorization is recommended, however, for a callback and certainly for a screen test.

Before a reading, Rubin suggests asking questions about motivation, plot, and pronunciations. He may not answer them until after the reading if he wants to get a sense of an actor's instincts. He also recommends reacting to the reader as you would to another actor. "Your reactions are just as important as your own line readings." If you think you've blown the reading, you may or may not get another shot at it. "Very often I can get more positive impressions from a botched but interesting attempt than from a slick, perfected one. I am entirely process-oriented in that regard."

Rubin is always looking for a variation on a theme, so to speak. In *Men Don't Leave*, writer-director Paul Brickman had written an oddball neighbor into the script with an extremely unusual and inscrutable vocal pattern and world view. "Some very fine actresses attempted to simulate the off-rhythms of Jody, but when Joan Cusack began to read, the skies parted, the sun beamed down, and we had found someone whose unique comic timing perfectly matched and even enhanced Brickman's vision."

To Rubin, the difference between a fine actor and a movie star lies in an ineluctable quality, "a force of personality that a camera picks up, that engages an audience almost regardless of what the actor is doing on screen." Occasionally, he adds, one can get a sense of that luminous quality sitting in a room, but the only true test is from camera to screen. "I firmly believe that 95 percent of the time, a script is better served by the casting of fine actors than by the inclusion of one of the handful of 'stars' for its own sake."

Because David Rubin is one of the busiest casting directors in Hollywood, he rarely has time to chat with actors, even those he admires. "But what I try to make clear to actors is that while they may not hear from me for years, when they do come in, chances are it's because they're right for the role, and odds are they'll land it."

*David Rubin accepts pictures, resumés, and videotapes; he rarely holds generals.*

# Joan Sittenfield

## VICE PRESIDENT OF TALENT AND CASTING, UNIVERSAL TELEVISION

T he casting philosophy at MCA Universal is to look for the best people available for the part, "people we want in our living rooms, whom the audience will take to, week after week." So says Joan Sittenfield who, prior to joining MCA, was the casting director for "Taxi" and "The Jeffersons." "Basically, the way my staff and I work is that we meet as many people as it takes to find the cream of the crop." She also realizes that the decision is not ultimately hers, but that of the producers. "I think that's something more casting directors and actors should be aware of. Casting directors are glorified employment agents. I'm a personnel director. I can let producers know what I think, and I can introduce them to someone I think is exciting, but I didn't write the words that appear on the page."

Despite her modesty when it comes to the decision-making process, Joan does influence much of the casting that goes on at Universal, and what impresses her the most is an actor with the proper training. "It's the thing I look for first in a resume. I respond best to people who come from a four-year theater program more than I respond to anything else." This attitude stems from Joan's own background. "I'm a product of university theater. I was an actress who later went on to teach on the university level for nearly five years. When I see good training, it makes me relax. It makes me feel

SPECIALTY:
TV series (cast by her staff) and TV pilots

CREDITS INCLUDE:
"Murder She Wrote"
"Quantum Leap"
"Columbo"
"Coach"
"Major Dad"
"Uncle Buck"
"Law and Order"
"Harry and the Hendersons"

this is a person who knows how to approach the material." She finds this essential when dealing with episodic television because of the nature of the medium. There's little time to rehearse and hone your skills on the set. You have to be precise on a grueling schedule, week after week.

In order to achieve this professionalism, Sittenfield believes an actor must study. "Your acting's like a muscle, and if all you're going to do is sit around waiting for auditions, the muscle will atrophy, and you may not be ready when that part comes. An actor," she adds, "should work that acting muscle in some way— whether it's through a formal class, or by getting together with a group of friends and working on scenes or monologues."

While monologues may be fine on an actor's own time, Sittenfield is opposed to them at her audition sessions. "I always cold-read on a general to get a sense of the actor. I hate prepared monologues because they've got nothing to do with what they are going to do at an audition. It doesn't show me how they can do scripted dialogue, and it doesn't show me how they interrelate with other people." What Sittenfield appreciates from actors at auditions, whether general or specific, is an attitude of openness, enthusiasm, and preparation. As far as dressing for the part, "I have enough imagination," offers Sittenfield. "If they feel that a three-piece suit will help them get close to the character, they should do it. If they don't, then they should wear what makes them feel comfortable."

Joan Sittenfield doesn't want energy from an actor unless it's appropriate for the part. "It's being appropriate to what's called for by the medium. Acting is a hear, think, and speak process. I like to see a reading that reflects someone who's listening to what's being said, is thinking about it, and who then responds in a straight-from-the-face way."

Several casting directors at Universal attend acting showcases, but Joan primarily attends comic showcases to find new faces for the pilots on which she's working. For instance, she discovered Kevin Meaney, the star of "Uncle Buck," at Catch A Rising Star in New York. "I look for somebody who's a breakthrough, somebody that you'd want to develop a show around." When she introduced Kevin to the producers, they, too, knew he was perfect for "Uncle Buck" and put him under contract.

While Sittenfield tries to get to the theater as much as possible, she refuses to attend workshops that charge a fee to actors because, number one, she doesn't believe they are good vehicles for honing one's craft. And number two, she thinks that "for the most part,

they're done as money-making propositions for the people running them. I think if you want to hone your craft, get in a play. I
don't think that doing a little bitty scene constructed for two or
three minutes shows me anything."

Another place to be discovered by this particular casting director
is at a school like Juilliard or Yale. "The only times I really see people who aren't represented by agents are when I go to the annual
graduations of classes at these drama schools." Joan found Jane
Atkinson ("Parenthood") and Chris Noth ("Law and Order") at
such institutions.

Some words of wisdom to the aspiring actor: "Talent alone is not
the answer," cautions Sittenfield. "I think you have to be real honest
with yourself. I have friends in their forties who do maybe three or
four episodic roles a year, and they're still trying to continue. I think
that's sad. They're never getting on with their lives." Leading a full
life is what Joan recommends, whether or not you decide to pursue
your dreams. "It helps you in an acting sense, because you see,
you're only as good as your own personal history."

---

*Joan Sittenfield does not accept outside submissions; she will only sched-
ule generals during summer hiatus.*

# Stanley Soble

## MARK TAPER FORUM

**H**aving cast a variety of television productions, Stanley Soble is acutely aware of the difference between camera and stage acting. Though he admits there are many actors who can comfortably switch between the two media, there are others who can't. "There are just some actors who've done so much television and film, they've learned to act only for the camera, and when it comes to stage, they really have to work on their vocal skills to bring their voices back up to fill the house."

When Stanley conducts his auditions, they're usually in a rehearsal hall, a large room where actors must project to be heard. "We push the actors all the way to the back wall, so that they have to come out of themselves. They often get frightened by that. I've seen more than one actor who's been in television for a long time come back to do an audition for us, and they just can't cut it. They've lost the technique. On the other hand, there are those actors who make sure that every year, no matter where they are, they do some theater."

Training for a stage actor is, to Soble, as important as training for a violinist or pianist. "In film, a good director takes enough shots so that he can edit and cover himself, but when you're dealing with theater, an actor goes on stage and there's nothing to help him, no sound, no editing, nothing to save that person. He's out there, exposed, and has to deal with the situation. That's why technique is so important."

Actors who are used to doing

SPECIALTY:
Theater

CREDITS INCLUDE:
*An Early Frost*
*The Atlanta Child Murders*
*Big River*
*The Human Comedy*
*Pirates of Penzance*
*The Mystery of the Rose Bouquet*
*Who's Afraid of Virginia Woolf?*
Joseph Papp's Public Theatre
"Search for Tomorrow" (TV)

film auditions and who find themselves in a rehearsal hall at the Mark Taper Forum may not be able to pull out of the intimate technique they've developed for film. "And what we're looking for is somebody who can use a technique designed especially for the stage to project the character, the voice, everything."

At his typical audition, Stanley provides a chair for the actor. Other than that, it's up to the actor how to handle the scene. "We just say the space is yours, do with it as you will. If they want to move, they should feel free. When they're ready to start, they start. I try to make it as comfortable for the actor as possible. My feeling is that an actor comes into a room to audition. He really feels he has no allies, especially if he's coming into a room where there's a producer, a director, and maybe even a designer, the author, and the casting director. It's hard. They walk through that door and need to feel there's someone on their side."

Anyone who sends a photo and resumé to Soble gets seen by the casting director. He looks through them all. If he finds an interesting face with some good training, it's likely that individual will be called in for a general audition. "I ask actors to prepare two contrasting monologues for me. If one is contemporary, the other should be classic. If one is funny, the other should be more serious. The actor should try to show as many facets of his or her talent as possible." And what is Stanley looking for at these auditions? "Talent. I want an actor who is capable of coming in and not giving a finished performance, but giving enough of a performance that it will interest me, the director, and the producer. That's what we're looking for."

The other thing he's looking for is quality. "People go through their lives acquiring a certain knowledge about themselves and the ability to reflect; that, in an audition, is what I call quality. I think we're all looking for that. It's the person who can take the subtotal of what he is and what he's learned and what he's been through, and project that through his reading. That person is the much more interesting actor."

The first audition is usually just between Soble and the actor. The first callback will include the director, followed by a third reading that may include other actors in the cast. "What we try to do is give actors at least a week's notice so that they can get a copy of the script from their agent, take it home with them, read it, and work on the scene." He doesn't expect an actor to memorize the scene; in fact, he's very much opposed to that practice. He feels it's detrimental, "because I know what happens. An actor will often memorize the material, and mind you, it's only the lines, so he doesn't know how the actor reading with him is going to deliver his cues. I think it's far better to be familiar with the material, but to keep the script in hand. It gives you a certain amount of security. You're not thinking about the next line." Of course he expects actors to make eye contact and not be buried in the script, but he feels learning the lines should come after the actor has been given the role.

One of the ways an actor can get seen by Stanley Soble is to be a part of one of his many open calls; he conducts two a month. One is for Equity actors, the other for non-Equity players. About thirty actors are seen during each session. Equity auditions are preset; actors are asked to call ahead of time to schedule an appointment. The non-Equity calls are first come, first served, from 10:00 A.M. to noon. "We feel that it's important that the community has at least a chance to be seen without an agent."

Because he's working in Los Angeles, Stanley realizes that not every actor will be amenable to reading for him. Film actors are used to being cast without auditioning for the role, and Soble finds it difficult to get some of them to agree to read for a play, even though their stage experience is limited. There are times, however, when star talent will read for the director. "When we were doing *Mystery of the Rose Bouquet*, we were interested in Jane Alexander and Anne Bancroft. Those two didn't have to read per se, but what we did is a reading of the play with them. After that, they made the decision whether or not they wanted to do it."

Stanley spends as much time with the minor characters as he does with the stars. "You're putting together a group of actors, a chain that's only as strong as its weakest link. So we are as careful with the smaller roles as we are with the leading players." He's also responsible for casting the understudies. Most of those hired are not members of the original cast, unless it's a repertory company or the production is so huge that it's feasible to use one of the other players. And sometimes an actor gets lucky. Soble recalls one instance where they hired someone for a leading role and she turned out to be so awful they had to use the understudy in the lead, just two weeks into rehearsal. At first, the producers were reluctant to even hire the actress as the understudy, but they were delighted when she turned out to be much better than the person they originally expected would lead the cast.

Performing on stage in L.A. is different from New York. Soble admits most actors who work the L.A. stage are doing it for the exposure. They're on the West Coast to break into TV or film, and hope they'll be discovered by casting directors who often attend the theater scouting new faces. Does it bother Stanley Soble? Not at all—he's proud of the productions with which he's involved. "The most important thing to say is that the well-rounded actor is aware of the particular field he's working in and learns to audition for each area in its own specific technical way. I really feel that unless you have a technique, a background, you're not what you call yourself—an actor."

*Stanley Soble accepts photos and resumés; he schedules generals and open calls.*

# Lynn Stalmaster

**I**f there is one name in casting that everyone knows, even those not in the business, it's Lynn Stalmaster. Lynn was the first independent casting director on the West Coast in the mid-1960s. Prior to that, he was an actor. "At the outset, I thought acting was the answer," he admits. "And then I think, as all actors know, the rejection and lack of control influenced me in deciding that perhaps there was another way to express myself." And he obviously found the right path.

The Stalmaster philosophy has been with him from the beginning: "Trying to find actors who have not necessarily appeared in a lot of films and would bring a certain reality to the screen, or giving an opportunity to an actor who has been identified with one sort of character the chance to demonstrate his capacity to do something else." That's what Lynn claims originally turned him on to casting: "Trying to bring something unexpected to each character."

Many top directors rely on the Stalmaster technique. He's frequently called upon by the same cinematic heavyweights to lend his expertise to their films, among them Sidney Pollack, Hal Ashby, Brian DePalma, Ted Koch, and Mark Rydell. He also travels extensively, unlike many other casting directors who rely on associates in other cities to help with the chore. "I personally have read thousands of actors in cities all over the world, including Vancouver, San Juan, Santo Domingo,

SPECIALTY:
Feature film and TV miniseries

CREDITS INCLUDE:
*Bonfire of the Vanities*
*Taking Care of Business*
*Havana*
*Tootsie*
*The Right Stuff*
*10*
*Harold and Maude*
*An Officer and a Gentleman*
*Coming Home*
*The Graduate*
*The Rose*
*Roots*
*The Thorn Birds*

and London, and I've seen as many as a hundred and fifty people in a day. I've had open calls in places like North Carolina and Montana where literally fifteen hundred people have shown up."

One fond memory was in Asheville, North Carolina, when Lynn was casting *Winter People*. He was looking for a little girl to play Kurt Russell's daughter. "I think it was on one of those cattle calls where I spotted a young lady hiding in the background. Something about her caught my eye, and through a series of readings and tapings, she got the part. Oddly enough, she probably came there with her mother on a lark, and she may never work again." Casting children is one of Lynn Stalmaster's specialties. "It's something I enjoy a great deal," he admits. "I think it's not only an enormous challenge, but also a test of concentration and discipline in terms of trying to continually be alert as you meet all these youngsters until you find the one that fits the director's image."

Stalmaster is also ever on the alert for promising minorities. When he cast *Havana* he had to explore the Hispanic market all over the world since the film took place in Cuba. He found himself up at 5:00 A.M. most mornings, traveling from New York to Santo Domingo to Miami to Puerto Rico. The biggest challenge in that project was finding someone who not only fit the bill, but also spoke enough English to make himself understood on camera. Authenticity is a primary concern to Stalmaster. "I'll make every effort to cast actors who either have the exact ethnic background or are of a similar heritage."

He also spends as much time on one-line roles as he does on the leads. "I even cast reactive roles that have no dialogue if the director requests an actor rather than an extra, and I agonize over those parts as much as I do the larger roles." Why? "Because I'm paranoid about that kind of care and detail."

Although Lynn Stalmaster recoils at the word "discovered," he has nonetheless been responsible for many careers, including that of Geena Davis, whom he hired for *Tootsie*. He was the one who recognized Richard Dreyfuss's potential when he appeared briefly in *The Graduate*, and he cast Andy Garcia in *Eight Million Ways to Die* before he went on to greater success in *The Untouchables*.

An actor is lucky to get a reading not only for but *with* Lynn Stalmaster. He can truly empathize with an actor since he's been in his shoes. "I know the nerves and tension and what an actor goes through, and I just want to play to the actor and react as much as I can to give him as much to relate to as possible." He's so good at reading that many a director has offered him a role. He's never accepted, however. "It isn't proper, and it isn't fair to take a role from an actor who makes his livelihood acting."

If you have the opportunity to meet Lynn Stalmaster it will definitely be a memorable experience. Getting to read for the "master" is reason alone, but his office is a treasure trove of memorabilia from his numerous excursions abroad. Confesses Stalmaster, "I love to collect knicknacks and actors."

*Lynn Stalmaster accepts photos and resumés but no videocassettes; he holds generals occasionally when time allows.*

# Stanzi Stokes

**W**hen entering Stanzi Stokes's office one can't help but notice a height chart prominently displayed on the wall adjacent to the door. No, she doesn't measure every actor she interviews. It's there for the children she cast in "Lassie." Sometimes, she says, it's important that a guest star isn't inches taller or shorter than the series' regulars. The difference in height could look peculiar, hence the wall chart.

Stanzi is great with kids. "You need to have a good rapport with children, to be able to put them at ease. Some of them come in, and they're scared. They don't really want to be there. They want to be on the baseball field." What Stanzi does is get down on the floor with the kids and talk to them on their level. She'll even do the readings on the floor if necessary. "You have to catch that moment," she explains. "They may do a whole scene, but one line might be the perfect thing. A casting director has to see that certain something that gives us an idea of what we have to work with."

Training, she feels, isn't as important for children as it is for adults. In fact, the leading youngster in "Lassie" had virtually no experience. "We wanted a real little boy, and a lot of kids we read were good, but they had already done a lot of TV, had already been trained, and they came out of that school of TV acting where everything was studied and every reaction was predictable." Will Nipper was just a natural little boy. "He had this cute little face and these expressions that were just so real." They ended up having to work diligently with him to

SPECIALTY:
Feature film and TV

CREDITS INCLUDE:
Bill and Ted's Excellent Adventure
The Terminator
Casual Sex
It's Your Funeral
Grey Men
Feds
"The New Lassie"

152

improve his line readings, since he'd had little training, but it paid off. Not only was he adorable on camera, but he worked extremely well with Lassie. "A lot of kids said they had dogs and loved animals, but when Lassie would be in the room with them, they'd flinch and that sort of thing."

There had been another contender for the lead in "Lassie," as Stanzi recalls. "One boy was so precious. He was an adorable little redhead, and he got so excited when he met Lassie. He kept going, 'Oh my God! Oh my God!' It was like he was starstruck. He kept staring at Lassie, and unfortunately, he ended up blowing his reading totally." Casting children may be fun and challenging, but it certainly isn't easy.

When it came to casting "Lassie," Stokes used her own extensive files. She utilized Breakdown Services when she had the time, but she rarely had the time. "I had to cast every episode in three or four days," she says with exasperation in her voice. "At the beginning of the season I put a lot of breakdowns out, but soon I just had time to scan my files and immediately set up auditions." Stokes kept her "Lassie" submissions an entire season, actors she knew wanted to work on a syndicated TV series and were willing to work for lower wages than they might have gotten on network TV or feature films.

That's one of the difference Stanzi notes between casting features and television. "I don't usually have to coax people into coming in for feature film auditions. Everybody wants to do features." And she won't hesitate to cast the same actors she hired for "Lassie" in upcoming movies on which she's working. "If I thought they were good enough for 'Lassie,' I think they're good enough for features, too." One of the reasons is that "Lassie" was shot on film, not videotape. It didn't require a broad performance from an actor. The acting is subtle and real, as in film. If she were casting sitcoms, she admits, she might not be able to hire the same actors. In fact, she does suggest that stage or video actors who want to do features should take courses in acting for the camera. "It's so important to get some film technique to see what you're doing. It really helps to play it back and see if your acting is too big, and if you need to work on pulling it back a bit." She also suggests that actors ask their agent before an audition if the TV show for which they're auditioning is filmed or taped, and if the producers want it broad or subtle. And she recommends, "If you're going up for a series, watch at least one episode to see what it's like."

Stanzi Stokes does not always read actors before she takes them in to meet the producers. "The more I've gotten confident in myself, the less people have to read for me. I used to make people who had read for me many times still come in and read if it was a different part. Now, if they've done a good job once, I just call them, explain the part to the agent, and take them right in to the producers."

Stanzi has discovered many young people at the theater, which she attends several times a week. When she was an assistant casting person on *I Wanna Hold Your Hand*, she spotted Wendy Jo Sperber doing a musical at a small theater. She immediately brought her to Robert Zemeckis, who was having a lot of trouble casting one particular role. Wendy Jo got the part, and went on to costar in *Back to the Future* and "Bosom Buddies."

When auditioning for Stokes, an actor should come in as himself and then assume the character for the reading. Stokes, as well as the producers, want to see the transition as well as the performance itself. There are exceptions to this rule, of course. Stanzi recalls bringing in an Aussie actor with a heavy accent for a role requiring some French speaking ability. "There wasn't much dialogue, but he had to do a very heavy French accent. It didn't bother me that he had an Australian accent, but I asked him if just this once he could come in to the producers with a French accent, because I thought it would be less confusing." It worked: he got the job.

Stokes will usually have actors read from the script, but if there isn't much dialogue, she may have them prepare monologues or read someone else's lines just to get an idea of how they handle the material. It's important that an actor be as comfortable as possible. Nerves don't make the actor look good, nor does it make the casting person look good. "That's what the producers remember—the nerves, not the reading." Classes might be one way of learning to overcome these jitters. The more practice an actor gets in front of people, the easier auditions become.

Stanzi Stokes wants actors to know she's on their side. "I love actors. When they come in for me, I put out as much positive energy as possible, because they're only going to make me look better if they're doing well. My philosophy is to be nice to the actors because they've got enough pain, and I was once in their shoes. I did theater and stuff. I know what they're going through!"

---

*Stanzi Stokes accepts photos and resumés but will only consider videotapes from actors she's already auditioned; she does not hold generals.*

# Juliet Taylor

Although Juliet Taylor is best known for her casting work on all of Woody Allen's features since *Bananas*, she doesn't feel that she's typecast, since she works on at least two other features each year. Her relationship with Allen, however, is her most cherished. "I think people would be surprised," reveals Taylor, "that Woody's film persona of a neurotic, compulsive character is quite different from his work style. He's really a dream to work for: very clear, has no ego problems whatsoever, never loses his temper. You can deliver the worst news, and he bounces right back!" Taylor adds that it's also impossible for Allen to do something he doesn't believe in.

As far as his casting philosophy, she says he works very intuitively "so that people, in a way, fulfill his vision. He's not always swayed by the same people others are swayed by. He responds to a certain quality about an actor very quickly. He meets actors for a very short time, like minutes, so it hardly affords him the time to get to know them, and yet he knows almost immediately when someone walks into the room whether they're right." That, says Taylor, puts the burden on her to make sure the actors to which he responds are capable of doing the job. "Sometimes I'll say I'm concerned that they may not be able to do a large part, and I'll recommend he read them, which he doesn't care to do very much, but he will." Woody Allen also has an aversion to theatricality, according to Taylor. "So, if I like someone who has a theatrical edge to him, I sometimes like for Woody to hear him, so I know there's not a disparity in our feelings about that person."

SPECIALTY:
Feature film

CREDITS INCLUDE:
Woody Allen's films
*Working Girl*
*Mississippi Burning*
*Dangerous Liaisons*
*Shoot the Moon*
*Julia*
*The Exorcist*
*Pretty Baby*

When Juliet Taylor casts a film she keeps in mind what her mentor, Marion Dougherty, taught her: graciousness. "For instance, when we have readings, unless we're absolutely pressed into it, we would never have actors in to ready for the same roles back to back. It's very unnerving for an actor to hear someone working on a part you're about to read. It's anxiety-provoking to know your competition." Another thing she learned from Dougherty is to give directors as much information about the actors they're going to meet, and to give actors as much information as possible about the material.

Taylor hasn't the time to meet every actor in New York, but she does go through all the photos that come in, and she says she gets at least thirty unsolicited pictures a day. "I have a Woody Allen section because Woody tends to use more unusual, humorous faces, and I always know where to go." If she likes someone's picture, she'll then set up a general interview to get a feel for that person, and when a role comes up that's appropriate, she may call him in for an audition. She also relies on agents and the players guides for discovering new talent.

When Juliet calls an actor in for a reading, she prefers her own scripts to monologues. "I find that monologues are simply out of context. People tend to pick very high-pitched scenes, throwing themselves against the wall and collapsing into a puddle of tears. I'd rather read them in the material I'm working on."

When Taylor is casting a film, she'll sometimes resort to a street search, as happened when she was looking for interesting faces for *Broadway Danny Rose*. Even the lounge singer in the film, Nick Apollo Forte, was an inexperienced actor from Waterbury, Connecticut. "We were going through all the male vocalists at the Colony Record Store in Manhattan, when we came across this guy's album. We called him, and he came in, and he had a lot of confidence and pizzazz. We had the sense he was fearless about the whole thing. He was perfect."

Taylor has also discovered a number of actors who have gone on to greater success, although she doesn't like the term "discovered." She was responsible for finding Brooke Shields for *Pretty Baby*, Linda Blair for *The Exorcist*, Meryl Streep for *Julia*, William Hurt for the PBS production *The Best of Families*, John Malkovich for *The Killing Fields*, and Jeff Daniels for *Terms of Endearment*. Juliet had seen Jeff in a Lanford Wilson play in New York and called him in to read for a part in a movie he didn't get. "I thought he should have. I was so impressed by his reading that I got all excited about him." She was more insistent when it came to casting Melanie Griffith in *Working Girl*. "The producers didn't believe they'd ultimately give her the lead because they didn't have an awareness of what her quality would be. So we had her fly in from L.A. and read for it, and that was it. Mike Nichols fell in love with her." Juliet Taylor is obviously very much in love with her job. She's equally adept at casting comedy and serious film. "I do love to cast wonderful characters. I love the opportunity to be a little outrageous!"

*Juliet Taylor accepts outside submissions; she will schedule generals when time allows.*

# Mark Teschner

## ABC DAYTIME TELEVISION

Daytime drama is one of the best vehicles for getting a start in television, and because "General Hospital" has one of the largest casts in daytime TV, it would behoove an actor to keep in contact with casting director Mark Teschner. "I'm looking for any actor who's right for a particular role," states Teschner, and if he or she happens to be a non-union player, it's not a problem for Mark. They can always join the union after they secure the part. "If an actor sends me a photo, and I want to read him for a role, I certainly will do so. Everybody has been non-union at some point or other in their lives, and most have gotten their union cards by working."

When Mark was casting "Loving," he recalls hiring Terri Polo as a contract player. "It was her first audition, but she had wonderful instincts. There was something very special about her despite her lack of credits." In fact, they created a part for her because they were so impressed with her ability.

It's not unusual for producers of soaps to create roles based on the discovery of unique talent. Teschner says it recently happened on "General Hospital." Brad Lockerman, one of the central characters on the show, had originally read for the part of Duke. "We didn't hire him for that," explains Mark, "but we knew we wanted him to be on the show and envisioned something coming up in the not-too-distant future." So they kept tabs on him, and when they had a suitable role, he was hired.

Casting for daytime drama is not very different from casting any other form of television, except that it's twice as hectic. Mark gets in every morning at 8:30, has his coffee, and sits down with the scripts to see what's coming up and what slots have to be filled. There are currently over

SPECIALTY:
Daytime drama

CREDITS INCLUDE:
"General Hospital"
"Loving"

thirty contract players on "General Hospital," along with six or seven recurring characters, about a dozen day players and a similar number of under-fives, not to mention anywhere from twenty to a hundred extras per week. "So it's continuous," sighs Mark. "The casting process never stops, because there are so many actors, there's no such thing as inactivity when you're casting daytime."

After perusing the scripts and determining what roles need to be cast for the week, Mark will open up his phone lines to agents. If he's auditioning for a contract role, he will probably see thirty-five to forty actors a day. Following the auditions, he'll decide whom to call back and what roles need additional searches.

"General Hospital" has a phone line check-in for those actors who have already worked the show as extras, and who want to know what's coming up. Unlike in film, AFTRA handles both speaking and non-speaking actors, and they all go through Mark Teschner's office. If an actor wants to work as an extra, Mark suggests submitting a photo and resumé, and if it passes muster, the actor will then be called in to work. Mark also likes to bring in a lot of actors for each role he's casting. For example, if he's looking for a major cast member, he may see three hundred people, bringing back up to forty to read for the producer. There are often two callbacks with the producer. "Sometimes we change the audition scene in the callback process to show a side of the character that wasn't present in the first scene." A screen test is the final step in the casting process. During the screen test, the actor will be paired with the character on the show with whom he'll be playing opposite, to test the dynamics and chemistry of the situation.

It's not necessary, says Mark, that an actor know the story line as well as a fan might, but he does think it's wise to watch a few episodes and become familiar with the characters. Of course, if the role being cast is part of a new story line, it's less important, and the producers themselves may not know exactly where they're going with the new character. "The bottom line," he explains, "is that an actor still has to make choices as that character in terms of what he or she is going for, and what's going to happen or not happen, regardless of his or her familiarity with the show."

Why is it that everyone on daytime TV looks so "perfect"? "Yes," admits Teschner. "Daytime does have a tendency to hire very attractive people, because it's about romance and our perceptions of romance and passion, but I do think we're slowly getting away from that antiquated concept. Lots of people can be very pretty but not very sexy. I think that sexuality and beauty are things that often stem from within. That's the way it is in real life. If you look carefully, you'll see that there is a much greater range today than there ever was in terms of the look of daytime. There are much fewer plastic-looking people than ten or fifteen years ago—at least I hope so."

Mark has been a firm believer in casting against type since he started doing daytime drama. During his stint on "Loving," he came across an actor who had a quality that appealed to him, even though physically the man was wrong for the part. "Even his reading was a little unfocused, but he was so very interesting and compelling that as soon as I dismissed him, I ran out to the elevator and asked him to come back and try again." Teschner worked on the scene with him and called the producer to explain the situation. "I asked the producer to please pay a lot of attention to him and give him the benefit of the doubt." That actor ended up getting the part. "He found a way to make the role work and made us rethink the role."

Mark is always on the lookout for good talent, frequenting the theater as often as three times a week. "I'll see an actor I like, and then a really interesting day player or recurring role comes along, and I can hire him. It's a very satisfying and creative feeling to see an actor whose work you've admired, and be able to call him the next day and say there's a part I'd like him to read for."

Teschner advises actors who audition for him not to try too hard. "Don't feel you have to sell yourself. We want to see who you are, not what you think we're looking for." If an actor works too hard, he says, it can pull him out of the scene. Another piece of advice: "Only act if you have to, not for fame or fortune. Ninety percent of union actors don't work. If during the periods you're not working, you still have the passion for what you do, continue. Do it only if it's what you must do, because it's just too difficult otherwise."

---

*Mark Teschner accepts photos, resumés, and videocassettes; he does not hold generals.*

# Bonnie Timmerman

**B**onnie Timmerman is one of the most respected names in casting, having worked on some of the most accredited and successful films of the last twenty years. She's also responsible for altering the look of television with the casting of "Miami Vice." "I think with 'Miami Vice' I single-handedly changed the face of TV. Television before 'Miami Vice' was mostly in California. There wasn't much activity in New York. I didn't even want to do TV, but Michael Mann called me and said, 'I'm going to put you in New York with a camera and an office, and you won't have to work with a director except by telephone. Just put your choices down on tape, and we'll leave a lot of this up to you.'"

Timmerman took the plunge on this amazing job opportunity, casting actors who had TV experience as well as people who had never appeared on TV before. Equating "Miami Vice" with today's music videos, Bonnie describes how she hired musicians like Glenn Frey, Miles Davis, and Eartha Kitt simply because of their incredible personas. "You read an article about somebody, and the personality affects you. We took parts that were supposed to be one way, and we changed them. We put Eddie Olmos in a role nobody would have imagined. It was very ethnic, very New York. It was a group you'd never seen on television before." As for the casting of Don Johnson, that was the producers' choice. It was Timmerman's responsiblity to challenge that choice, and come up with other interesting actors as competition. Johnson, obviously, triumphed.

SPECIALTY:
Feature film, TV, theater

CREDITS INCLUDE:
*State of Grace*
*Fast Times at Ridgemont High*
*Gangsters*
*The Stand*
*Midnight Run*
*Bull Durham*
*Dirty Dancing*
*Trading Places*
"Miami Vice"
"Crime Story"

Others who got started on their skyrocketing careers via "Miami Vice" and Bonnie Timmerman were Julia Roberts, Bruce Willis, and Liam Neeson. "Liam came to town," she recalls. "He was visiting Robert DeNiro, who asked me if I would meet a friend of his. He came to the office, and I thought, 'What an interesting person he is.' We talked about his life and where he's from. He sent me some tapes, and we cast him." So actors who thumb their noses at television may be doing themselves an injustice. "TV is very good for actors just starting out," suggests Bonnie. "Stage is better, but TV is good too, because you can experiment."

Theater is an excellent training ground for actors not only because they can hone their craft on the stage, but because it's where many casting directors discover new faces. That, is in fact, where Timmerman found Sean Penn. At the time she was casting *Fast Times at Ridgemont High*, Sean was appearing at the Phoenix Theatre playing a retarded child. He was fifty pounds lighter and had shaved his head. Timmerman was so impressed with his acting that she asked him to come in for an interview. "I was mesmerized by him, and there was no way of stopping me from trying to help him any way I could, to get him an agent, to be his friend. I think when people love you and bring you in for things and support you, it always helps, because actors are basically insecure, but when they're cared for and nurtured, they're less insecure."

There was also something about Ellen Barkin that caught Bonnie's trained eye. Ellen was trying to make ends meet by waitressing at a New York restaurant. "We happened to be looking for a young, striking lady for a play I was doing at the Phoenix Theatre called *Shout Across the River*. Ellen had a powerful presence, and I brought her in to read. She pulled it off—she was discovered in a restaurant!"

Bonnie finds actors through all sorts of channels. When she was doing *Dirty Dancing* she held open calls, went to Rockefeller Center, put an ad in the newspaper, visited a number of ballet companies, attended acting classes, and talked to coaches. The stars of the film, however, were sent to her through agents.

Actors should be wary of agents, in Timmerman's opinion. They can be wonderful and boost an actor's career, but they can also be a hindrance if an actor isn't careful. "Sometimes they outprice an actor and stop him from getting a job. I also think actors should read scripts themselves and not rely on their agents; read *everything* before turning it down. Sometimes an actor can see a creative side to a script that maybe an agent can't. Sometimes agents will think financially even though a smaller-budget film may have a better script."

If there's one point Bonnie Timmerman likes to stress to actors, it's to keep studying. "You should be reading. You should be the smartest person you can be. You're not an actor because you're getting paid—you're an actor because you're an actor." And when should an actor think about calling it quits? "Never, never." she says. "Just keep trying. If you love this business, just keep going."

*Bonnie Timmerman accepts photos and resumés but no unsolicited videotapes; she schedules generals when casting a specific project.*

# Joy Todd

**J**oy Todd teaches private classes for actors in New York. The former actress/stand-up comic understands the process of performing and tries to pass her knowledge of auditioning on to actors. "I only take ten in a class and usually only do it once a year." She says the main thrust of her instruction is positive thinking. "If you're not a positive thinker," she advises, "you may as well get out of the business."

Some of the things she teaches to her students are the do's and don'ts of auditioning. Do come prepared. Do come on time. Don't wear a lot of jewelry that rattles on your wrists, and don't wear your hair hanging in your face. "They're so busy brushing their hair from their eyes, they can't concentrate. Pin it back, for God's sake. Let me see what's going on in your face. I don't care that you're not coiffed. I don't care if you come in sans make-up, sans wardrobe. I just want to see what's in your heart and in your soul, what your talent's about." Joy also gets annoyed with certain irritating habits. "There was one actress who came in," she recalls. "She had a ballpoint in her hand and kept clicking it for a long time. I said, 'Have you any idea what you're doing? I haven't heard one word that you've said. Give me that pen, and I'll show you what you were just doing.' And when I showed her she was shocked." What Joy Todd does not want an actor to do is to distract her from the business at hand. "It's what I call dissipating your energy. You've got to be focused."

She also believes that an actor should be pliable, flexi-

SPECIALTY:
Feature film; occasional TV projects and commercials

CREDITS INCLUDE:
*Q&A*
*Scenes From a Mall*
*Prince of the City*
*Moscow on the Hudson*
*Someone to Watch Over Me*

ble, and able to "go with the flow." "Sometimes something may happen within the casting director's office over which he or she has no control. If I'm in the middle of a session, and my producer calls and keeps me on the phone for half an hour, I can't tell him I've got people waiting, so I may wind up thirty minutes behind schedule." She hopes an actor will understand that these things happen. "I think there should be seminars that explain what happens to the actor at auditions."

Todd finds her actors by submitting to Breakdown Services and getting the usual onslaught from agents. But she also has her own files, and it's first come, first served, as she says. "As the pictures and resumés come in, we open them up and look at every single picture; I sit with my staff, go through them very quickly, and decide whom to call in." She adds that she never spends much time on an individual photo. "I make snap decisions, because you might have fifty submissions in one day, and we can't afford to pore over every single one."

Often it's the picture itself that pops out at her. Other times, it's the resumé. If the actors have trained with admirable teachers or have an impressive body of work, she'll bring them in. She believes that an actor trained in the classics has a definite edge. "I find that very often when an actor has done the classics, it seems to give him a very strong foundation." As for looks, "It's something in the eyes, something that makes me sit up and pay attention. There are some faces," she insists, "that demand to be brought in." That's not to say she's looking for classic beauty, but what she does not want to see is the "Don Johnson look." "I'm getting real tired of looking at guys who need a shave. That look is out!"

Joy enjoys casting real people. She even went to gay bars to scout transvestites for one early film. "I like to cast people who are wonderful, people who are extraordinary." One such person was Holly Hunter, whom she'd spotted at a showcase. Todd was working on a film for Ulu Grosbard and thought he should take a look at her. "I described her as a little Georgia Cracker with a thick Southern accent, but when she comes on stage, you cannot take your eyes off of her. The place lights up." Hunter wasn't right for Grosbard's film, but the director happened to be doing a Beth Henley play next, and as soon as he met her, he had the same reaction as Todd, and the actress was cast. The play folded, but Holly got raves and her career took off shortly thereafter.

There have also been times when Todd was so impressed by a particular actor that the director altered the script to accommodate the talent. Michael Gross, who portrayed the father on "Family Ties," had come in to read for Joy when she was looking for a hotshot agent type. "I thought, 'Is he wrong for this!' He came in dressed like a bank auditor, and I said, 'Michael, I have to tell you physically you are wrong for this role, but why don't you read anyway.' It was a very small part, but I was so impressed with him that I brought him to Sidney Lumet, who changed the role to fit Michael."

While many casting directors distinctly avoid monologues, Joy Todd encourages actors to prepare these solo scenes so she can see an actor at his or her best. "I cast *Prince of the City* that way," she confesses. "When an actor's doing a monologue, this is something he uses for audition purposes. He's worked on it, he's sorted it out. If someone does a monologue for me and it's boring, I'm going to know for sure that this is not an actor I'm going to cast." Joy always asks actors to prepare monologues when a script is structured in such a way that the dialogue is very sporadic, with maybe three lines of dialogue for six or seven scenes. "How do you get anybody to read that?"

Having been an actress herself, Joy Todd knows precisely how it feels to audition. "My job is not to sit and judge an actor. My job is to help the actor as much as I can, to give him as much as I can when I'm reading with him. Do I expect an actor to come in and do a performance? No. But I do expect an actor to come in and be prepared."

---

*Joy Todd accepts photos and resumés, but accepts videotapes only for a specific project; she rarely schedules generals.*

# Ronnie Yeskel

## INDEPENDENT

There are two things that set Ronnie Yeskel apart from most casting directors: first, she hires readers to assist actors with their auditions; and second, she accepts phone calls. "I love actors," she confesses. "I was an actor for about five minutes, so I know what a high you get when it's really working, and I know how hard it is for you to audition and try to land something in five minutes." Ronnie admits she's one of the most accessible casting people in the business. She also feels it's vital that actors are in an environment that's comfortable to them.

Yeskel hires readers as a way of making actors feel more at home. Most of the readers she employs are actor friends who usually wind up getting a role in the project at hand. The reader not only reads the scene with the actor who's auditioning, but he or she will also work with the actor, helping to make adjustments before the audition. The reader is used during callbacks for the producer and director. The only time Ronnie expects an actor to memorize a scene is when it's being taped, so that his face isn't buried in the script.

Yeskel requires that all actors coming in for auditions fill out a form that asks the standard questions, including how to contact them or their agents, although to land a role with Ronnie it's not necessary to have an agent or be a member of SAG. She'll also ask actors about prior experience and with whom they've studied. During the auditioning process, Ronnie encourages actors to ask questions. "This is their time to find out about the character. And if they're in the middle of a reading, and it's not going well, I also encourage them to stop and, if need be, to leave the room." She realizes it

SPECIALTY:
"L.A. Law" and feature film

CREDITS INCLUDE:
"L.A. Law"
The Marrying Man
Partners in Life
Little Feet

may be their only shot, and she doesn't want them to throw it away needlessly.

As for what she expects in the way of dress, Yeskel prefers an actor to look the part as much as possible without donning a nurse's uniform or a G-string. "Sometimes people aren't creative enough to see beyond what's in front of them," she explains. "They see what's there, and that's all."

What's more important than dress to Yeskel, however, is an actor's behavior. "I like an actor who's really natural and who's funny. And I love actors who take risks . . . who are dangerous and don't know what they're going to do . . . who are not afraid to make asses of themselves." Just how can an actor take risks? "When an actor has really done his homework and gives the character life, color, and depth," she offers. She believes that when an actor plays it safe, it's boring.

Casting against type is also important to this casting director, "because it's more interesting. It's unpredictable, and you don't want to go for what's predictable." For "L.A. Law" Ronnie tries to find unusual characters, and they're always seeking a significant number of minorities to fill the bill.

To Ronnie Yeskel "star quality" is more than just a presence. It's an eccentricity. Maybe an offbeat look. And definitely humor. "I think if you're funny you can go very, very far. People love to laugh." It's obvious that Yeskel loves people, especially those in front of the camera, and she'll give her all to see that everyone gets a fair shot. "We go through every single picture that comes into this office." Just another example of her respect for actors. "Hey— without actors, we're without jobs!"

---

*Ronnie Yeskel accepts photos, resumés, and videocassettes; she does schedule general meetings and auditions. She does not attend workshops, but prefers local theater.*

**PART TWO**

# The Casting Process

# Family Planning:

## THE PROCESS OF PEOPLING *PARENTHOOD*

### BY JANE JENKINS AND JANET HIRSHENSON

**I**t's hard enough to cast your basic two-character buddy movie, but when an ensemble piece like *Parenthood* crosses your desk with its nine marquee roles and forty-three minor speaking parts, a log of the casting process is a must. Jane Jenkins and Janet Hirshenson of the Casting Company (*Willow, When Harry Met Sally., Tucker, Reds, Beetlejuice*) share a diary of their work on Ron Howard's comedy.

August 1, 1988
We meet with Howard, who tells us he'd prefer that every major part be played by a "name" performer.

August 1-15
We compile a list of possible performers for each of the main adult characters, keeping in mind the overall budget. We select about twenty possibilities for each character. The list for Gil, the leading man, includes Steve Martin (the eventual choice), Robin Williams, Richard Dreyfuss, Bruce Willis, Danny DeVito, Bill Murray, and Howard himself.

August 17
Howard and his partner, Brian Grazer, meet with us to discuss the lists. We eliminate several names and come up with shorter rosters of perhaps five or six names.

October 4
We check the availability of each actor to pare down the lists even further. We call the actors' agents and tell them we're starting a film for Ron Howard and that we're holding readings in December.

October 10

A breakdown of every role in the immediate family, including the adults and older children, is released by Breakdown Services, a company that acts as an intermediary between casting directors and agents. The service describes all the characters in a script and lists them in order of importance, even indicating on which page a character enters the script. The breakdown goes out to all franchised agents who subscribe.

October 16

We start going through the photographs and resumés that are sent in by agents, and set up a schedule of auditions.

October 24

A breakdown for the other characters in the script (thirty-six in all) is released.

October 25-27

Howard comes into L.A. to meet with some of the stars being considered for leading roles. Agents at ICM, William Morris, and other major talent agencies arrange these introductions.

October 27

We read actors for the part of Susan (Gil's sister), seemingly the most difficult part to cast. Most of the other adult leads are set. Actresses read for Karen and Helen, but none who audition get the parts. Mary Steenburgen and Dianne Wiest land the roles, having met with the director only to determine if they see eye-to-eye. Jason Robards turns down Grandpa, saying he doesn't see any humor in the part. Howard pleads with the actor's agent to just have him come in and discuss it. Robards agrees to a meeting, and Howard is able to convince him to come aboard. Howard and Grazer negotiate terms with the principals' agents, allowing us to finish casting the younger set.

October 29

Keanu Reeves and Martha Plimpton come to the Imagine Films office to read for the teen roles. They are first on the list of likely candidates and are eventually approved by Howard.

November 2-December 16

We start seeing hundreds of other young actors to portray the eight children in the script. Most are under 10, some with little or no experience. One of the characters is only 2½, and Jane can't read someone that young the way she would read an older actor. She creates a game, asking the children to repeat everything she says. All of these children are represented by Hollywood agents, even the toddlers. Sometimes they're seen in groups to observe the chemistry between them. The children who seem most appropriate are videotaped. The tapes are then sent to Connecticut for Howard's evaluation.

November 3-5

Howard comes into town to meet with those who've already auditioned for us and who are being considered for the roles of Susan and some of the older children. The other leads are now out of the casting director's hands. Stars of the caliber of Steve Martin are handled by the producer or director, who contacts the agent and sets up a meeting to discuss the project.

November 15-18

Howard again comes to Los Angeles to meet the contenders for the roles of the school principal, Dianne Wiest's boyfriend, and Steve Martin's boss. At this point, it's certain that Martin is the star of the film.

November 28

Jane heads to Florida to cast the day players [most location films hire local actors for the smaller parts to avoid travel expenses]. She works with Ellen Jacoby, an Orlando casting agent, who sets up auditions for various roles, including the grandmother and Gil's boss. Jane spends several days in Miami videotaping actors, then goes to Orlando. The tapes are sent to Howard in Connecticut.

December 16

Harley Kozak is recommended by her agent for the role of Susan. Jane is delighted to know she's available and tapes her audition.

December 18

Howard loves Kozak's audition and decides to hire her for the role, amending his original conviction that all leads should mean something on the marquee.

December 23
We begin calling agents and setting the deals for those actors earning $38,000 or less. The Screen Actors Guild calls this the "money break." Deals for more than $38,000 are handled by attorneys in the business affairs department.

December 28
We and the actors' agents finish the contracts: salaries, per diem expenses, billing (credits on the screen), travel expenses, and parent or guardian transportation. Now begins the tedious process of drawing up twenty individual contracts.

January 16, 1989
Filming for *Parenthood* gets underway in Orlando. We now have to make sure that the actors show up on schedule and that they're in good standing with their union when they do.

# Musical Chairs:

## CASTING AND THE WORLD GOES 'ROUND
### BY JOSEPH ABALDO

April 18, 1991
*And the World Goes 'Round: The Songs of Kander and Ebb,* currently at the Westside Theatre, was originally presented at the Whole Theatre in Montclair, New Jersey, as *The World Goes 'Round* in June 1989. Casting director: Joseph Abaldo. Casting associate: Laura Richin.

August 25
Director Scott Ellis calls from L.A. to let me know that *The World Goes 'Round* may get picked up for an Off-Broadway run.

August 22
Scott Ellis called again from L.A., more excited. *The World Goes 'Round* is looking very strong for an Off-Broadway opening this season. He reminded me not to get too excited but wanted me to be prepared in case it was to happen soon. Laura and I got my notes ready from the last call and alphabetized all the names of the actors already seen—those who were liked and called back, and those who were not—just in case.

September 7
Scott called from New York City this time. It's definite—we're a go. Peter Neufeld should be calling to make it official. The fact that Scott's in New York makes all this sound real, but there's nothing we can do till I'm officially hired. Laura suggests we prepare an idea list just for ourselves. We do—it's a good list!

September 12
Peter Neufeld and I begin negotiating. It looks like this is really going to happen. I ask for a meeting to discuss making offers to

those in the original cast. Peter assures me that this is already being discussed. I start checking availabilities on the five actors.

September 17
Scott calls to bring me up to date on his casting ideas. In a meeting with Susan Stroman [the choreographer] and David Thompson [the co-author], the decision is made and approved by Kander and Ebb that the show would be stronger if we did some nontraditional casting and should encourage this idea in all breakdowns sent out. Fortunately, Laura and I anticipated this, and are able to read him a list of possibilities, both male and female.

September 24
Peter Neufeld and I decide that since one of our former actors is already unavailable and some of the others have other offers, we must consider all roles open till contracts are signed. Scott has been in touch with all the actors to keep them up to date and see if they are truly interested.

September 28
I meet with Karen Ziemba to discuss her moving to L.A. and why I feel she should postpone it, since she needs to be reviewed in New York. She's uncertain and has already accepted another job. Luckily she has a four-week out and we have some time. She's promised to keep thinking it over and keep me informed.

October 9
12:30: Susan Stroman calls to say that everyone in the show must move well. She reminds me that they all have to roller skate.
3:00: Susan calls again, this time to remind me that playing the banjo is essential for all five actors. She said we could teach them. She also stressed that we could teach them to roller skate, too.

October 26
Scott wants Laura and me to write the breakdown, keeping it as simple as possible, stressing the vocal. I remind him that the male understudy has to sing, dance (tap and jazz), roller skate, play the banjo, and also play the piano. I tell him this won't be easy. He says he trusts me; I laugh. I suggest a potential breakdown to read: "Seeking actors who can roller skate, dance, and play the banjo. Singing a plus." He laughs.

November 7
Laura handles the open call, which goes well. We find actors for our own file and have decided to bring some in to sing for Scott and Susan.

November 13-14
Each actor is told what we want them to sing, and the black actresses are asked to sightread *And the World Goes 'Round*. All actors are told to bring their music in case Kander and Ebb want to hear additional material. The actors are excited to be singing for Kander and Ebb but also quite nervous. I tell them to relax—both Kander and Ebb are delightful.

November 16
The callbacks go very smoothly. The actors are extremely well-prepared. Every actress who sang *And the World Goes 'Round* sang it differently but very well. Toward the end of the day Adriane Lenox, an actress who was called back, asks to speak to me. She tells me to look around the Equity lounge. I do. Then she says, "If a bomb went off in this building, every diva in New York City would be dead." A few of the other actors hear her and say the casting of this would be tough. They all seem happy to be there.

Later, at the casting session, we knew we were making offers to Karen Mason, Jim Walton, and Karen Ziemba, all of whom had done the show for us last year. We narrow the ethnic female role to eight. Discussion begins; we cut to five. Discussion continues; we cut to three. Kander and Ebb decide they can cut no further and will leave the decision to Scott. I insist they give us their opinion and they do. The male role wasn't any easier; we were down to two and couldn't decide. Peter suggested we take the weekend to think it over—we agree. The understudy issue isn't easy, either. We postpone the male understudy decision but decide to offer the female understudy to Andrea Green.

November 20
After much discussion, the roles are offered to Brenda Pressley and Bob Cuccioli, and the male understudy to George Dvorsky. Everyone seems happy. Scott calls to thank us and say how excited he is. Within hours Peter calls to say that all conflicts—and there have been many—have been worked out and everyone has accepted. Laura and I are finished, and the work on the show can now begin.

# Casting Directors State by State

## ALABAMA

Shirley Crumley
1654 County Rd 40 W.
Piratville, AL 36067
Phone: (205) 361-1147
Specialty: Commercials

Elizabeth Lane Fischer
2940 Old Farm Rd.
Montgomery, AL 36111
Phone: (205) 263-4658
Specialty: Film and TV

Mary Gaffney
RT4 5021 Cole Dr. W.
Mobile, AL 36619
Phone: (205) 661-0599
Specialty: location casting for film
and TV

Marie Prater Casting Services
2642 O'Neal Circle
Birmingham, AL 35226
Phone: (205) 822-8135
Specialty: Advertising

## ARIZONA

Irene Levitt
9707 E. Mountain View Dr., #2407
Scottsdale, AZ 85258
Phone: (602) 860-4188
Alternate phone (Santa Fe): (505) 983-2330
Specialty: Film and TV

## ARKANSAS

The Agency
910 W. 6th St.
Little Rock, AR 72201
Phone: (501) 374-6447
Casting Director: Sarah Tackett
Specialty: Film and TV

## CALIFORNIA

Mercedes Alberti-Penny
5000 Lankershim Blvd. #3
North Hollywood, CA 91601
Phone: (818) 509-1026
Specialty: Theater, features, and TV
(union and non-union)

Ridgely Allison
Allison and Associates
6960 Vesper
Van Nuys, CA 91405
Phone: (818) 782-3676
Specialty: Features, TV, music videos

Julie Alter
8721 Sunset Blvd., Suite 210
Los Angeles, CA 90069
Phone: (213) 652-7373
Specialty: TV and feature film

Donna Anderson
Independent
c/o Casting Society of America
6565 Sunset Blvd. #306
Los Angeles, CA 90028
Phone: (213) 463-1925
Specialty: Features and TV

Mei-Ling Andreen
New Star Casting
P.O. Box 2626
Beverly Hills, CA 90213
Phone: (213) 858-6778
Specialty: Feature film

Jeanne Ashby
Barbara Remsen and Assoc.
650 N. Bronson, #124
Los Angeles, CA 90004
Phone: (213) 464-7968
Specialty: Feature film and TV

Maureen Arata
Viacom Productions
100 Universal City Plaza
Bldg. 69, Room 103
Universal City, CA 91608
Phone: (818) 777-7821
Associate: Tammy Tirgrath
Specialty: TV movies and series

Anthony Barnao
CBS-TV
Director of Talent and Casting
7800 Beverly Blvd., #284
Los Angeles, CA 90036
Phone: (213) 852-2835
Specialty: TV

Rick Barsh
Long/Barsh Casting
8564 Wilshire Blvd.
Beverly Hills, CA 90211
Phone: (213) 652-2414
Partner: Carrie Long
Specialty: Features, TV and theater

Mary Ann Barton
930 N. Westbourne
Los Angeles, CA 90069
Phone: (213) 854-6635
Specialty: Features and TV

Deborah Barylski
Sunset-Gower Studios
1438 N. Gower St.
Casting Bldg., Room 1406
Los Angeles, CA 90028
Phone: (213) 460-7375
Associate: Julie Pernworth
Specialty: TV series

Fran Bascom
Columbia Pictures TV
Columbia Plaza East Room 148
Burbank, CA 91505
Phone: (818) 972-8332
Fax: (818) 972-0423
Specialty: TV

Pamela Basker
1071 N. La Cienega Blvd., 2nd floor
Los Angeles, CA 90069
Phone: (213) 652-8617
Associate: Sue Swan
Specialty: Film and TV

Cheryl Bayer
CBS-MTM
4024 Radford
Studio City, CA 91604

Phone: (818) 760-5278
Specialty: TV

BCI
6565 Sunset Blvd., #412
Los Angeles, CA 90028
Phone: (213) 466-3943
Casting Director: Barbara Claman
Associate: Vicki Goggin
Specialty: Feature film and TV

Elza Bergeron
P.O. Box 1489
La Canada, CA 91012
Phone: (818) 790-9832
Specialty: Features and TV

Chemin Bernard
8306 Wilshire Blvd., #7072
Beverly Hills, CA 90211
Phone: (213) 281-8558
Specialty: Film and TV

Sharon Bialy
Pagano/Bialy Casting
1680 N. Vine St., #904
Hollywood, CA 90028
Phone: (213) 871-0051
Partner: Richard Pagano
Associates: Debbi Manwiller, Mary
Margiotta, and Anne Morgan
Specialty: Features, TV, and theater

Tammy Billik
1438 N. Gower St., #1407
Los Angeles, CA 90028
Phone: (213) 460-7266
Associate: Steven Craig
Specialty: Features and TV

Lacy Bishop
Independent
No address listed
Phone: (213) 660-8961
Specialty: Theater

Susan Bluestein
Susan Bluestein Casting
4063 Radford Ave., #105
Studio City, CA 91604

Phone: (818) 505-6636
Associate: Marsha Shoenman
Specialty: Features and TV

Eugene Blythe
Disney Studios
500 S. Buena Vista
Burbank, CA 91521
Phone: (818) 560-7625
Associate: Steven O'Neil
Specialty: TV features

Deedee Bradley
Deedee Bradley Casting
11684 Ventura Blvd., # 195
Studio City, CA 91604
Phone: (818) 954-2015
Specialty: TV series

Risa Bramon
Bramon and Hopkins
183 N. Martel, #210
Los Angeles, CA 90036
Phone: (213) 937-0153
Partner: Billy Hopkins (New York)
Associate: Heidi Levitt
Specialty: Theater and feature film

Megan Branman
Universal Television
100 Universal City Plaza
Universal City, CA 91608
Phone: (818) 777-1744
Specialty: TV

Jacov Bresler
5330 Lankershim #203
North Hollywood, CA 91601
Phone: (818) 760-1391
Associate: Becky Richardson
Specialty: Features

Jackie Briskey
Briskey/Chamian Casting
3701 W. Oak St., Bldg. 4
Burbank, CA 91505
Phone: (818) 954-5418
Partner: Denise Chamian
Specialty: TV series and feature film

Ross Brown
Brown/West Casting
7319 Beverly Blvd., #10
Los Angeles, CA 90036
Phone: (213) 938-2575
Fax: (213) 938-2755
Partner: Mary West
Specialty: Feature film, movies of the
week, and miniseries

Mary Buck
Buck/Edelman Casting
4051 Radford Ave., Bungalow B
Studio City, CA 91604
Phone: (818)506-7328
Specialty: Movies of the week
and pilots
Partner: Susan Edelman

Perry Bullington
Macdonald-Bullington Casting
3000 W. Olympic Blvd., #1437
Santa Monica, CA 90404
Phone: (213) 315-4774
Partner: Robert Macdonald
Specialty: Feature film

Jackie Burch
c/o CSA
6565 Sunset Blvd., #306
Los Angeles, CA 90028
Phone: (213) 463-1925
Specialty: Feature film

Tom Burke
CBS-TV
7800 Beverly Blvd., #284
Los Angeles, CA 90036
Phone: (213) 852-2835
Specialty: TV

Victoria Burrows
Burrows Casting
5555 Melrose Ave.
Billy Wilder Bldg., #210
Los Angeles, CA 90038
Phone: (213) 956-5921
Specialty: TV movies and series

Irene Cagen
Liberman Hirschfeld Casting
1438 N. Gower, #1410
Los Angeles, CA 90028
Phone: (213) 460-7258
Specialty: Features and TV

Randy Callahan
PAS Casting
8235 Santa Monica Blvd., #214
West Hollywood, CA 90046
Phone: (213) 656-4400
Specialty: Film and TV
(union and non-union)

Gail Camacho
CBS-TV
7800 Beverly Blvd., #305
Los Angeles, CA 90036
Phone: (213) 852-2803
Specialty: Daytime TV

Reuben Cannon
Reuben Cannon and Associates
100 Universal City Plaza, Bldg. 466
Universal City, CA 91608
Phone: (818) 777-7801
Partner: Carol Dudley
Specialty: Feature film and TV

Alice Cassidy
Steven Bochco Productions
10201 W. Pico Blvd., Pico Apts. #5
Los Angeles, CA 90035
Phone: (213) 203-1127
Specialty: TV series

Lucy Cavallo. *See* Peter Golden

Denise Chamian
Briskey/Chamian Casting
3701 W. Oak St., Bldg. 4
Burbank, CA 91505
Phone: (818) 954-5418
Partner: Jackie Briskey
Specialty: TV series and feature film

Fern Champion
Fern Champion Casting
7060 Hollywood Blvd., # 808

Hollywood, CA 90028
Phone: (213) 466-1884
Associate: Dori Zuckerman
Specialty: Features and TV

Barbara Claman. *See* BCI

Lori Cobe
Independent
10351 Santa Monica Blvd.,
Suite 410
Los Angeles, CA 90025
Phone: (213) 277-5777
Fax: (213) 556-3821
Specialty: Low-budget features
and syndicated TV

Andrea Cohen
Warner Bros. Television
4000 Warner Blvd.
Burbank, CA 91522
Phone: (818) 954-1621
Specialty: TV movies, pilots
and series

David Cohn
David Cohn Casting
9060 Santa Monica Blvd., #202
Los Angeles, CA 90069
Phone: (213) 859-4812
Specialty: Feature film and movies of
the week; occasional theater

Annelise Collins
Annelise Collins Casting
1103 El Centro Ave.
Los Angeles, CA 90038
Phone: (213) 962-9562
Specialty: Feature film and TV

Ruth Conforte
Ruth Conforte Casting
P.O. Box 4795
North Hollywood, CA 91617
Phone: (818) 760-8220
Specialty: Feature film and TV

Eleanor Cooke
14120 Ventura Blvd., # 456
Sherman Oaks, CA 91423

Phone: (818) 995-3717
Specialty: Feature film (independent) and miniseries (national and international casting)

Cara Coslow. *See* Jeff Greenberg and Associates

Allison Cowitt. *See* Fenton and Taylor Casting

Steven Craig
Tammy Billik Casting
1438 N. Gower St., #1407
Los Angeles, CA 90028
Phone: (213) 460-7266
Specialty: Features and TV

Creative Casting
1680 N. Vine St., #709
Hollywood, CA 90028
Phone: (213) 466-7319
Associates: Curt Pilz and Andrea Curtis
Specialty: Feature film and TV (union and non-union)

Anne Cummings
5750 Wilshire Blvd., #276
Los Angeles, CA 90036
Phone: (213) 965-1500
Specialty: Feature film and TV

Billy DaMota
Billy DaMota Casting
P.O. Box 4635
Glendale, CA 91222
Phone: (818) 243-1263
Specialty: Feature film

Eric Dawson
Ulrich/Dawson Casting
Universal Studios
100 Universal City Plaza
Bungalow 466
Universal City, CA 91608
Phone: (818) 777-7802
Partner: Robert Ulrich
Specialty: TV

Sally Dennison
Dennison/Selzer Casting
Phone: (213) 652-7528
Partner: Julie Selzer
Specialty: Feature film

Patricia De Oliveira
c/o Midnight Caller Prods.
2200 Army St.
San Francisco, CA 94124
Phone: (415) 285-5001
Specialty: Film and TV

Elina DeSantos
2461 Santa Monica Blvd., Suite C-131
Santa Monica, CA 90404
Phone: (213) 829-5958
Specialty: Daytime consultant for ABC-TV; feature film and theater

Diane Dimeo
Dimeo and Associates
12725 Ventura Blvd., #H
Studio City, CA 91604
Phone: (818) 505-0945
Specialty: Feature film and TV

Dick Dinman
c/o Casting Society of America
6565 Sunset Blvd. # 306
Hollywood, CA 90028
Phone: (213) 469-2283
Specialty: Feature film and TV movies

Pam Dixon
Independent
P.O. Box 672
Beverly Hills, CA 90213
Specialty: Feature film

Donna Dockstader
Universal Television
100 Universal City Plaza
Universal City, CA 91608
Phone: (818) 777-1961
Specialty: TV

Christy Dooley
7800 Beverly Blvd., #3371
Los Angeles, CA 90036
Phone: (213) 852-4501
Specialty: "The Bold and the
Beautiful" daytime serial

Kim Dorr
The Arthur Company
100 Universal City Plaza, Bldg. 447
Universal City, CA 91608
Phone: (818) 505-1200
Specialty: TV series and feature film

Maryann Drake
Universal Television
100 Universal City Plaza
Universal City, CA 91608
Phone: (818) 777-1527
Specialty: TV series and movies
of the week

Carol Dudley
Reuben Cannon and Associates
100 Universal City Plaza, Building
466
Universal City, CA 91608
Phone: (818) 777-7801
Alternate address: 29 Cumberland
Place
London, England W1H7LF
Phone: (071) 262-5692
Partner: Reuben Cannon
Associate: Monica Swann
Specialty: Feature film and TV

Jonell Dunn
Penny Ellers Casting
4063 Radford Ave., # 109
Studio City, CA 91604
Phone: (818) 505-6660
Specialty: TV

Nan Dutton
Nan Dutton and Assoc.
5555 Melrose Ave.
Clara Bow Bldg., Room 217
Los Angeles, CA 90038
Phone: (213) 956-1840
Associate: Donna Larsen

Specialty: TV movies and series
Susan Edelman
Buck/Edelman Casting
4051 Radford Ave., Bungalow B
Studio City, CA 91604
Phone: (818) 506-7328
Specialty: Movies of the week
and pilots
Partner: Mary Buck

Penny Ellers
Penny Ellers Casting
4063 Radford Ave., # 109
Studio City, CA 91604
Phone: (818) 505-6660
Associate: Jonell Dunn
Specialty: TV

Cody Ewell
c/o CSA
6565 Sunset Blvd., #306
Los Angeles, CA 90028
Phone: (213) 463-1925
Specialty: TV

Rachelle Farberman
The Kushner Locke Company
11601 Wilshire Blvd., 21st floor
Los Angeles, CA 90025
Phone: (213) 445-1111
Specialty: TV

Mike Fenton
Fenton and Taylor Casting
100 Universal City Plaza,
Bungalow 477
Universal City, CA 91608
Phone: (818) 777-4610
Partner: Judy Taylor
Associates: Valorie Massalas and
Allison Cowitt
Specialty: Feature film, cable TV film,
and pilots

Steven Fertig
Independent
205 N. Canon Dr.
Beverly Hills, CA 90210
Phone: (213) 276-6267
Associates: Toni Livingston and

Pamela Sparks
Specialty: Theater; occasional film
and TV projects

Sharon Howard Field
Warner Bros.
4000 Warner Blvd.
Burbank, CA 91522
Phone: (213) 954-1495
Specialty: Feature film

Mali Finn
Independent
c/o Breakdown Services
Phone: (213) 276-9166
Specialty: Feature film

Eddie Foy
Eddie Foy Casting
3003 W. Olive Ave.
Burbank, CA 91505
Phone: (818) 841-3003
Associates: Dina Foy and Christo-
pher Holmes
Specialty: Features and TV

Nancy Foy
Vice President of Casting
Paramount Studios
5555 Melrose Ave.,
Dressing Room Bldg. #330
Los Angeles, CA 90038
Phone: (213) 956-5444
Specialty: Feature film

Jerold Franks
Onorato/Franks Casting
1717 N. Highland Ave., #904
Los Angeles, CA 90028
Phone: (213) 468-8833
Fax: (213) 468-9172
Partner: Al Onorato
Specialty: Feature film, movies
of the week, and TV series

Carrie Frazier
Frazier/Ginsberg Casting
Paramount
5555 Melrose Ave.
Freeman Bldg., Room 213

Los Angeles, CA 90038
Phone: (213) 956-4813
Partner: Shani Ginsberg
Specialty: Feature film

Lisa Freiberger
Director of Talent and Casting
CBS-TV
7800 Beverly Blvd., #284
Los Angeles, CA 90036
Phone: (213) 852-2335
Associates: Christopher Gorman,
Margaret McSharry, and Tom Burke
Specialty: TV

Jean Frost
6565 Sunset Blvd.
Suite 306
Los Angeles, CA 29028
Phone: (213) 463-1925
Specialty: Unspecified

Melinda Gartzman
Paramount Television
5555 Melrose Ave.
Von Sternberg Bldg., #204
Los Angeles, CA 90038
Phone: (213) 956-4373
Specialty: TV series

Jeff Gerrard
Jeff Gerrard Casting
10661 Whipple St.
Toluca Lake, CA 91602
Phone: (818) 508-8665
Specialty: Feature film and TV

Shani Ginsberg
Frazier/Ginsberg Casting
Paramount
5555 Melrose Ave.
Freeman Bldg., Room 213
Los Angeles, CA 90038
Phone: (213) 956-4813
Partner: Carrie Frazier
Specialty: Feature film

Jan Glaser
Independent/associated with MGM
1000 W. Washington Blvd.

Culver City, CA 90232
Phone: (213) 280-6238
Specialty: TV series and feature film

Susan Glicksman
12001 Ventura Place #400
Studio City, CA 91604
Phone: (818) 766-2610
Specialty: Movies of the week

Vicki Goggin. *See* BCI

Peter Golden
Vice President of Talent and Casting,
Cannell Productions
7083 Hollywood Blvd., 1st floor
Hollywood, CA 90028
Phone: (213) 856-7576
Associates: Lisa Miller, Lucy Cavallo,
and Susan Scuyler
Specialty: TV series

Louis Goldstein
Paradoxe Casting
7441 Sunset Blvd., #204
Los Angeles, CA 90046
Phone: (213) 851-6110
Specialty: Feature film and TV (union
and non-union)

Elisa Goodman
Independent
P.O. Box 67217
Los Angeles, CA 90067
No phone calls
Specialty: Film and TV

Christopher Gorman
CBS-TV
7800 Beverly Blvd., #284
Los Angeles, CA 90036
Phone: (213) 852-2975
Specialty: TV

Jeff Greenberg and Associates
Independent/office at Paramount
5555 Melrose Ave.
Marx Bros. Building ,#102
Los Angeles, CA 90038
Phone: (213) 956-4886

Associates: Sheila Guthrie and
Cara Coslow
Specialty: Feature film, TV series,
and theater

Michael Greer. *See* Teri Tunder

Al Guarino
2407 Wilshire Blvd., #1014
Santa Monica, CA 90403
No phone calls
Specialty: Feature film

Sheila Guthrie. *See* Jeff Greenberg
and Associates

Linda Hack
Affiliated Models, Inc.
28860 Southfield Rd., #100
Southfield, MI 48076
Phone: (313) 559-3110
Specialty: Film

Renee Haines
913 E. Delaware Rd.
Burbank, CA 91504
Phone: (818) 846-7910
Specialty: Feature film, TV,
and commercials

Ted Hann. *See* Barbara Miller

Bob Harbin
Vice President Talent and Casting
Fox Broadcasting Company
10201 W. Pico Blvd., #335
Los Angeles, CA 90035
Phone: (213) 203-3847
Specialty: TV series

Michael Heit
L.A. Casting
2000 W. Magnolia Blvd., #209
Burbank, CA 91506
Phone: (818) 845-9041
Specialty: Features and TV

Karen Hendel
Director of Casting,
HBO/nonexclusive

2049 Century Park East,
Suite 4100,
Los Angeles, CA 90067
Phone: (213) 201-9309
Specialty: Feature film and TV movies

Cathy Henderson
Henderson/Tarzia Casting
12140 W. Olympic Blvd., #1
Los Angeles, CA 90025
Phone: (213) 447-3609
Partner: James Tarzia
Specialty: Feature film

Marc Hirschfeld
Liberman/Hirschfeld Casting
1438 N. Gower St., #1410
Los Angeles, CA 90028
Phone: (213) 460-7258
Partner: Meg Liberman
Associates: Irene Cagen, Michael
Katcher, and Therese Lang
Specialty: Feature film and TV

Janet Hirshenson
The Casting Company
8921 Venice Blvd., Suite B
Los Angeles, CA 90034
Phone: (213) 842-7551
Partner: Jane Jenkins
Associate: Roger Mussenden
Specialty: Feature film

Alan Hochberg
Geri Windsor and Assoc.
4500 Forman Ave., #1
Toluca Lake, CA 91602
Phone: (818) 509-9993
Specialty: TV

Bobby Hoffman
6311 Romaine St., #7327
Hollywood, CA 90038
Phone: (213) 463-7986
Specialty: TV

Christopher Holmes
Eddie Foy Casting
3003 W. Olive Ave.
Burbank, CA 91505

Phone: (818) 841-4004
Specialty: Features and TV

Judith Holstra
Independent
4043 Radford Ave.
Studio City, CA 91604
Phone: (818) 761-9420
Specialty: TV pilots, cable movies,
and feature film

Bill Hooey
Latino Talent Directory
P.O. Box 46123
Los Angeles, CA 90046
Phone: (213) 934-6465
Specialty: Features and TV (union
and non-union)

Dava Horwitz. *See* Nancy Lara-Hansch

Vicki Huff
Ohlmeyer Communications
962 N. La Cienega Blvd.
Los Angeles, CA 90069
Phone: (213) 659-8557
Specialty: Feature film and TV

Elaine Huzzar. *See* Johanna Ray

Beth Hymson
11846 Ventura Blvd.
Studio City, CA 91604
Phone: (818) 763-5508
Specialty: TV series and MOWs

Rick Jacobs
Senior Vice President of Talent and
Casting
Columbia Pictures Television
3400 Riverside Dr., #856
Burbank, CA 91505
Phone: (818) 972-8591
Associate: Nancy Perkins
Specialty: TV series, miniseries, and
movies of the week

Steven Jacobs
Steven Jacobs Casting
3000 W. Olympic Blvd., #1422

Los Angeles, CA 90404
Phone: (213) 315-4813
Specialty: Film and TV
Justine Jacoby
Aurora Productions
8642 Melrose Ave.
Los Angeles, CA 90069
Phone: (213) 854-6900
Specialty: Feature film

Jane Jenkins
The Casting Company
8925 Venice Blvd., Suite B
Los Angeles, CA 90034
Phone: (213) 842-7551
Partner: Janet Hirshenson
Associate: Roger Mussenden
Specialty: Feature film, TV movies,
and pilots

Sharon Jetton. *See* Sana Landsburg

Ed Johnston
Manager of Feature Film Casting
Disney Studios
500 S. Buena Vista St.
Burbank, CA 91521
Phone: (818) 560-7875
Specialty: Film

Caro Jones
Independent
5858 Hollywood Blvd., #220
Hollywood, CA 90028
Phone: (213) 464-9216
Fax: (213) 962-9866
Associate: Jack Jones
Specialty: Feature film and TV

Karen Kalensky
Director of Casting
L.A. Theater Center
514 S. Spring St.
Los Angeles, CA 90013
Phone: (2130 627-6500
Specialty: Theater

Darlene Kaplan
Raleigh Studios, 650 N. Bronson
East Office Bldg., 3rd floor

Los Angeles, CA 90004
Phone: (213) 960-4503
Specialty: Episodic TV
Judi Keppler
1134 N. La Brea
Hollywood, CA 90038
Phone: (213) 466-1195
Specialty: Feature film (non-union)

Lee Sonja Kissik
Magic Casting
7201 Melrose Ave.
Los Angeles, CA 90046
Phone: (213) 933-0287
Specialty: Feature film
(union and non-union)

Beth Klein
Director of Casting
Viacom Productions
10 Universal City Plaza, 32nd floor
Universal City, CA 91608
Phone: (818) 505-7661
Specialty: TV

Marsha Kleinman
Marsha Kleinman and Associates
704 N. Gardner St., #2
Los Angeles, CA 90046
Phone: (213) 852-1521
Fax: (213) 852-1936
Associate: Marion Levine
Specialty: Movies of the week

Eileen Knight Casting
4024 Radford Ave.
Studio City, CA 91604
Phone: (818) 760-5855
Specialty: Film and TV

Joanne Koehler. *See* Barbara Miller

Larry Kogan
6221 Wilshire Blvd., #207
Los Angeles, CA 90048
Phone: (213) 285-7817
Specialty: Film and TV

Annamarie Kostura
Director of Daytime Casting

NBC-TV
3000 W. Alameda #233
Burbank, CA 91523
Phone: (818) 840-4410
Specialty: Daytime TV

L.A. Casting
2000 W. Magnolia Blvd., # 209
Burbank, CA 91506
Phone: (818) 845-9041
Casting Directors: Michael Heit and
Robert John Teitelbaum
Specialty: Features and TV

Sana Landsburg
Universal Studios
100 Universal City Plaza
Bldg. 506, #129
Universal City, CA 91608
Phone: (818) 777-3497
Associate: Sharon Jetton
Specialty: TV

Doreen Lane
c/o Breakdown Services
Phone: (213) 276-9166
Specialty: Feature film

Jason La Padura
6205 Temple Hill Dr.
Los Angeles, CA 90068
Phone: (213) 957-1624
Fax: (213) 957-9328
Specialty: Feature film and TV

Nancy Lara-Hansch
8200 Wilshire Blvd., #307
Beverly Hills, CA 90212
Phone: (213) 966-5651
Associate: Dava Horwitz
Specialty: Feature film

Donna Larsen
Nan Dutton and Assoc.
5555 Melrose Ave.
Clara Bow Bldg., Room 217
Los Angeles, CA 90038
Phone: (213) 956-1840
Specialty: TV movies and series

Latino Talent Directory
P.O. Box 46123
Los Angeles, CA 90046
Phone: (213) 934-6465
Casting Director: Bill Hooey
Specialty: Features and TV (union
and non-union)

Geraldine Leder. *See* Barbara Miller

Carol Lefko
P.O. Box 84509
Los Angeles, CA 90073
Phone: (213) 397-7790
Specialty: Theater, feature film,
and TV

Kathleen Letterie
761 N. Cahuenga Blvd.
Los Angeles, CA 90038
Phone: (213) 466-7655
Associate: Pat Melton
Specialty: TV

Elizabeth Leustig
6565 Sunset Blvd., #306
Los Angeles, CA 90028
No phone calls
Specialty: Feature film

John Levey
Director of Casting and Talent
Warner Bros. Television
4000 Warner Blvd.
Building 3A, Room 26
Burbank, CA 91522
Phone: (818) 954-4080
Fax: (818) 954-6709
Associate: Patricia Noland
Specialty: TV series, miniseries,
and TV movies

Marion Levine
Marsha Kleinman and Associates
704 N. Gardner St., #2
Los Angeles, CA 90046
Phone: (213) 852-1521
Fax: (213) 852-1936
Specialty: Movies of the week

Heidi Levitt. *See* Risa Bramon

Meg Liberman
Liberman/Hirschfeld Casting
1438 North Gower St.
Los Angeles, CA 90028
Phone: (213) 460-7258
Partner: Mark Hirschfeld
Associates: Irene Cagen, Michael
Katcher, and Therese Lang
Specialty: TV series

Terry Liebling
8407 Coreyell Place
Los Angeles, CA 90046
(213) 656-6803
Specialty: Feature film

Robin Lippin
Disney Studios
500 S. Buena Vista,
Zorro #5
Burbank, CA 91521
Phone: (818) 560-2700
Associate: Bonnie Weeks
Specialty: Features and TV

Leslie Litt
NBC-TV
3000 W. Alameda Ave., #231
Burbank, CA 91523
Phone: (818) 840-4142
Specialty: TV sitcoms

Toni Livingston
Toni Livingston Casting
P.O. Box 2472
Toluca Lake, CA 91610
Phone: (818) 969-1673
Specialty: Features and TV

Lauren Lloyd
Paramount
5555 Melrose Ave.
Los Angeles, CA 90038
Phone: (213) 956-8565
Specialty: Feature film

Lisa London
Sunset Gower Studios
Box 6
1438 N. Gower St.
Los Angeles, CA 90028
Phone: (213)962-8070
Specialty: Feature film and TV

Carrie Long
Long/Barsh Casting
8564 Wilshire Blvd.
Beverly Hills, CA 90211
Phone: (213) 652-2414
Partner: Rick Barsh
Specialty: Feature film, TV,
and theater

Molly Lopata
4043 Radford Ave.
Studio City, CA 91604
Phone: (818) 753-8086
Specialty: TV pilots, movies of
the week, and miniseries

Junie Lowry
20th Century-Fox
10201 W. Pico Blvd.
Los Angeles, CA 90035
Phone: (213) 203-3233
Associate: Ron Surma
Specialty: Features and TV

Ray Lucero
Rapid Casting
1918 N. Main St., #203
Los Angeles, CA 90031
Phone: (213) 223-5734
Specialty: Feature film
(union and non-union)

John Lyons
Independent
c/o C.S.A.
6565 Sunset Blvd.
Los Angeles, CA 90028
(213) 463-1925
Specialty: Feature film and theater

Valerie McCaffrey
Director of Feature Casting

MCA/Universal
100 Universal City Plaza
Universal City, CA 91608
Phone: (818) 777-7581
Specialty: Feature film

Susan McCray
10202 W. Washington Blvd., #223
Culver City, CA 90232
Phone: (213) 280-4449
Specialty: Film and TV

Robert Macdonald
Macdonald-Bullington Casting
3000 W. Olympic Blvd., #1437
Santa Monica, CA 90404
Phone: (213) 315-4774
Partner: Perry Bullington
Specialty: Feature film

Amanda Mackey
Mackey/Sandrich Casting
9155 Sunset Blvd.
Los Angeles, CA 90069
Phone: (213) 278-8858
Partner: Cathy Sandrich
Specialty: Feature film

Margaret McSharry
CBS-TV
7800 Beverly Blvd., #284
Los Angeles, CA 90036
Phone: (213) 852-2862
Specialty: TV

Magic Casting
7201 Melrose Ave.
Los Angeles, CA 90046
Phone: (213) 933-0287
Casting Director: Lee Sonja Kissik
Specialty: Feature film
(union and non-union)

Joyce Maio
Paradoxe Casting
7441 Sunset Blvd., #204
Los Angeles, CA 90046
Phone: (213) 851-6110
Specialty: Feature film and TV
(union and non-union)

Francine Maisler
NBC TV
3000 W. Alameda Ave., #231
Burbank, CA 91523
Phone: (818) 840-4410
Specialty: TV

Ann Manners
Barbara Remsen and Assoc.
650 N. Bronson, #124
Los Angeles, CA 90004
Phone: (213) 464-7968
Specialty: Features and TV

Debbie Manwiller. *See* Richard
Pagano

Jackie Margie
Imagine Entertainment
1925 Century Park East, 23rd floor
Los Angeles, CA 90067
Phone: (213) 277-1665
Specialty: Feature film and TV

Mary Margiotta. *See* Richard Pagano

Irene Mariano
Vice President of Casting
Lorimar
300 S. Lorimar Plaza
Bldg. 140, 1st floor
Burbank, CA 91505
Phone: (818) 954-7646
Specialty: TV

Mindy Marin
Casting Artists, Inc.
5300 Melrose Ave., #305D
Hollywood, CA 90038
Phone: (213) 960-4992
Fax: (213) 960-4537
Associate: Allison Bauer
Specialty: Feature film

Jan Marlyn
Marlyn/Turco Casting
c/o Adam Hill's Actors Studio
8517 Santa Monica Blvd.
Los Angeles, CA 90069
Phone: (818) 783-6433

Partner: Lisa Turco
Specialty: Feature film, TV,
and theater

Jerry Marshall
Supervisor/Manager of Talent
ABC Television Network
2040 Ave. of the Stars, 5th floor
Los Angeles, CA 90067
Phone: (213) 557-7777
Specialty: TV series and movies of
the week

Valorie Massalas. *See* Fenton and
Taylor Casting

Pat Melton. *See* Kathleen Letterie

Jeff Meschel
NBC-TV
3000 W. Alameda Ave., #231
Burbank, CA 91523
Phone: (818) 840-4729
Specialty: TV

Ellen Meyer
Witt/Thomas/Harris Productions
11811 West Olympic Blvd.
Los Angeles, CA 90064
Phone: (213) 444-1818
Fax: (213) 444-4918
Associate: Bonnie Shane
Specialty: Sitcoms, movies of the
week, and miniseries

Adriana Michel
Saban Entertainment
4000 W. Alameda, 5th floor
Burbank, CA 91522
Phone: (818) 972-4800
Specialty: Features and TV

Barbara Miller
Senior Vice President of Talent
Lorimar
300 S. Lorimar Plaza
Bldg. 140, 1st floor
Burbank, CA 91505
Phone: (818) 954-7645
Specialty: Television

Associates: Irene Mariano, Tony
Sepulveda, Joanne Koehler,
Geraldine Leder, Mark Saks, Eliza
Simon, and Ted Hann

Karen Miller. *See* Lynn Stalmaster

Lisa Miller
Cannell Prods.
7083 Hollywood Blvd, 1st floor
Hollywood, CA 90028
Phone: (213) 856-7576
Specialty: TV series

Ed Mitchell
23901 Civic Center Way, #348
Malibu, CA 90265
Phone: (213) 456-2095
Associate: Robyn Ray
Specialty: Feature film

Patricia Mock
c/o CSA
6565 Sunset Blvd., #306
Los Angeles, CA 90028
No phone calls
Specialty: Feature film

Anne Morgan. *See* Richard Pagano

Bob Morones
Independent
733 N. Seward St., #7
Los Angeles, CA 90038
Phone: (213) 467-2834
Specialty: Feature film and TV

Helen Mossler
Vice President of Talent and Casting
Paramount Television
5555 Melrose Ave.
Los Angeles, CA 90038
Specialty: TV

Roger Mussenden. *See* Janet Hirshenson

Robin Nassif
ABC-TV
2040 Ave. of the Stars, 5th floor
Los Angeles, CA 90067

Phone: (213) 557-7777
Specialty: TV sitcoms

Debi Nathan. *See* Susan Vash

Nationwide Talent Casting
6362 Hollywood Blvd., #320
Hollywood, CA 90028
Phone: (213) 463-4401
Specialty: Feature film (non-union)

Nancy Nayor
Vice President of Feature Casting
Universal Studios
100 Universal City Plaza
Universal City, CA 91608
Phone: (818) 777-3566
Specialty: Feature film

Debra Neathery
Debra Neathery Casting
4820 N. Cleon Ave.
North Hollywood, CA 91601
Phone: (818) 506-5524
Specialty: Feature film

Jeffrey Newman
Melissa Skoff Casting
11684 Ventura Blvd., #5141
Studio City, CA 91604
Phone: (818) 760-2058
Specialty: TV movies

New Star Casting
P.O. Box 2626
Beverly Hills, CA 90213
Phone: (213) 858-6778
Casting Director: Mei-Ling Andreen
Specialty: Feature film

Patricia Noland
Warner Bros. TV
4000 Warner Blvd.
Bldg. 3A, Room 26
Burbank, CA 91522
Phone: (818) 954-4080
Specialty: TV movies and series

Steven O'Neil
Disney Studios

500 S. Buena Vista
Burbank, CA 91521
Phone: (818) 560-6566
Specialty: TV features

Pauline O'Con
ABC-TV
2040 Ave. of the Stars, 5th floor
Los Angeles, CA 90067
Phone: (213) 557-7777
Specialty: TV dramatic series

Meryl O'Laughlin
Imagine Entertainment
1925 Century Park East, 23rd floor
Los Angeles, CA 90067
Phone: (213) 277-1665
Specialty: TV movies, miniseries,
and pilots

Al Onerato
Onerato/Franks Casting
1717 N. Highland Ave., #904
Los Angeles, CA 90028
Phone: (213) 468-8833
Partner: Jerold Franks
Specialty: Feature film, TV,
and theater

Lori Openden
Vice President of Talent and Casting
NBC-TV
3000 W. Alameda Ave., #231
Burbank, CA 91523
Phone: (818)840-3774
Specialty: TV

Fern Orenstein
Southgate Entertainment
7080 Hollywood Blvd., #307
Hollywood, CA 90028
Phone: (213) 962-8530
Specialty: Feature film

Michael Orloff. *See* Lynn Stalmaster

Pat Orseth
Propaganda Films
1145 N. McCadden Place
Los Angeles, CA 90038

Phone: (213) 957-1663
Specialty: TV series

Gregory Orson
Sunset-Gower Studios
1438 N. Gower, #1406
Los Angeles, CA 90028
Phone: (213) 460-7593
Specialty: TV

Jessica Overwise
17250 Sunset Blvd., #304
Pacific Palisades, CA 90272
Phone: (213) 459-2686
Associate: Mona Wilde
Specialty: Feature film, TV,
and theater

Richard Pagano
Pagano/Bialy Casting
1680 N. Vine St., #904
Hollywood, CA 90028
Phone: (213) 871-0051
Partner: Sharon Bialy
Associates: Debbi Manwiller, Mary
Margiotta, and Anne Morgan
Specialty: Feature film, TV,
and theater

Paradoxe Casting
7441 Sunset Blvd., #204
Los Angeles, CA 90046
Phone: (213) 851-6110
Casting Directors: Louis Goldstein
and Joyce Maio
Specialty: Feature film and TV
(union and non-union)

Jennifer Part
Universal Studios
100 Universal City Plaza
Building 507, Suite 4F
Universal City, CA 91608
Phone: (818) 777-5013
Specialty: TV series, movies of
the week, and pilots

Cami Patton
Hollywood Center Studios
1040 N. Las Palmas

Bldg. 17, East Suite
Los Angeles, CA 90038
Specialty: TV

Don Pemrick
Don Pemrick Casting
3939 Lankershim Blvd.
Universal City, CA 91604
Phone: (818) 505-0555
Specialty: Feature film and TV

Nancy Perkins
Director of Talent and Casting
Columbia Pictures Television
1438 N. Gower St.
Los Angeles, CA 90028
Phone: (213) 460-7254
Specialty: TV

Julie Pernworth
Deborah Barylski Casting
1438 N. Gower
Casting Bldg., Room 1406
Los Angeles, CA 90028
Phone: (213) 460-7375
Specialty: TV series

Shancy Pierce
Slate Please Casting
948 N. Fairfax Ave.
Los Angeles, CA 90046
Phone: (213) 654-2103
Specialty: Feature film (Union and
non-union)

Bonnie Pietila
20th Century-Fox
10201 W. Pico Blvd., Trailer 732
Los Angeles, CA 90035
Phone: (213) 203-3632
Specialty: Feature film and TV

Pam Polifroni
New World TV
3000 W. Alameda, Stage 11
Burbank, CA 91523
Phone: (818) 840-4641
Associate: Jan Powell
Specialty: "Santa Barbara"

Producers Casting Agency
P.O. Box 1527
Pacific Palisades, CA 90272
Casting Director: Gabrielle Schary
Phone: (213) 459-0229
Specialty: Feature film

Rapid Casting
1918 N. Main St., #203
Los Angeles, CA 90031
Phone: (213) 223-5734
Casting Director: Ray Lucero
Specialty: Feature film
(union and non-union)

Johanna Ray
Independent
c/o Propaganda Films
941 N. Mansfield St.
Hollywood, CA 90038
Phone: (213) 463-0451
Associate: Elaine Huzzar
Specialty: Feature film and
special TV projects

Robyn Ray
10960 Wilshire Blvd., 10th floor
Los Angeles CA 90024
Phone: (213) 653-5603
Specialty: Feature film and
TV features

Karen Rea
Independent
c/o CSA
6565 Sunset Blvd., #306
Los Angeles, CA 90028
Phone: (213) 463-1925
Specialty: Feature film

Robbi Reed
Independent
8306 Wilshire Blvd., #429
Beverly Hills, CA 90211
Phone: (213) 281-8302
Specialty: Feature film and TV

Joe Reich
NBC Productions
3000 W. Alameda, Studio 9

Burbank, CA 91523
Phone: (818) 840-3244
Specialty: "Generations"

Barbara Remsen
Barbara Remsen and Assoc.
650 N. Bronson, #124
Los Angeles, CA 90004
Phone: (213) 464-7968
Associates: Ann Manners and
Jeanne Ashby
Specialty: Feature film and TV

Gretchen Rennell
Vice President of Feature Film Casting
Disney Studios
500 S. Buena Vista St.
Burbank, CA 91521
Phone: (818) 560-7510
Specialty: Feature Film

Becky Richardson
5330 Lankershim, #203
North Hollywood, CA 91601
Phone: (818) 760-1391
Specialty: Features

Vicki Rosenberg
Sunset-Gower Studios
1438 N. Gower, #1406
Los Angeles, CA 90028
Phone: (213) 460-7593
Associate: Gregory Orson
Specialty: TV

Donna Rosenstein
Vice President of Talent and Casting
ABC-TV
2040 Ave. of the Stars, 5th floor
Los Angeles, CA 90067
Phone: (213) 557-6532
Specialty: TV pilots, series, and
movies of the week

Marcia Ross
Vice President of Talent, Warner
Bros. TV
North Administration Bldg. R. 25
4000 Warner Blvd.
Burbank, CA 91522

Phone: (818) 954-1123
Associates: John Levey, Andrea Cohen, and Deedee Bradley
Specialty: Series, pilots, and movies of the week

Renée Rousselot
Director Feature Film Casting
Disney Studios
500 S. Buena Vista
Casting Bldg. 6, Room 5
Phone: (818) 560-7509
Specialty: Feature film

Ben Rubin
5750 Wilshire Blvd., #276
Los Angeles, CA 90036
Phone: (213) 965-1500
Associate: Anne Cummings
Specialty: Feature film and TV

David Rubin
David Rubin Casting
c/o Casting Society of America
6565 Sunset Blvd., Suite #306
Los Angeles, CA 90028
Phone: (213) 463-1925
Associate: Debbie Zane
Specialty: Feature film

Debra Rubinstein
Culver Studios
9336 W. Washington Blvd.
Culver City, CA 90230
Phone: (213) 202-3490
Specialty: TV series

Doris Sabbagh
3400 Riverside Dr., Suite 1071
Burbank, CA 91505
Phone: (818) 972-8339
Specialty: Daytime TV

Mark Saks. *See* Barbara Miller

Cathy Sandrich
Mackey/Sandrich Casting
9155 Sunset Blvd.
Los Angeles, CA 90069
Phone: (213) 278-8858

Partner: Amanda Mackey
Specialty: Feature film

Ellen Lubin Sanitsky
Universal Television
100 Universal City Plaza
Universal City, CA 91608
Phone: (818) 777-3023
Specialty: TV

Gabrielle Schary
Producers Casting Agency
P.O. Box 1527
Pacific Palisades, CA 90272
Phone: (213) 459-0229
Specialty: Feature film

Jean Scoccimaro
6565 Sunset Blvd., Suite 306
Los Angeles, CA 29028
Phone: (213) 463-1925
Specialty: Unspecified

Brien Scott
Wilson Scott Associates
425 S. Fairfax Ave.
Los Angeles, CA 90036
Phone: (213) 934-6150
Specialty: Feature film and TV

Susan Scudder. *See* Peter Golden

Joe Scully
c/o Jack Armstrong Productions
12700 Ventura Blvd., #130
Studio City, CA 91604
Phone: (818) 753-8010
Specialty: Feature film

Susan Scuyler. *See* Peter Golden

Lila Selik
Lila Selik Casting
1551 S. Robertson, #202
Los Angeles, CA 90035
Phone: (213) 556-2444
Specialty: Feature film
(union and non-union)

Julie Selzer
Dennison/Selzer Casting
Phone: (213) 652-7528
Partner: Sally Dennison
Specialty: Feature film
Tony Sepulveda. *See* Barbara Miller

Bonnie Shane
Ellen Meyer Casting
11811 W. Olympic Blvd.
Los Angeles, CA 90064
Phone: (213) 444-1818
Specialty: TV

Bill Shepard
14155 Magnolia Blvd., #1
Sherman Oaks, CA 91423
Phone: (818) 789-4776
Specialty: Feature film

Tony Shepherd
Vice President of Talent
Aaron Spelling Productions
5700 Wilshire Blvd., 5th floor
Los Angeles, CA 90036
Phone: (213) 965-5718
Specialty: TV

Marsha Shoenman
Susan Bluestein Casting
4063 Radford Ave., #105
Studio City, CA 91604
Phone: (818) 505-6636
Specialty: Features and TV

Eliza Simon. *See* Barbara Miller

Clair Sinnett
937 N. Beverly Glen Blvd.
Bel Air, CA 90077
Phone: 470-8641
Specialty: Feature film and TV

Joan Sittenfield
Vice President of Talent and Casting,
Universal Television
100 Universal City Plaza
Building 500, 12th floor
Universal City, CA 91608
Phone: (818) 777-3211

Casting staff: Ron Stephenson
(director), Maryann Kohler, Megan
Branman, Ellen Lubin Sanitsky, Dava
Waite, and Donna Dockstader
Specialty: TV series (cast by her staff)
and TV pilots

Melissa Skoff
Melissa Skoff Casting
11684 Ventura Blvd., #5141
Studio City, CA 91604
Phone: (818) 760-2058
Associate: Jeffrey Newman
Specialty: TV movies

Mary Jo Slater
10000 W. Washington Blvd., #4011
Culver City, CA 90232
Phone: (213) 280-6128
Specialty: Feature film and TV series

Lisa Snedeker
ABC-TV
4151 Prospect Ave.
Los Angeles, CA 90027
Phone: (213) 557-5542
Specialty: "General Hospital"

Stanley Soble
Mark Taper Forum
135 N. Grand Ave.
Los Angeles, CA 90012
Phone: (213) 972-7374
Specialty: Theater

Pamela Sparks. *See* Steven Fertig

Lynn Stalmaster
Independent
9911 West Pico Blvd., Suite 1580
Los Angeles, CA 90035
Phone: (213) 552-0983
Associates: Michael Orloff and Karen
Miller
Specialty: Feature film and
TV miniseries

Sally Steiner
c/o CSA
6565 Sunset Blvd., #306

Los Angeles, CA 90028
Phone: (213) 463-1925
Partner: Lisa Mionie
Specialty: Feature film and TV

Ron Stephenson
Director of Casting
MCA
Universal Studios Bldg. 463,
Room 106
Universal City, CA 91608
Phone: (818) 777-3498
Specialty: TV

Stanzi Stokes
Independent
Universal Studios
Building 506, Room 123
Universal City, CA 91608
Phone: (818) 777-4021
Fax: (818) 508-9304
Specialty: Feature film and TV

Ron Surma
Junie Lowry-Johnson Casting
20th Century-Fox
10201 W. Pico Blvd.
Los Angeles, CA 90035
Phone: (213) 203-3233
Specialty: Feature film and TV

Sue Swan. *See* Pamela Basker

Monica Swann
Reuben Cannon and Associates
100 Universal City Plaza, Bldg. 466
Universal City, CA 91608
Phone: (818) 777-7801
Specialty: Feature film and TV

James Tarzia
Henderson/Tarzia Casting
12140 W. Olympic Blvd., #1
Los Angeles, CA 90025
Phone: (213) 447-3609
Partner: Cathy Henderson
Specialty: Feature film

Judy Taylor
Fenton and Taylor Casting

100 Universal City Plaza,
Bungalow 477
Universal City, CA 91608
Phone: (818) 777-4610
Partner: Mike Fenton
Associates: Valorie Massalas and
Allison Cowitt
Specialty: Feature film, cable TV film,
and pilots

Robert John Teitelbaum
L.A. Casting
2000 W. Magnolia St., #209
Burbank, CA 91506
Phone: (818) 845-9041
Specialty: Feature film and TV

Mark Teschner
ABC Daytime Television
4151 Prospect Ave.
Los Angeles, CA 90027
Phone: (213) 557-5542
Associate: Lisa Snedeker
Specialty: Daytime drama

Tammy Tirgrath
Viacom Productions
100 Universal City Plaza
Bldg. 69, Room 103
Universal City, CA 91608
Phone: (818) 777-7821
Specialty: TV movies and series

David Tochterman
Independent
12001 Ventura Place
Studio City, CA 91604
Phone: (818) 760-5201
Specialty: TV

TIna Treadwell
Tina Treadwell Casting
835 N. Fuller, #13
Los Angeles, CA 90046
Phone: 9213) 653-2740
Specialty: Feature film and TV

Teri Tunder
Teri Tunder Casting
1438 N. Gower St., Bldg. 42

Los Angeles, CA 90028
Associate: Michael Greer
Specialty: TV

Tony Turano
Bobbi Morris Casting
8150 Beverly Blvd., #204
Los Angeles, CA 90048
Phone: (213) 653-4031
Specialty: Feature film, TV,
and theater

Lisa Turco
Marlyn/Turco Casting
c/o Adam Hill's Actors Studio
8517 Santa Monica Blvd.
Los Angeles, CA 90069
Phone: (818) 783-6433
Partner: Jan Marlyn
Specialty: Feature film, TV,
and theater

Susan Tyler
Susan Tyler Casting
3859 Lankershim Blvd.
Studio City, CA 91604
Phone: (818) 506-0400
Specialty: Film and TV

Robert Ulrich
Ulrich/Dawson Casting
Universal Studios
100 Universal City Plaza,
Bungalow 466
Universal City, CA 91608
Phone: (818) 777-7802
Partner: Eric Dawson
Specialty: TV

Susan Vash
Paramount
5555 Melrose Ave.
Von Sternberg Bldg., #207
Los Angeles, CA 90038
Phone: (213) 956-4049
Associate: Debi Nathan
Specialty: Feature film and TV

Dava Waite
Universal Studios

100 Universal City Plaza
Bldg. 463, #104
Universal City, CA 91608
Phone: (818) 777-1114
Specialty: TV

April Webster
Independent
Warner Bros. TV
4000 Warner Blvd.
Administration Bldg. 25
Burbank, CA 91522
Phone: (818) 954-1123
Specialty: TV

Bonnie Weeks
Robin Lippin Casting
Disney Studios
500 S. Buena Vista, Zorro #5
Burbank, CA 91521
Phone: (818) 560-2700
Specialty: Features and TV

Mary West.
Brown/West Casting
7319 Beverly Blvd., #10
Los Angeles, CA 90036
Phone: (213) 938-2575
Fax: (213) 938-2755
Partner: Ross Brown
Specialty: Feature film, movies of
the week, and miniseries

Mona Wilde
Jessica Overwise Casting
17250 Sunset Blvd., #304
Pacific Palisades, CA 90272
Phone: (213) 459-2686
Specialty: Film, TV, and theater

Nick Wilkinson
ABC-TV
2040 Ave. of the Stars, 5th floor
Los Angeles, CA 90067
Phone: (213) 557-7777
Specialty: Movies of the week

Kim Williams
2049 Century Park East, 41st floor
Los Angeles, CA 90067

Phone: (213) 201-9402
Specialty: Film and TV

Geri Windsor
Geri Windsor and Assoc.
4500 Forman Ave., #1
Toluca Lake, CA 91602
Phone: (818) 509-9993
Associate: Alan Hochberg
Specialty: TV

Jerry Wolfe
Gerrie Wormser Casting
P.O. Box 6449
Beverly Hills, CA 90210
Phone: (213) 277-3281
Specialty: Film and TV

Gerrie Wormser
P.O. Box 6449
Beverly Hills, CA 90210
Phone: (213) 277-4381
Associate: Jerry Wolfe
Specialty: Film and TV

Ronnie Yeskel
Independent
10201 W. Pico Blvd., Pico Apts. #6
Los Angeles, CA 90035
Phone: (213) 203-2662
Specialty: "L.A. Law" and
feature film

Diane Young
Independent
Aaron Spelling Prods.
5700 Wilshire Blvd., 5th floor
Los Angeles, CA 90036
Phone: (213) 965-5888
Specialty: TV

Joanne Zaluski
Joanne Zaluski Casting
9348 Civic Center Dr., #407
Beverly Hills, CA 90210
Phone: (213) 456-5160
Specialty: Feature film

Debbie Zane
David Rubin Casting

c/o CSA
6565 Sunset Blvd., #306
Los Angeles, CA 90028
Phone: (213) 463-1925
Specialty: Feature film and TV

Lisa Zarowin
Mark Taper Forum
135 N. Grand Ave.
Los Angeles, CA 90012
Phone: (213) 972-7374
Specialty: Theater

Gary Zuckerbrod
6565 Sunset Blvd.
Suite 306
Los Angeles, CA 29028
Phone: (213) 463-1925
Specialty: Unspecified

Dori Zuckerman
Fern Champion Casting
7060 Hollywood Blvd., #808
Hollywood, CA 90028
Phone: (213) 466-1884
Specialty: Feature film and TV

## COLORADO

Colorado Casting Association
1441 York, #102
Denver, CO 80206
Phone: (303) 355-5888
Casting Directors: Peggy Larson, Ted
Ferrari, and Denise Miller
Specialty: Film and TV

## FLORIDA

Ed Arenas. *See* Unique Casting

Barbara DiPrima
Barbara DiPrima Casting
3390 Mary St., Penthouse J
Coconut Grove, FL 33133
Phone: (305) 445-7630
Alternate address: 7200 Lake Ellenor
Dr., #135
Orlando, FL 32809

Phone: (407) 240-4718
Casting Director: Herb Mandell
Specialty: Film and TV

Vonit Hamer. *See* Unique Casting

Amie Heitz
Heitz/McClean Casting
112 Annie St.
Orlando, FL 32806
Phone: (407) 649-8686
Partner: Jan McClean
Specialty: Film and TV

Ellen Jacoby
Ellen Jacoby Casting International,
Ltd.
420 Lincoln Rd., #210
Miami Beach, FL 33139
Phone: (305) 531-5300
Specialty: Film and TV

Melvin Johnson
Melvin Johnson and Associates
Universal Studios
1000 Universal Plaza
Bldg. 22, Suite 235
Orlando, FL 32819
Phone: (407) 363-8582
Associate: Patricia Thomas
Specialty: Film and TV

Jan McClean
Heitz/McClean Casting
112 Annie St.
Orlando, FL 32806
Phone: (407) 649-8686
Partner: Amie Heitz
Specialty: Film and TV

Beverly McDermott
Beverly McDermott Casting
923 N. Golf Dr.
Hollywood, FL 33021
Phone: (305) 625-5111
Associate: Aimee O'Real
Specialty: Film and TV

Herb Mandell. *See* Barbara DiPrima

Lynne Marks. *See* Unique Casting

Candy Milford. *See* TLC Casting

Lisa O'Connor. *See* TLC Casting

Aimee O'Real. *See* Beverly McDermott

Terri Rand. *See* TLC Casting

TLC Casting
DuPont Plaza Center
200 Biscayne Blvd. Way, 12H
Miami, FL 33131
Phone: (305) 539-1945
Casting Directors: Terri Rand, Lisa
O'Connor, and Candy Milford
Specialty: Film and TV

Patricia Thomas. *See* Melvin Johnson

Unique Casting
540 NW 165th St., #110
Miami, FL 33169
Phone: (305) 947-9339
Fax: (305) 947-0713
Casting Directors: Yonit Hamer, Ed
Arenas, and Lynne Marks
Specialty: Film and TV

---

## GEORGIA
Don Slaton Casting
572 Armour Circle
Atlanta, GA 30324
Phone: (404) 885-1334
Specialty: Commercials

---

## IDAHO
Artists Agency, Inc.
2346 Roanoke
Boise, ID 83712
Phone: (208) 345-0038
Casting Director: Tamara Thomson
Specialty: Film

Lynn Bishop
P.O. Box 2790

Sun Valley, ID 83353
Phone: (208) 726-7722
Specialty: Film and TV

Idaho Casting Company
Route 1, Box J-56
McCall, ID 83638
Phone: (208) 634-8335
Casting Director: Christina Wintergate
Specialty: Film and TV
(non-union)

Jennifer Rahr
P.O. Box 411
Ketchum, ID 83340
Phone: (208) 774-3369
Specialty: Film and TV (union and
non-union)

Tamara Thomson. *See* Artists
Agency, Inc.

Christina Wintergate. *See* Idaho
Casting Company

## ILLINOIS

Jane Alderman
190 N. State St., 7th floor
Chicago, IL 60601
Phone: (312) 899-4250
Specialty: Film, TV, and theater

Jane Brody
Jane Brody Casting
20 W. Hubbard
Chicago, IL 60610
Phone: (312) 527-0665
Specialty: Film and TV

Jane Heitz
Jane Heitz Casting Services, Inc.
920 N. Franklin #205
Chicago, IL 60610
Phone: (312) 664-0601
Associates: Lynne Levinson and
Cynthia Pighini
Specialty: Film and TV

Dennis Hitchcock
P.O. Box 3784
Rock Island, IL 61201
Phone: (309) 786-2667
Specialty: Theater and film

Ted Hoerl. *See* Beth Radedeau Casting

Knutsen-Satterlee
919 N. Michigan
Suite 3011
Chicago, IL 60611
Phone: (312) 649-1167
Specialty: Film

Lynne Levinson. *See* Jane Heitz

Tara Lonzo. *See* Beth Radedeau Casting

Cherie Mann Casting
1540 N. LaSalle
Chicago, IL 60610
Phone: (312) 751-2927
Specialty: Commercials

Cynthia Pighini. *See* Jane Heitz

Beth Rabedeau
Beth Radedeau Casting
225 W. Ohio
Chicago, IL. 60610
Phone: (312) 222-0181
Associates: Tara Lonzo and
Ted Hoerl
Specialty: Film, TV, and theater
(Goodman)

## IOWA

Art Breese
Complete Casting Service
1940 68th St.
Des Moines, IA 50322
Phone: (515) 276-0170
Specialty: Film and TV

Rodney Franz
P.O. Box 1842
Fairfield, IA 52556

(515) 472-8384
Specialty: TV and commercials

J. Thomas Jacobs
1607 W. 12th
Davenport, IA 52804
Phone: (319) 326-9343
Specialty: TV and radio

Susan Riedel
282 Kellys Bluff
Dubuque, IA 52001
Phone: (319) 556-4367
Specialty: Theater

## KANSAS
Joyce Cavarozzi
1544 Matlock Drive
Wichita, KS 67208
Phone: (316) 683-4896
Specialty: Film and TV

Linda Connaghan
RT3 Box 124B
Tonganoxie, KS 66086
Phone: (913) 724-1527
Specialty: Commercials

## KENTUCKY
Mina Davis
1120 Julia Ave.
Louisville, KY 40204
Phone: (502) 459-2807
Specialty: Film and TV

Eben Henson
Pioneer Playhouse
840 Stanford Rd.
Danville, KY 40422
Phone: (606) 236-2747
Specialty: Theater

Merry Kay Poe
K Casting
P.O. Box 22927
Louisville, KY 40222
Phone: (502) 426-7008

Associate: Richard Sirianni
Specialty: Film and TV

Richard Sirianni. *See* Merry Kay Poe

## LOUISIANA
Richard Castleman
Production Service
202-30 Fifth Ave.
Covington, LA 70433
Phone: (504) 892-2628
Specialty: Film and commercials

Dolly Dean Modeling and
Career Network
3535 S. Sherwood Forest Blvd.
Baton Rouge, LA 70816
Phone: (504) 292-2424
Casting Director: Brenda P.
Netzberger
Specialty: Film and TV

Miriam Fontenot
200 Arceneaux St.
Lafayette, LA 70506
Phone: (318) 235-6906 or 981-7386
Specialty: Film,TV, and theater;
also Cajun casting

Wilma Francis
2925 Clifford Dr.
Metairie, LA 70002
Phone: (504) 835-9047
Specialty: Film and TV

Rick Landry
P.O. Box 51244
New Orleans, LA 70151
Phone: (504) 454-8000
Specialty: Film and TV

Anne Massey
P.O. Box 640697
Kenner, LA. 90064
Phone: (504) 464-9889
Specialty: Theater, film, and TV

Brenda Netzberger. *See* Dolly Dean Modeling and Career Network

## MASSACHUSETTS
Ann Baker
6 Wheeler Rd.
Newton, MA 02159
Phone: (617) 964-3038
Specialty: TV

Madelyn J. Burns
1361 Cambridge St.
Cambridge, MA 02139
Phone: (617) 492-8688
Specialty: Film and TV

Cameo Agency
437 Boylston St.
Boston, MA 02116
Phone: (617) 536-6004
Casting Director: Estelle Davids
Specialty: Film and TV

## MICHIGAN
Emily Schreiber
3870 Sobieski
Detroit, MI 48212
Phone: (313) 893-9431
Specialty: Film and TV

The Talent Shop
30100 Telegraph
Suite 116
Burmingham, MI 48025
Phone: (313) 644-4877
Specialty: Film, commercials,
and radio

## MISSOURI
Carrie Houk
6300 Northwood
St. Louis, MO 63105
Phone: (314) 862-1236
Specialty: Film and TV

Laura Nelson
P.O. Box 30157
Kansas City, MO
Phone: (816) 444-2254
Specialty: Film and TV

## NEBRASKA
Actors Etc.
16812 N. Circle
Omaha, NE 68135
Phone: (402) 896-9908
Casting Director: Lisa Falk
Specialty: Film and TV

Jackie Beavers
Jackie Beavers and Group 0
315 S. 9th St., #220
Lincoln, NE 68508
Phone: (402) 476-0779
Specialty: Film and TV

Lisa Falk. *See* Actors Etc.

John Jackson. *See* Talent Pool, Inc.

Talent Pool, Inc.
206 S. 44th
Omaha, NE 68134
Phone: (402) 553-1164
Casting Director: John Jackson
Specialty: Film and TV

## NEVADA
Christine O'Rourke. *See* Spectrum Services

April Ann Pope. *See* Spectrum Services

Spectrum Services
810 S. 7th St.
Las Vegas, NV 89101
Phone: (702) 388-7557
Casting Directors: Christine O'Rourke and April Ann Pope
Specialty: Film and TV

## NEW JERSEY
Prime Time Casting
91 Monmouth St.
Red Bank, NJ 07701
Phone: (201) 747-8228
Fax: (201) 747-6221
Casting Directors: Eddy Howard,
Christine Lynn, and Steven A. Levine
Specialty: Film and TV

## NEW MEXICO
Lisa Law
Lisa Law Casting
1624 Ben Hur Dr.
Santa Fe, NM 87501
Phone: (505) 988-2917
Associate: Jyette Lockvig
Specialty: Film and TV

Jyette Lockvig. *See* Lisa Law

Monica McDowell
P.O. Box 88
Chama, NM 87520
Phone: (505) 756-2389
Specialty: Extras for film

## NEW YORK
Joseph Abaldo
Independent
450 W. 42nd St., Suite 2F
New York, NY 10036
Phone: (212) 947-3697
Fax: (212) 268-5501
Associate: Laura Richin
Specialty: Regional theater

Amerifilm
95 Delancy St., #206
New York, NY 10002
Phone: (212) 353-3118
Casting Director: Meredith Jacobson
Specialty: Feature film (union and
non-union)

Bob Anthony
Bob Anthony Casting

1 Times Square, 17th floor
New York, NY 10036
Phone: (212) 575-9087
Associate: Ray Normandeau
Specialty: Film, theater, and TV

Deborah Aquila
Independent
1633 Broadway, 18th floor
New York, NY 10019
Phone: (212) 664-5049
Fax: (212) 215-1760
Associates: Alison Zimet, Jane Shan-
non, and Schulla Van Buren
Specialty: Feature film and TV pilots

Alycia Aumuller
330 W. 89th St.
New York, NY 10024
Phone: (212) 877-0225
Specialty: Film, TV, and theater

Christina Avis-Krauss
Gross-Jacobson Prods.
767 3rd Ave., 15th floor
New York, NY 10017
Phone: (212) 644-6909
Fax: (212) 355-3178
Specialty: TV

Baby Wranglers Casting
666 West End Ave., #17N
New York, NY 10025
Phone: (212) 769-0910
Casting Director: John Hicks
Specialty: Film and TV

Lisa Bankert. *See* Poco Casting

Jeff Barber. *See* CTP Casting

BCI Casting
151 W. 25th St.
New York, NY 10001
Phone: (212) 627-7300
Casting Directors: Billy Serow, Paula
Sindlinger, and Linda Godlove
Specialty: Theater, film, and TV

Breanna Benjamin
Independent
1600 Broadway, Suite 306
New York, NY 10019
Phone: (212) 541-9067
Specialty: Feature film and theater

Ricardo Bertoni
Navarro/Bertoni Casting
101 W. 31st St.
New York, NY 10001
Phone: (212) 736-9272
Partner: Esther Navarro
Specialty: Feature film

Jay Binder
Jay Binder Casting
513 W. 54th St., Suite 2
New York, NY 10019
Phone: (212) 586-6777
Partner: Jack Bowdan
Associate: Barbara Hipkiss
Specialty: Broadway, TV,
regional theater, and occasional
Off-Broadway

Jeff Block. *See* Bonnie Timmerman

Jimmy Bohr. *See* Betty Rea

Jack Bowdan
Jay Binder Casting
513 W. 54th St., Suite 2
New York, NY 10019
Phone: (212) 586-6777
Partner: Jay Binder
Associate: Barbara Hipkiss
Specialty: Broadway, TV,
regional theater, and occasional
Off-Broadway

Jane Brinker
51 W. 16th St.
New York, NY 10011
Phone: (212) 924-3322
Specialty: Theater, film , and TV

Bryan Brooks. *See* Roelfs and
Carroll Casting

Deborah Brown
Deborah Brown Casting
250 W. 57th St., #2608
New York, NY 10107
Phone: (212) 581-0404
Specialty: Film, TV, and theater

Kate Burton
Kate Burton Casting
39 W.19th St.
New York, NY 10011
Phone: (212) 929-0948
Fax: (212) 627-3977
Specialty: Film, TV, and theater

Theresa Carroll. *See* Roelfs and
Carrol Casting

Kit Carter
Kit Carter Casting
160 W. 95th St., #1D
New York, NY 10025
Phone: (212) 864-3147
Specialty: Theater, film, and TV

Aleta Chapelle
Independent
250 W. 57th St., Suite 1527
New York, NY 10107
No phone calls
Specialty: Feature film

Brian Chavanne
Chavanne/Mossberg Casting
165 W. 46th St., Suite 514
New York, NY 10036
No phone calls
Partner: Julie Mossberg
Associate: Marnie Waxman
Specialty: Feature film, TV, and
theater

Claire Casting
333 Park Ave. South
New York, NY 10010
Phone: (212) 673-7373
Casting Directors: Claire Shull and
Nancy Kagen
Specialty: Feature film and TV

Richard Cole. *See* McCorkle

Alan Coleridge. *See* Professional Casting Associates

Aisha Coley. *See* Billy Hopkins

Collier Casting
1560 Broadway #509
New York, NY 10036
Phone: (212) 719-9636
Casting Director: Lisa Weiss
Specialty: Film and TV
(union and non-union)

David Conaway. *See* Poco Casting

Contemporary Casting
P.O. Box 1844
FDR Station
New York, NY 10022
Phone: (212) 838-1818
Fax: (212) 371-6468
Casting Director: Mark Reiner
Specialty: Theater, film, and TV

CTP Casting
22 W. 27th St.
New York, NY 10001
Phone: (212) 696-1100
Casting Director: Jeff Barber
Specialty: Film and TV

Judy Courtney
Courtney and Newton Casting
205 W. 54th St.
New York, NY 10019
(No visits)
Phone: (212) 246-0986
Fax: (212) 489-6388
Partner: D. L. Newton
Specialty: Film and TV

Wendy Dana
221 W. 82nd St.
New York, NY 10024
Phone: (212) 580-1871
Specialty: Theater

Donna DeSeta
525 Broadway
New York, NY 10012
Phone: (212) 274-9696
Associates: Lucy Tyler, Lori Gunty, and Patti Kelly
Specialty: Film and TV

Lou DiGiaimo
Independent
513 W. 54th St.
New York, NY 10019
Phone: (212) 713-1884
Specialty: Feature film in U.S. and Italy

Joan D'Inecco
Cap Cities/ABC
320 W. 66th St.
New York, NY 10023
Phone: (212) 496-3354
Associate: Jean Rohn
Specialty: Daytime TV

Stephanie Dioczi. *See* Wendy Ettinger

Jerome DuMaurier
245 W. 107th St.
New York, NY 10025
Phone: (212) 663-8533
Specialty: TV, film, and theater

Jeffrey Dunn Casting
857 Ninth Ave.
New York, NY 10019
Phone: (212) 245-3166
Specialty: European musical tours

Fleet Emerson. *See* Sylvia Fay

Wendy Ettinger
Wendy Ettinger Casting
95 5th Ave., 8th floor
New York, NY 10003
Associate: Stephanie Dioczi
Specialty: Theater and film

Sylvia Fay
Independent
71 Park Ave.

New York, NY 10016
Phone: (212) 889-2707
Associates: Fleet Emerson and
Tim McDowell
Specialty: Extras/bits for feature
film and TV

Howard Feuer
Independent
c/o CSA
311 W. 43rd St., #700
New York, NY 10036
Phone: (212) 242-4430
Specialty: Feature film

Alan Filderman
188 Columbus Ave #4RS
New York, NY 10023
Phone: (212) 580-3213
Specialty: Theater and TV

Leonard Finger
Independent
1501 Broadway
New York, NY 10036
Phone: (212) 944-8611
Fax: (212) 869-4826
Associates: Anne Byrne and
Stephanie Klapper
Specialty: Feature film and TV;
occasional theater

Alexa Fogel
Director, Prime Time Casting
ABC-TV
40 W. 66th St., 3rd floor
New York, NY 10019
Phone: (212) 887-363
Associates: Bob Huber and
Benjamin Lipton
Specialty: TV

Paul Fouquet. *See* Elissa Myers

Maureen Fremont
641 W. 59th St.
New York, NY 10019
Phone: (212) 541-4710
Specialty: Film, TV, and theater

Ginger Friedman
Actor's Outlet Theater
120 W. 28th St.
New York, NY 10001
Phone: (212) 807-1590
Specialty: Theater

Jessica Gilburne. *See* Julie Hughes

Maria Gillen
Talent Coordinator Primetime,
CBS-TV
51 W. 52nd St.
New York, NY 10019
Phone: (212) 975-3851
Specialty: TV

Linda Godlove. *See* BCI

Pat Golden
Golden Casting Company
133 W. 72nd St., 16th floor
New York, NY 10023
Phone: (212) 496-0146
Fax: (212) 721-9581
Associate: John McCabe
Specialty: Feature film; occasional TV
and theater

Alixe Gordin
129 W. 12th St.
New York, NY 10011
Phone: (212) 627-0472
Specialty: Feature film

Maria Greco Casting
630 Ninth Ave.
New York, NY 10036
Phone: (212) 247-2011
Specialty: Camera casting

Lori Gunty. *See* Donna DeSeta

Carol Hanzel
Hanzel and Stark Casting, Inc.
1261 Broadway, #505
New York, NY 10001
Phone: (212) 779-0966
Partner: Elsie Stark
Specialty: Feature film and TV

Olivia Harris. *See* Phyllis Huffman

Natalie Hart
ABC-TV
56 W. 66th St., 2nd floor
New York, NY 10023
Phone: (213) 887-3580
Associate: Judy Wilson
Specialty: "One Life to Live"

Susan Haskins
Haskins Casting
426 Broome St.
New York, NY 10013
Phone: (212) 431-8405
Specialty: Theater, film, and TV

Judy Henderson
Judy Henderson and Associates
330 W. 89th St.
New York, NY 10024
Phone: (212) 877-0225
Associate: Alycia Aumuller
Specialty: Theater, film and TV

John Hicks. *See* Baby Wranglers Casting

Barbara Hipkiss. *See* Jay Binder Casting

Billy Hopkins
Lincoln Center Theater
150 W. 65th St.
New York, NY 10023
Phone: (213) 362-7600
Partner: Risa Bramon (Los Angeles)
Associates: Suzanne Smith and Aisha Coley
Specialty: Theater and feature film

Stuart Howard
Stuart Howard Associates
22 W. 27th St., 10th floor
New York, NY 10001
Phone: (212) 725-7770
Associates: Amy Schecter and Howard Meltzer
Specialty: Theater, film, and TV

Bob Huber. *See* Alexa Fogel

Phyllis Huffman
Vice President, Warner Bros.
Television Casting
75 Rockefeller Plaza, 23rd floor
New York, NY 10001
Phone: (212) 484-6371
Fax: (212) 484-6657
Specialty: Feature film, movies of the week, and pilots

Julie Hughes
Hughes Moss Casting
311 W. 43rd St., #700
New York, NY 10036
Phone: (212) 307-6690
Partner: Barry Moss
Associate: Jessica Gilburne
Specialty: Theater, film, and TV

Sara Hyde-Hamlet
Hyde-Hamlet Casting
311 W. 43rd St., #903
New York, NY 10036
Phone: (213) 767-1842
Associate: Valerie Ramer
Specialty: Theater, film, and TV

Amy Introcaso-Davis
Director, Prime Time Casting,
East Coast
CBS-TV
51 W. 52nd St., 23rd floor
New York, NY 10019
Phone: (212) 975-3851
Specialty: TV

Donna Isaacson
Donna Isaacson Casting
453 W. 16th St., 2nd floor
New York, NY 10011
Phone: (212) 691-8555
Specialty: Feature film and theater

Meredith Jacobson. *See* Amerifilm

Sheila Jaffe
Walken/Jaffe Casting
235 W. 76th St., #2A
New York, NY 10023
Phone: (212) 877-4025

Partner: Georgianne Walken
Specialty: Theater and film

Rosalie Joseph
1501 Broadway
Suite 2605
New York, NY 10036
Phone: (212) 921-5781
Specialty: TV and feature film

Nancy Kagen. *See* Claire Casting

Patti Kelly. *See* Donna DeSeta

Lynn Kressel
Independent
111 W. 57th St., #1422
New York, NY 10019
Phone: unlisted
Associate: Suzanne Ryan
Specialty: Feature film and TV

Avy Kaufman
40 Barrow St.
New York, NY 10014
No phone calls
Specialty: Feature film and TV

Jodi Kippermann
39 W. 19th St., 12th floor
New York, NY 10011
No phone calls
Associate: Barri Kippermann
Specialty: Theater, film, and TV

Stephanie Klapper
Stephanie Klapper Casting
19 W. 44th St., #1715
New York, NY 10036
Specialty: Feature film and theater

Fran Kumin
Simon and Kumin Casting
1600 Broadway, #609
New York, NY 10019
Phone: (212) 245-7670
Partner: Meg Simon
Specialty: Feature film, theater,
and TV

Hanina Levin
408 W. 57th Street
New York, NY 10019
Phone: (212) 247-8060
Specialty: Film, TV, and commercials

Ellen Lewis. *See* Juliet Taylor

Liz Lewis
Lewis/Shepp Partners
39 W. 19th St., 12th floor
New York, NY 10011
Partner: Evan Shepp
Specialty: Film, theater, and TV

Vince Liebhart
CBS-TV
524 W. 57th St., #5330
New York, NY 10019
Phone: (212) 757-4350
Specialty: TV ("As the World
Turns"), features, and theater

Benjamin Lipton. *See* Alexa Fogel

Pat McCorkle
264 W. 40th St., 9th floor
New York, NY 10018
Phone: (212) 840-0992
Associate: Richard Cole
Specialty: Theater

Tim McDowell. *See* Sylvia Fay

Abigail McGrath
Abigail McGrath, Inc.
1501 Broadway #1310
New York, NY 10036
Phone: (212) 768-3277
Fax: (212) 768-3279
Associate: Ava Zilberfain
Specialty: Theater, feature film,
and TV

Howard Meltzer. *See* Stuart Howard

Ross Mondschain *See* Bernard Telsey

Barry Moss
Hughes Moss Casting

311 W. 43rd St., #700
New York, NY 10036
Phone: (212) 307-6690
Partner: Julie Hughes
Associate: Jessica Gilburne
Specialty: Theater, film, and TV

Julie Mossberg
Chavanne/Mossberg Casting
165 W. 46th St., Suite 514
New York, NY 10036
No phone calls
Partner: Brian Chavanne
Associate: Marnie Waxman
Specialty: Feature film, TV, and theater

Elissa Myers
33 W. 52nd St.
New York, NY 10019
Phone: (212) 315-4777
Associate: Paul Fouquet
Specialty: Theater, feature film,
and TV

D. L. Newton
Courtney and Newton Casting
205 W. 54th St.
New York, NY 10019
(No visits)
Phone: (212) 246-0986
Fax: (212) 489-6388
Partner: Judy Courtney
Specialty: Film and TV

Ray Normandeau. *See* Bob Anthony

Ellen Novack
Ellen Novack Casting
20 Jay St., #9B
New York, NY 10013
Phone: (212) 431-3939
Specialty: Theater, film, and TV

Esther Navarro
Navarro/Bertoni Casting
101 W. 31st St.
New York, NY 10001
Phone: (212) 736-9272
Partner: Ricardo Bertoni
Specialty: Feature film

Michele Ortlip
311 W. 43rd St., 4th floor
New York, NY 10036
Phone: (212) 459-9462
Specialty: Theater, film, and TV
Jeffrey Passero
47 Perry St., Suite 1D
New York, NY 10014
No phone calls
Specialty: Theater, film, and TV

Sally Perle. *See* Lisa Scott

Nancy Piccione
New York Shakespeare Festival
425 Lafayette St.
New York, NY 10003
Phone: (212) 598-7124
Specialty: Theater

Poco Casting
Radio City Station
P.O Box 628
New York, NY 10101-0628
Phone: (212) 581-5536
Partners: David Conaway and
Lisa Bankert
Specialty: Film and TV

Professional Casting Associates
P.O. Box 1944
Murray Hill Sta.
New York, NY 10156
Phone: (212) 953-2478
Casting Director: Alan Coleridge
Specialty: Theater

Valerie Ramer. *See* Sara Hyde-Hamlet

Betty Rea
222 East 44th St.
New York, NY 10017
Phone: (212) 986-5330
Associate: Jimmy Bohr
Specialty: Daytime TV ("Guiding
Light")

Mark Reiner. *See* Contemporary
Casting

Shirley Rich
Independent
200 E. 66th St.
New York, NY 10021
Phone: (212) 688-9540
Specialty: Feature film, TV features,
and theater

Judy Richter. *See* Joy Weber

Toni Roberts
Toni Roberts Casting, Ltd.
150 Fifth Ave.
New York, NY 10011
Phone: (212) 627-2250
Specialty: Theater, film, and TV

Christine Roelfs. *See* Roelfs and
Carrol Casting

Roelfs and Carroll Casting
379 W. Broadway
New York, NY 10012
Phone: (212) 431-3131
Partners: Christine Roelfs and
Theresa Carroll
Associate: Bryan Brooks
Specialty: Theater, film, and TV

Jean Rohn. *See* Joan D'Incecco

Charles Rosen
32 Gramercy Park South
New York, NY 10003
Phone: (212) 254-2080
Specialty: Theater and film

Suzanne Ryan. *See* Lynn Kressel

Amy Schecter. *See* Stuart Howard

Lisa Scott
Lisa Scott Assoc.
206 E. 85th St.
New York, NY 10028
Phone: (212) 772-3300
Associate: Sally Perle
Specialty: Feature film

Sherie L. Seff Casting
400 W. 43rd St.
New York, NY 10036
Phone: (212) 947-7408
Specialty: Commercials

Billy Serow. *See* BCI

Jane Shannon. *See* Deborah Aquila

Barbara Shapiro
111 W. 57th St.
New York, NY 10019
Phone: (212) 582-8228
Specialty: Film, TV, and theater

Evan Shepp
Lewis/Shepp Partners
39 W. 19th St., 12th floor
New York, NY 10011
Partner: Liz Lewis
Specialty: Film, theater, and TV

Claire Shull. *See* Claire Casting

Marcia Shulman
270 Lafayette St., #610
New York, NY 10012
Phone: (212) 219-1010
Specialty: Film and TV

Paula Sindlinger. *See* BCI

Mark Simon
228 W. 10th St., #2A
New York, NY 10014
No visits
Phone: (212) 929-7863
Specialty: Theater

Caroline Sinclair
720 Greenwich St., #7J
New York, NY 10014
Phone: (212) 675-4094
Specialty: Film and TV

Suzanne Smith. *See* Billy Hopkins

Elsie Stark
Hanzel and Stark Casting, Inc.

1261 Broadway, #505
New York, NY 10001
Phone: (212) 779-0966
Partner: Carol Hanzel
Specialty: Feature film and TV

Irene Stockton. *See* Susan Willett

Kari Strom
Warner Bros.
1325 Ave. of the Americas
New York, NY 10019
Phone: (212) 636-5060
Specialty: Feature films

Daniel Swee
Playwrights Horizons
416 W. 42nd St.
New York, NY 10036
Phone: (212) 564-1235
Specialty: Theater

Helyn Taylor
Helyn Taylor Casting
140 W. 58th St.
New York, NY 10019
No phone calls
Specialty: Theater, film, and TV

Juliet Taylor
Independent
130 W. 57th St., #12E
New York, NY 10019
Phone: (212) 245-4635
Associate: Ellen Lewis
Specialty: Feature film

Bernard Telsey
Bernard Telsey Casting
442 W. 42nd St.,
2nd floor
New York, NY 10036
Phone: (212) 239-9033
Associate: Ross Mondschain
Specialty: Theater, TV, and film

Jordan Thaler
New York Shakespeare Festival
425 Lafayette St.
New York, NY 10003

Phone: (212) 598-7100
Specialty: Theater

Rosemarie Tichler
New York Shakespeare Festival
425 Lafayette St.
New York, NY 10003
Phone: (212) 598-7124
Associate: Nancy Piccione
Specialty: Theater

Bonnie Timmerman
Independent
c/o Casting Society of America
311 W. 43rd St., #700
New York, NY 10036
Phone: (212) 333-4552
Associate: Jeff Block
Specialty: Feature film, TV, and
theater

Joy Todd
Independent
37 E. 28th St., #700
New York, NY 10016
Phone: (212) 685-3537
Fax: (212) 684-7039
Associate: Grant Wilfley
Specialty: Feature film; occasional TV
projects and commercials

Lucy Tyler. *See* Donna DeSeta

D. Urell
Urell Casting
P.O. Box 993
Staten Island, NY 10312
No phone calls
Specialty: Film and TV
(union and non-union)

Schulla Van Buren. *See* Deborah Aquila

Georgianne Walken
Walken/Jaffe Casting
235 W. 76th St., #2A
New York, NY 10023
Phone: (212) 877-4025
Partner: Sheila Jaffe
Specialty: Theater and film

Marnie Waxman. *See* Brian Chavanne

Joy Weber
Joy Weber Casting
250 W. 57th St.
New York, NY 10107
Phone: (212) 245-5220
Associate: Judy Richter
Specialty: Theater, film, and TV
Lisa Weiss. *See* Collier Casting

Susan Willett
Susan Willett Casting
1170 Broadway
New York, NY 10001
Phone: (212) 725-3588
Associate: Irene Stockton
Specialty: Film, TV, and theater

Judy Wilson. *See* Natalie Hart

Liz Woodman
Liz Woodman Casting
311 W. 43rd St., #700
New York, NY 10036
Phone: (212) 787-3782
Specialty: Theater and TV

Ava Zilberfain. *See* Abigail McGrath

Alison Zimet. *See* Deborah Aquila

## NORTH CAROLINA
Fincannon and Associates
107 Front St.
Wilmington, NC 28401
Phone: (919) 251-1500
Casting Directors: Mark and
Craig Fincannon
Specialty: Film and TV

Martha Spainhour
Action Casting
7246 Wrightsville Ave.
Wilmington, NC 28403
Phone: (919) 256-9650
Specialty: Film and TV

## OHIO
Anita Daughtery
P.O. Box 6472
Cinncinatti, OH 45206
Phone: (513) 961-7607
Specialty: Principals and extras

## OREGON
Janet Barret
6533 N. Commercial
Portland, OR 97217
Phone: (503) 285-0708
Specialty: Commercials

## RHODE ISLAND
Roberta Bailey
1 Brook Farm Rd.
N. Providence, RI 02904
Phone: (401) 353-1878
Specialty: Film, TV, and theater

## TENNESSEE
Patsy Bruce
P.O. Box 120428
Nashville, TN 37212
Phone: (615) 255-5711
Specialty: Feature film

Tess Carrier
P.O. Box 11862
Memphis, TN 38111
Phone: (901) 278-7454
Specialty: Film and TV

Jo Doster
P.O. Box 120641
Nashville, TN 37212
Phone: (615) 385-3850
Specialty: Film and TV

Linda S. Dotson
123 Waltor Ferry Rd., 2nd floor
Hendersonville, TN 37075
Phone: (615) 824-1947
Specialty: Film and TV

Jim Kup
P.O. Box 1632
Madison, TN 37116
Phone: (615) 383-6345
Specialty: TV

Darilyn S. Mason
138 Jackson Trace
Hermitage, TN 37076
Phone: (615) 885-5122
Specialty: Feature film

**TEXAS**
Barbara Blanchette
P.O. Box 551-383
Dallas, TX 75355
Phone: (214) 348-5190
Specialty: Commercials and
industrials

**WASHINGTON, D.C.**
Bonnie Schwartz Casting Association
4200 42nd Street NW
Washington, D.C. 20016
Phone: (202) 362-1860
Specialty: Film and video